# THE BEST
# OF GOLF

# THE BEST OF GOLF

## Peter Alliss
## and Bob Ferrier

**PARTRIDGE PRESS**

LONDON · NEW YORK · TORONTO · SYDNEY · AUCKLAND

TRANSWORLD PUBLISHERS LTD
61-63 Uxbridge Road, London W5 5SA

TRANSWORLD PUBLISHERS (AUSTRALIA) PTY LTD
15-23 Helles Avenue, Moorebank, NSW 2170

TRANSWORLD PUBLISHERS (NZ) LTD
Cnr Moselle and Waipareira Aves,
Henderson, Auckland

Published 1989 by Partridge Press
a division of Transworld Publishers Ltd
Copyright © Robert Ferrier and Peter Alliss 1989

Designed by Peter Phillips

British Library Cataloguing in Publication Data

Alliss, Peter, *1931–*
    The best of golf.
    1. Golf
    I. Title    II. Ferrier, Bob
    796.352

    ISBN 1–85225–077–1

Printed in Great Britain
by Mackays of Chatham Plc, Letchworth

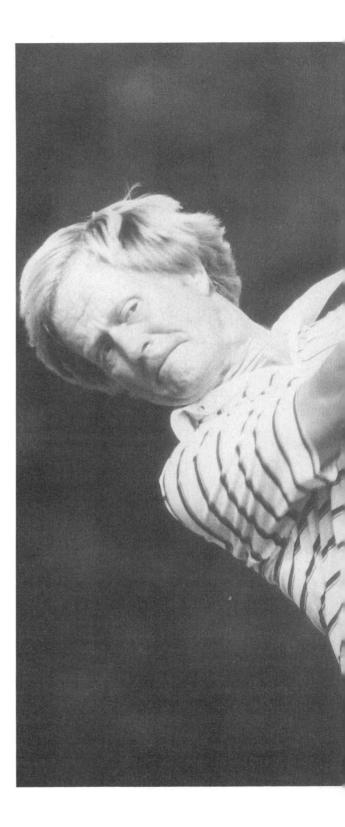

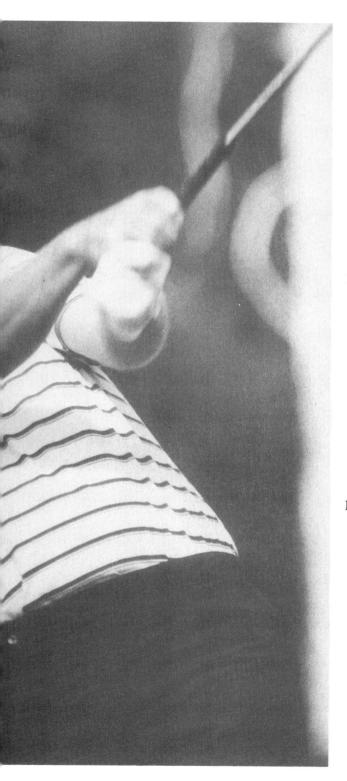

# CONTENTS

# INTRODUCTION

*Golf – the most beautiful game.*

**T**he game of golf has enriched our lives. To one degree or another, we have experienced between us almost every aspect of the ancient game which is 'deceptively simple, endlessly complicated' – as club member, club professional, tournament player, international championship player; in tournament management, golf course design and construction and management; and in the various elements of media – the written word, film, radio, and television.

We have tried to set down how things were in our time, and, as well as may be, before our time, and have tried to look at the changes that have come along, and the long lines of personalities, intriguing and otherwise, which have marched through the long decades of the game.

# Part I
# THE GAME

*1ST Hole*

# THE NATURE OF GOLF

## Its Allure

*"I love the place. I love the feel of it.*
*The smell of it, the taste of it.*
*I love the turf, the feel of my spikes in it.*
*I love the people."*
**Tom Watson, Muirfield, 1987.**

**W**hat is it, this game, this most beautiful of games? It is all things to all men. All human life, all human experience, is here. It is not a matter of life and death. It is not that important. But it is a reflection of life, and so the game is an enigma wrapped in a mystery impaled on a conundrum.

It is magnificent, and, to those who do not play it, meaningless. It has been called a mental disorder, a pernicious, habit-forming drug, a disease for which there is no cure, an obsession. It has been called "an indispensable adjunct of high civilisation", and, by every golfer who ever swung a club, "this benighted game". It is the most satisfying of games, the most infuriating of games, the most humbling of games, which is to say it is the most humiliating of games. Of course, no game analysed closely, looked at objectively, makes very much sense. One can imagine the question, in a Monty Pythonesque context, "What are these grown men doing, daddy?" And you might imagine trying to explain the thing to a group of newly-arrived Martians: "Well, you take this stick with a bulge on the end of it, and you take this ball, see, and stand it on this little splinter of wood, see, and you whack the ball with a stick across that field, see. And over there is a hole, a small hole, and you

**Ben Hogan a gentleman first, and next a golfer.**

have to knock the ball into it, see . . ." Bobby Jones, perhaps the greatest of all golfers, once pondered on the fame he had achieved "because of proficiency in the inconsequential performance of striking a golf ball". Ask any golfer why he plays and you'll have a hard time finding a rational answer. Usually it is a mumbled platitude – "for the exercise", "for the pleasure", "fresh air", "I'm too old for anything else", "the golf course is right by my house", and so on. The hard men may answer, eyeball to eyeball, "to win the monthly medal", with a grit in the teeth and a spark in the eye. They are the competitive ones, for whom victory is all. But all of them know that this is not good enough. They are in it and at it for the pleasure and the pain, the temperament and the temper, the delights and damnations, the heroic moment, the tragic moment, the intermittent glory, and for one of the game's abiding delusions – that our very best shot is our standard shot, our normal shot.

Perhaps the absolute basic allure of the game is that anyone can play it; a child can play it, a pensioner can play it. Yet in another of golf's seemingly endless paradoxes, it is neither a child's game nor an old man's game. It can begin when walking begins, end when walking ends. In a word, unlike almost all other sports, golf does not demand youth. It requires no particular athleticism, neither speed nor stamina, no highly-toned muscles, no excessive physical

**Bobby Jones, aged 14½.**

strength. All it needs is the leg power to cover 18 holes, or some four miles, in any other context no more than a pleasant walk.

The game is played by striking a stationary ball. The player initiates the action – the swing – from a stationary position. This swing will take little more than two seconds. The ball, from any shot with any club, has been measured to fly through the air for six seconds, no longer. Thus, the golf swing becomes an act of will as much as a physical act. And there's the rub. In the moving ball games, the player's mind is constantly in gear, providing running, jumping, throwing, catching, kicking, tackling data, and producing the required, instinctive reaction. Not so in golf. Golf's physical action is calculated and is not an instinctive act. Thus, another of the game's many paradoxes is that time is both friend and enemy. It is perhaps the most ignored and most critical element in the game, and therefore amongst the most intriguing. A round of golf goes along at a leisurely pace. It may take three hours, perhaps longer. And this

relaxed tempo allows the externals to intrude – the environment, the weather, the partner or opponent, with whom some conversation on the state of the nation or the infamies of government is unavoidable, and the like. And the mere presence of a partner, an opponent, throws the golfer in spite of himself into a continuing observation of the characteristics, the character, the personality, of the other man.

"Time" is described by the Shorter Oxford Dictionary as "a limited stretch or space of continued existence, the period through which an action, condition or state continues". The golfer's limited stretch or space of continued existence, may be several minutes between strokes, yet by contrast the period through which his action continues is a mere two seconds, furiously brief. Thus the golfer must do all this thinking about his action BEFORE it takes place, then create that action almost without thinking of it – thus the almost act-of-will. Inevitably, this puts him into "memory", the fickle companion of time and space. How to hit that static, innocent ball? How did he do it *last time*? Yet the swing must exist in the present, the permanent present – NOW. Paradox, paradox, irresistible allure!

The evolution of the golfer demands that he learns how to hit the ball, how to advance the ball, how to reach the fairway. He must learn to control the hit so that the ball will land in a certain, pre-selected part of the fairway. He will then learn how to hit the ball consistently from the fairway to the green, then to a certain area of the green, ignoring at all times the perils to hand – the wind, the rain, the cold, the heat, the bunker, the burn, the lake, the lone tree in the fairway. And he will learn to putt, and become a golfer, all this with much play and practice.

But what kind of a golfer is he; how good will he be; how good *is* he? One of the blessings of the game, one of its greatest single attractions, is the handicapping system. Our golfer will be allotted a handicap in keeping with his proven standard of play that will enable him to play with, score as well as, and possibly even beat, say, Jack Nicklaus. As with all handicapping systems, that is the theory. The practice, inevitably, is somewhat different. If Nicklaus played our golfer on a course with a standard score of 72 (Standard Scratch Score is the expected standard score of an expert player on that course, its length, degree of difficulty and other factors having been taken into account), the 18-handicap player, the *average* player, would expect to score the course in 90 strokes, Jack Nicklaus in 72 strokes. Two reservations immediately arise. First, in order to score the course in 90 strokes, the average player must play every stroke perfectly by his standards. Second, Jack Nicklaus is more than an expert player – he is an outstanding champion who is likely to score the course in fewer than 72 strokes. So, apart from the sheer terror of actually playing with Nicklaus, the 18-handicap player is not likely to match him, much less beat him. Nevertheless, the fact that he can do it, in theory, in the abstract, and the fact that he might finish within a few strokes of Nicklaus, and, even more important, the fact that the handicapping system can allow them to have a pleasant game together, are just a few of the many delights which abound in this most absorbing of sports. The handicapping system can almost be made to prove that there is no such thing as a *bad* golfer, which does wonders for the ego. It may well persuade our Mr Average that, had life given him a little more time for it, why, he'd be just as good a golfer as Nicklaus.

Furthermore, the average golfer can actually play in the same majestic arenas as do Nicklaus and all the other great players. Few tennis players experience play on the Centre Court at Wimbledon, but any golfer can play, for example, on the famous Old Course at St Andrews because it is a public course. And, with a little help from his friends, a nod, a nudge and a wink, and a little of the connivance that life demands, Mr Average will be able to walk in the footsteps of the gods at many another great championship course. If he does, he will experience yet another of the game's unending seductions – the infinite variety of the arenas. Play at Royal Lytham and St Annes, a truly great championship course, and the golfer will be surrounded by suburbia. Play at Muirfield, Ballybunion, Royal County Down and, for most of his round, he will see almost nothing that is man-made. This temporary separation from the world is one of the game's greatest delights.

Golf flatters, disappoints, elates, dispirits. It is irritating to the nerves, trying to the temper. It is a mosaic of moments of ecstasy shattered by nightmares. Yet it is simply more fun than other games. The golf swing demands a sequence of elementary physical movements and usually the sequence fails. Yet the golfer remains undismayed. He is bolstered by a sublime, ignorant confidence that *next time* all will be well and the sequence will succeed. This is the imperishable dream of all golfers, including the most talented of them. Their failures are matters of degree, and it has been a persistent factor since the whole thing began. The addictive golfing potion is that it can always be better, that it will be better.

The fact that the sequence of movements that comprises a swing must start from a state of rest, and that the ball is stationary, introduces the inexorable complexity of the ego, the "conscious thinking subject". Subjectivity is the crucifixion of the golfer. It cannot exist in games of movement. In golf, the player must generate his own power, control it, apply it. The ball is inert. It cannot be compromised. There is no physical challenge from anyone to contemplate the action. The golfer – and this is one of the game's most powerful fascinations – is essentially playing against himself, his ego, his subjectivity. As he stands over the ball, he should be in a totally objective frame of mind. He seldom is. He is probably concerned with the details of his physical movements, the component parts of the swing – keeping the head still, transferring his weight, breaking his wrists, unbreaking his wrists, getting his foot movement right. He may be thinking of the bad luck he had on the previous hole, or the difficulty of the hole which is three ahead. He may already be contemplating the glass of beer he will have when it is all over, or why that idiot over there is wearing scarlet trousers. Just as likely, his head will be throbbing with Mahler chords, or the lyric to *itsy bitsy, teeny weeny, yellow polka dot bikini*. He will not truly be concentrating on the task at hand. What he should have done, of course, was to have completed his thinking before he stepped up to the ball so that he had a clear idea of his swing as a total entity, and when he does come to the physical action, he is all but empty-headed. He seldom does this. For one thing, he has not spent enough time practising the game. What we are talking about here is concentration. Jack Nicklaus has said, 'Every golfer should approach every shot with confidence and enthusiasm". Ah, confidence and enthusiasm! Too few of us practice our confidence, our concentration. Too few of us practice. Well, it's only a game.

Luck is critical in the game; it is one of its abiding conversation pieces. Gary Player, an outstanding bunker player, was once told by a fan that he was lucky, playing from the sand. "You're right," said Player, "and the funny thing is, the more I practise, the luckier I get." To the anguished cry "Oh, it isn't fair, it isn't fair" comes the classical, pointed response – "But it's not meant to be fair". Golf courses are not billiards tables. The game is played out of doors, in the wind and the weather, over ground that slopes and rises and falls and is occasionally "rough". The ball can strike an unseen stone, bounce every which way. The *lucky* bounce is immediately claimed as part of the skill and subtlety of the shot and is clearly what the golfer intended. The *unlucky* bounce (another delusion) is clearly the work of all the devils that ever were, and has

there ever been a man so persecuted, sobs the golfer.

The game is stiff with fantasies, with illusions, with self-delusion. A golfer believes – it is part of the game's holy writ – that next time it will be right, indeed that somewhere in his subconscious is the certainty that somehow he will be better than he ever can be, in spite of it all. One famous exception was the golfer who came off the course saying "I didn't play my best game today," then adding with bitter whimsy, "Come to think of it, I never play my best game." Golf is not an exact science. Improvement, enlightenment and revelation come in fits and starts, depending on how much work the golfer puts into his game, rather like learning a foreign language. Many people would claim that is exactly what the game is. And, in the search for golf's holy grail, there are sub-cultures. One is of vanity, that success can come from a dashing wardrobe, or new or changed equipment, as though salvation is to be found in a forest of shafts, heads, grips, putters, gloves, sweaters, slacks, shoes, books and now video films, packed into the professional's shop.

The game is rich in camaraderie. Play golf with a man, just one round, and you will never forget him, because here he reveals himself to the world at large. He cannot conceal himself from the gaze of the world – his style, his movement, his walk, his character, his personality, and, yes, many of his prejudices come out during an 18-hole walk. The game is self-regulatory. Except in major, organised, sophisticated competitions, there is no need for a referee, an umpire, a touch judge, a linesman. By and large the game is played by honest people. Cheating is not tolerated. This is not to say that golfers don't cheat. Golfers, after all, are people, and people do cheat. But cheating in golf is considered the worst of sins and blatant cheats are invited to resign from their club, an invitation they had better accept, there and then. The golfer plays against the par of the course, the weather, and, in match play, against one specific opponent. But, most of all, he plays against himself, against his own consciousness, ego, phobias, neuroses. The game is simple. It is also the most imperfect of games because the player makes it so.

The golfer is free to choose his own equipment and clothing. The game is oddly un-uniformed. The shortcomings of his own game can render the golfer into an object of uncontrolled passion, but his expletives are aimed at the course, the ball, his club, the weather, the greenkeeper, all the gods of creation, but, oddly, never at his opponent because the golfer knows perfectly well that the obligation which the game puts on him is to be master of his own fate. He

must play to the limit of his ability. He must produce his best, his best score, and offer it openly and publicly to be beaten. The game is full of minor riches, the arrangement of matches, the negotiations on the first tee, the pairings, the play, the putts, the conniving for starting times, the ribaldry on the course, the ecstasy of that one perfect shot, the fact that in play no one cares who is rich or poor, fat or thin, tall or short, young or old. Then there is the showering, the changing, the bar and the post-mortem and the "if onlys". And such is the variety of the ground in golf, such is the arbitrary flight of the ball, the fickleness of its bounce, that the Rules of Golf, which seek to cover all possible situations, run to 112 brochure pages – 34 rules with mountains of sub-divisions and interpretations. Added to all this may be several local rules, applying to the conditions on one golf course only, and all of this is manna to the disputatious, providing the pseudo barrister/golfer with an endless source of discussion and debate in the locker room, at the bar, and, not infrequently, on the golf course.

The magnet of improvement, the optimism that convinces the golfer that his game will get better, is one of the game's greatest attractions. It would be intriguing to establish what has given, over the centuries, the greatest pleasure to the greatest number of people – the works of William Shakespeare or of Wilbur Smith, Mozart, Wagner, Beethoven, or Johann Strauss, Cole Porter, the Beatles? Perhaps there is a case for Coca Cola. But golf, the most beautiful game, would be high on the list.

As Robert Forgan wrote, many years ago, claiming that "Good Golf is a State of Mind",

"Golf is deceptively simple, endlessly complicated.

A child can play it well, and a grown man can never master it.

Any single round of it is full of unexpected triumphs and seemingly perfect shots that end in disaster.

It is almost a science, yet it is a puzzle without an answer.

It is gratifying and tantalising, precise and unpredictable.

It requires complete concentration and total relaxation.

It satisfies the soul and frustrates the intellect.

It is at the same time rewarding and maddening – and it is without doubt the greatest game mankind has ever invented."

**Gary Player, one of the most determined of champions.**

15

# Its Anguish

*"This benighted Game."*
**The anonymous golfer.**

The golf swing is an essentially simple, and in fact a rather undemanding, physical movement. A child of ten years can do it perfectly well. And it may be that this very simplicity and the fact that the golfer starts the action from a state of rest, makes golf the most anguished of games, of all games, for everyone without exception who has ever tried to play. Indeed, and perversely, the intrinsic anguish of it all may be part of its powerful appeal. If the seductive allure of the game is based on the fact that striking the ball well repeatedly is so difficult, the anguish which this provokes emerges from the imperfections of man. The golfer creates his own frustration, because no other game generates such introversions. The game makes schizophrenics of us all.

Consider the average golfer on the first tee. Rather, first consider the average golfer. If it were possible to establish a global average golfer, we might find that he would be no better than 18 handicap, to which he will seldom play. He will not be able to score below 90, he will not be able to hit the ball more than 200 yards, and he will be inclined to slice his shots, that is hit the ball with a trajectory which sees it move from left to right through the air. Still, let us consider our man on the first tee. He simply has to swing the club and strike the ball. Nothing, no one, will interfere with his action. He has done it many times before. But the prospect of this simple action brings a dozen "outside agencies" flooding into his mind. Can he remember what to do? Will he do it properly? Is this teeing ground rather more muddy than usual? Does this glove fit quite as it should? Has he placed the ball correctly, high enough, low enough, on the teepeg? What are these people doing on the 18th green? Is the fairway ahead of him quite clear? Why doesn't his playing partner stand where he can be seen? What will all these people watching from the clubhouse window think if he foozles the shot? (As if two people watching, or 2000 lining the first fairway at an Open Championship, could have the slightest influence on how the ball should behave).

Thus the average good citizen, who is kind to animals, gentle with old ladies in the street, and is perfectly capable, even talented, at work, undergoes a strange and inexplicable change of personality. Of course, any single one of us is many things to many men, as many a playwright has examined. It depends on who is looking. Unreality surrounds us all. The golfer's natural personality survives off the course, away from the benighted game. If he is an adult, it will be firmly established. We speak here of temporary aberrations and of confidence, of nerve, of fear – fear of embarrassment, fear of incompetence, fear of consequences, fear of failure.

The golfer is asking himself to do something he has done perfectly well before, probably quite often. He should have the confidence to do it again, but this is the first stroke of yet another round, and perhaps nothing that has gone before quite relates to this. He stands in splendid isolation. Nerve, like energy, may of course wane with the years. A man of 25 will be more adept at parking a car in a confined space than a man of 65, and it may be that nerve and energy are finite, not rechargeable. But nerve, an intangible, indescribable element in the human persona, is needed to get that ball away to the fairway, without fear of consequences. If the golfer is playing, let us say, a straightforward, routine par-4 hole, driving the ball into the fairway will give him a fair chance of hitting his next shot to the green, taking two putts for a regulation score on the hole, surely always a satisfactory start to a round. But if he pulls the ball to the left, why, he may well go out of bounds, over yonder fence. If he pushes the ball to the right, he may become tangled among yonder trees. Either way, he'll do well to score six on the hole, a rather unsatisfactory start. All of this may be in his mind when it should not be, yet fear, of consequences, of failure, of mis-hitting the shot, is a source of powerful embarrassment, even if the golfer is beyond sight of the clubhouse and of witnesses, because it is self-inflicted. He did it, nobody else.

Nowhere does the anguish of the game leave a more bitter taste than on the putting green, a critical area of the field since in general putting may take up much as 50 per cent of the strokes used in a round of golf. It appears that there can fall upon a man, an ex-

The agony and the ecstasy: all golfers have experienced both.
Bernhard Langer, 1987 Ryder Cup.

**Sam Snead, taking extreme steps to overcome the *yips*.**

cellent putter forsooth, a time when he can no longer putt. He may well stand over the ball from here to eternity and he cannot, *cannot*, move the putter blade away from the ball, much less return it to the ball. This is known as a case of the *yips*. Its cause is beyond explanation and beyond the understanding of those not afflicted, rather like going to a funeral and saying to a friend, "I'm sorry your father has died – I know how you feel". You don't know how he feels, and you will never know how he feels. The burden of the *yips* is clearly a phobia, a fear or aversion "especially of a morbid character" and it has afflicted many of the greatest players of the game – Vardon, Sarazen, Snead, Cotton, Byron Nelson (for a few seasons certainly the greatest of his time), Palmer. Snead at one time took to putting from between his legs, until that was forbidden, then putted facing the hole, feet together, putting side-saddle as it were.

Arnold Palmer still complains. In the US PGA Seniors Championship of 1988, after a third round

of 76, he declared "I missed five times from inside five feet – once from two feet. I have a serious case of the yips." Palmer, one of the greatest names in the history of the game, was complaining – at the age of 58! This persecution complex is not confined to putting. It can happen with the simple pitch shot over a bunker, the chip shot from just short of the green. At bridge or at poker in the club, "Frank" was a hard man who would win the money most of the time – he was an excellent card player – so much so that, in the nature of things, he was not for some the most popular member. Frank was a fine golfer, but the chipshot from just off the green was his damnation. He could have *air shots* (complete misses). He could hack up a divot behind the ball big enough to cover it. He tried playing the shot left-handed, one-handed, left hand below right. He had a club made only 18 inches long. He'd try the shot using a putter from 30 yards short of the green and have an air shot with that. His mental trauma might start from more than 100 yards away, when he realised his approach shot to the green had left the ball short, and he would have to face a chip shot. He said, "It was as though someone had switched off an electric light, and I was left in the dark, knowing I'd have to face that damned shot. A torrent of thoughts would race through my mind so that I could not think of one single thing, of only one thing, the brain working at such a speed that there was no picture any more, no picture of anything around me." Frank had no such problem with any other shots.

David Thomas, an outstanding international golfer who was plainly unlucky, twice, in not winning the Open Championship - in a play-off with Peter Thomson at Lytham in 1958, and again in finishing second to Jack Nicklaus at Muirfield in 1966 – suffered the yips with pitching. He couldn't get the club back. He might get it back about a foot, then have a flick or squirt at the ball. He tried everything; he took to taking tremendous swipes with a sand iron for a time, trying to play it like a bunker shot and taking divots that would sit comfortably in a harvest festival. Once in a match play final at Turnberry, against John MacDonald, David was comfortably ahead with lots of holes to play. At one par-5 hole, his second shot was just short (David was a magnificent striker of the ball and very long) and left him with a little pitch shot over a bunker. He couldn't face it. He picked up the ball and conceded the hole rather than risk a fluff into the bunker. He went on to win the final handily, but, for a player of his class it was bewildering. One begins to think of cowardice here, but it is certainly not physical cowardice. On his best day, David Thomas would have gone hand in hand against a lion. Yet there is surely some element of mental terror in the *yips*. Some of the afflicted have tried psychoanalysis, without much success.

The irony is that these great players could still putt perfectly well in non-competitive situations. On the practice putting greens, they could make perfect strokes with the putter, hole out comfortably, and make perfect strokes even when not putting towards a hole, simply putting across the putting green. What psychical tangles have we here! *Yippers* have described how they have stood over a short putt, a nine inch putt, and frozen, the brain switched off so that no message gets to the hands and they don't even *see* the ball! Something must happen to the human chemistry. The condition can be described, but not explained. In the closing years of his competitive career, Ben Hogan would stand frozen over the ball and could not move his hands. He would stand for so long that it became almost as embarrassing for the spectators as it must have been for him. Interviewed later, around the time of his 75th birthday in the American magazine *Golf Digest*, he said, explaining why he stopped playing in public, "I didn't want to put myself on display any more. All the technique and practice in the world wasn't going to help me. It was a nerves situation, and it was embarrassing for me out there in front of people. I couldn't get the putter back."

Severiano Ballesteros, playing the 15th hole of the final round of the 1986 US Masters tournament, was faced with a 4-iron shot over the lake which guards the entire front of the green. For Ballesteros, an Open Champion, a previous Masters winner, a winner of major competitions around the world, leading money winner, leader of the order of this, that and the other, a seasoned, indeed hardened, champion, this was a routine shot. He hit the ball into the water. How could that happen from such a player? Perhaps he hit the ball fat, perhaps this, perhaps that. He was leading the tournament at that moment, with four holes to play. He did not win it. Anguish for Ballesteros. Arnold Palmer once took six on the final hole of that same Augusta course when a par-4 would have won him the title. Sam Snead took eight on the final hole of a US Open Championship when six would have made him champion. Anguish for all of them. Perhaps the force simply left them. Yet the bewitching, democratic thought of the anguish of Ballesteros hitting into the water is that it was no less than the anguish of the average golfer doing exactly the same thing in the club's monthly medal. No less. No question of degree. The experience, the

emotion, the anguish, all are the same.

At the very top level of the game there are countless examples of self-inflicted anguish. Hale Irwin, in the Open Championship of 1983 at Birkdale, missed a half inch putt on the 14th green of the third round and finished the championship in second place just one shot (!) behind Tom Watson. Irwin had reached for the ball, two-handed, hitting left-handed. He missed the ball completely. But surely no man has suffered the cruel injustices of this game in the way that "Tommy" Nakajima of Japan has. In the 1978 Masters at Augusta, his second round was going along nicely at level par when he reached the 13th hole, a short par-5 which doglegs sharply to the left at around driving distance. A burn runs along the left side of the fairway, all the way to the green, then passes immediately in front of the green. Nakajima drove into the burn on the left, lifted out under penalty, then advanced the ball up the fairway with a 5-iron shot. He then pitched into the burn in front of the green – played four. He decided to play the ball as it lay, but popped it up in the air and, in falling, it struck his foot – further penalty, now score seven. But he also let his club touch the water in preparing for the next shot (grounding a club in a hazard) for another two stroke penalty. He then pitched the ball over the green, chipped back, two-putted and totalled 13 on the 13th hole – on Friday the 13th. Afterwards he said, 'It was a good lesson for me." It was a lesson quickly forgotten.

In the Open Championship at St Andrews three months later, Tommy had played well with 70–71 in the opening rounds and was in handy contact with the leaders, requiring to finish with two fours for a third round 71. At the 17th, the Road Hole, he hit two pretty shots just short of the green. He then putted into the fearsome Road Hole bunker. The pin was some 20 feet from the top rim of the bunker. He tried to splash out gently, four times, eventually taking two putts for a score of nine on the hole, which was immediately dubbed by the writers "The Sands of Nakajima". Tommy was not finished with the Open Championship. At Turnberry in 1986 he was partnered with Greg Norman who had a meagre single stroke advantage over him. Nakajima bunkered his second shot to the first hole, took three putts – his final miss was from 12 inches – and scored six. Norman made a par-4 for a three stroke lead, and won the championship. Nakajima finished eighth. Then it was the turn of the US Open in the following year, at the Olympic Club in San Francisco. Halfway, Nakajima was nicely placed with rounds of 68 and 70, only one stroke

**"The Sands of Nakajima": Tommy Nakajima in the bunker at the 17th, during the 1978 Open at St Andrews.**

behind the leader, Tom Watson. Coming to the final hole of the third round, Tommy pushed his drive a little and had to play his second over a tall pine tree. He didn't. The ball caught the top of the tree and stayed up there. A teenaged spectator shinned up the tree but couldn't find the ball. Nakajima had to play another ball, scored six for a 74 and finished ninth in the championship.

Chided with all these adventures, or disasters, Nakajima summoned up all his oriental inscrutability and said, 'I'll have to think about all that." And there is the well-testified, amply-witnessed example of the prominent London golfer, a low-handicap man, on the first tee one Sunday morning. Having teed his ball and addressed it, all ready to swing, he looked down and said in ringing tones, 'What the hell am I doing here? – I don't *want* to be here!" He picked up the ball, walked off the tee, and went home.

The effects that golf can have on a man, or a woman, are almost beyond belief. It can induce an almost mystical state of addiction to, of obsession with, the game. Consider the case of Ken Lane. Ken was not so much obsessed with golf as possessed by it, so much so that his wife Carol, after 14 years of marriage, sued for divorce. Carol, 41, mother of three children, told the court that, while she was left tending the home and minding the

family, Ken, 46, was either playing golf or drinking in the clubhouse. In her petition she cited excessive drinking, moodiness, neglect, and some incidences of violence. She said she had been driven to distraction by her film technician husband's obsession with golf. He worked nights and would go straight to the golf course without coming home, and when he did come home he would go straight to bed, then to work, thus completing the cycle. "He was fanatical," she said. "Golf was his mistress – there never was another woman. It took over his life." Ken, a county-class player, had a cupboard full of trophies and some 3500 golf balls at home. Carol said that on one of the rare occasions when she went to a tournament in which he was playing, she had said, "Remember me?" and his friends were astonished to learn that he had a wife. "He even played golf yesterday, the day before this court hearing," she said. Some two-and-a-half years earlier, Mrs Lane had moved out of the matrimonial bedroom. Ken argued that the marriage had not broken down and denied that golf was their problem. "I only played about twice a week," he said. "I went out around 5 pm on Saturdays and had a sit-down meal with friends afterwards. Then I'd go out on Sundays from 6 am to 9 am." It seems that Ken's memory was faulty – the divorce was granted.

20

Then there was the case of Mrs Sylvia Goff of Shrewsbury. Mrs Goff, who was attractive, 45, and the mother of two children, took court action against Shrewsbury Golf Club which had terminated her membership. She claimed £3000 damages from the club for the anxiety and distress caused by her expulsion for "improper conduct", and sought re-instatement as a member. Mrs Goff's preoccupation with the game brought her in five years from absolute beginner to a handicap of six and county standard, but oddly she was never selected for the club team. It seemed that Mrs Goff's "etiquette" was not to the liking of some other lady members, or, perhaps more pointedly, some of them felt that the shorts she wore on the course were altogether too short and that her "tops" were not topped enough. Mrs Goff had pretty legs. At all events, an 11-point petition, which included allegations of cheating, was passed from the lady members to the club captain and his all-male committee. The captain expelled Mrs Goff, and her legal action was also against him. The allegations included playing off wrong handicaps, signing an incorrect scorecard, replacing the ball in the wrong position, to name but a few. There were dark suggestions that lady members had spied on Mrs Goff, lurking in the undergrowth of the course to do it. If this was a storm in a Shrewsbury teacup, it had sinister undertones or overtones. The case had taken two years to get to court, and the judge in the first place declared that his court was no place for such a dispute. Perhaps more chauvinistic than judicial, he delivered the thought that Mrs Goff was seeking a cheap libel action, and he felt that it was wrong to use the court to drag members' names through the mud, and that the men's committee which had expelled her were "honest and just men". Cheating was not at issue. The question was whether she had been fairly treated. "She is not sincere," he said. "For reasons that I don't propose to examine any more, she has set out to do as much damage to that club and its members . . ." He ruled against her, and invited her to pay the costs of the action. Mrs Goff said afterwards that these might amount to £50,000. She was considering an appeal. She had not played golf since she was excommunicated from Shrewsbury Golf Club two years earlier. "My good name is at stake," she said, "and you cannot put a price on that." Oh, what a witch's brew of emotion is here – the jealousy, the vanity, the pride, the greed, and all the other deadly sins are here, not to mention that downtrodden race of womenfolk. Why should the Shrewsbury Golf Club's committee be exclusively male? The same persists in too many other clubs. But then the deadly sins are not in the game. They are in us. But the game seems to bring them out.

There is another scenario in golf, the one about the haunted hole, the hole which we never manage to play well, or moderately, or even routinely, no matter what. Perhaps it is that innocent little spinney on the left, perhaps that solitary and quite inoffensive tree on the right. It may be simply the general conformation of the fairway, the requirement to drive into an upslope, the lie of the land. It may be something that has happened in the past at the hole, a hooked shot, a slice, a socket, an *unlucky* bounce. The hole may be a straightforward par-3 with a flat, open green. It could be a routine par-4, wide fairway, not one single hazard, a drive and simple pitch hole, but there is something there, a presence which makes a man out of sorts on the tee and the hole unplayable. No matter how often, how carefully, the golfer plays it, no matter how much he lectures himself, no matter the promises he makes to himself, he never quite gets it right. This remains one of the abiding mysteries of a mysterious game. And there is an extension to this scenario, one of total, abject, anguished frustration. It comes when you hit a tee shot out of bounds, say, and *knew* you were going to do it. You knew perfectly well as you stood to the ball that you would drive it out of bounds, then went ahead and did precisely that. Then an inner voice will say, "Well, you never did play this hole very well." But you could have played the hole with different clubs – two shots with a 5-iron might have done just as well, but you didn't do it, did you? Now you'll be lucky to score six on the hole, instead of a possible four or five. And when the fury of frustration fades, you ask yourself feebly "Why did I do it?", and you will find no answer. If all of this is the product of stress, a common, even fashionable, element in modern life, it is well to remember that stress is man-made and anything man-made can surely be man un-made. In golf, the fault is seldom in our stars. We bring our own, personalised anguish with us, in the golf bag.

Memory, that foggy, foreign land, is another anguishing factor in this monstrous game. How did we do it last time? How can we remember all the component parts of the golf swing, an untaxing physical movement, and combine them into an effective, rhythmic whole? The golf swing, considered rationally, objectively, is a simple action. But its very simplicity makes it immensely difficult. And that very simplicity is the basis of the ultimate anguish in the game.

# Its Beauty

*"Ever charming, every new,*
*When will the landscape tire the view?"*
**John Dyer** (1699–1758)

**T**his old game is played in the deserts of Arizona, in the high places of Mexico City and Johannesburg, along the Melbourne sand strip, amid the exotica of Hong Kong, Singapore and Monte Carlo. It is played on the damp, hard shores of Fife, between the huddling towers of the Costa del Sol, through the tall pines of Georgia and along the teeming shore of the Eldorado called California. The game is played in the tropics and on the desert sands of Araby. The game is played everywhere.

And one of the compelling attractions of golf is that it is unbounded. Unlike other games it is not restricted by stadium, court, arena, by enclosing lines drawn on the ground. The golf course wanders freely - some critics of golf course designers would say aimlessly – over some 100 acres of land, and thus the environment becomes one of the most immediate and telling attractions of the game. All golf courses are the same in that they have tees, greens, fairways, hazards. But there the similarities end. Golf courses inhabit an infinite variety of environment, of landscape, moorland, heathland, linksland, parkland, and of seascape. They have been laid out on paddy fields, hewn out of mountainsides, devised artistically from plain farmland and on restored open-cast mining sites. Golf courses acquire their own personalities. Many golfers would describe the famous Carnoustie course, near Dundee, as "brutal". The equally famous Oakmont course near Pittsburgh has been called "a monster". And it would be a poor golfer who, on his first appearance on the first tee of the Old Course at St Andrews – the old course that is always new – did not suffer a twinge of "neurasthenic self-suppression", what with the oldest members at the window of the big room, only a few feet behind him, leering over their drinks; the inevitable citizenry drifting along the right side fence, savouring in advance the golfer's minor disaster to come; and, above all, the five centuries of history leaning on the poor man's shoulders. Yet, as the golfer escapes this purgatory and progresses out along the course, he will increasingly find himself separated from the works of man, communing if he so pleases with nothing but nature, save perhaps, if he also

pleases, for the distant and enchanting prospect of the old medieval town. There is the sheer pleasure of being "out", of being alone with your thoughts, or in good company, walking, thinking, dreaming, breathing, being part of the world, being alive.

This is not to claim that all golf courses are things of surpassing beauty. Some have been laid out within sight of looming prison walls, or coal bins, some in dense suburbia. Yet all of them represent an oasis of escape, the fantasy of being somehow back in an earlier time, for the urban and even suburban man. With almost all the cities of the world growing larger, the demand to escape from them, the quest for "leisure", grows larger. The golf course, and the game, have their place in this. And if it be a generalization, it would surly be true even if golf courses were built in Hyde Park, Central Park, the Bois de Boulogne. The golf course and the game provide this unique change of environment and nothing illustrates this more dramatically than the drive from the island of Manhattan to the Baltusrol Golf Club in New Jersey. Along the Hudson River shore, the Jersey shore, the roadway sweeps above a wasteland of docks, chemical plants and oil storage tanks, culminating in the forbidding industrial city of Newark – hardly "America the Beautiful". But a few miles beyond Newark, and quite suddenly, one is in lovely, rolling, wooded country, ripe and mature, and eventually the expansive, comfortable clubhouse at Baltusrol and an environment which, so divorced from the vast city and its detritus, inflicts upon the golfer, however fleetingly, a change of personality. The comparison in the UK would be the train journey from Liverpool to Southport, bursting out of the city and passing a necklet of lovely links courses such as West Lancs, Formby, Southport and Ainsdale, Hillside and Royal Birkdale, or the Glasgow experience by train down the west coast and the magical names of Barassie, Troon, Prestwick and Ayr.

In another sense, personality persists. The people, the types, the golfers themselves are a source of the joy of the game. There are the quick ones,

**Royal Melbourne, one of the world's finest courses.**

the impatient ones, usually late at the start, never time for a practice swing. There are the laid-back types, taking their time, probably pipe smokers – young bulls, old bulls. There is the other fellow who cannot quite shrug off his business instinct, who is always looking for the extra percentage point, the win-at-any-cost merchant. You feel that he might just cheat coming down the 18th hole, with a five needed to win the Captain's Prize, and his ball in the rough. Terrible thought, but you feel he might just improve the lie in there when no one is looking. There are no secrets on the golf course, no place to hide, and the physical movements of golfers reveal their personalities. There is the hungry lope of a Ballesteros, as though he cannot wait to get to the next shot. There is the magisterial progression of a Bobby Locke. There is a Lee Trevino, the compulsive talker, chattering to any unfortunate within earshot; the guardsman's stride of a Weiskopf; the brisk, business-like advance of a Nicklaus; and there is a Sean Connery, padding along with the silent intensity of a leopard.

The appurtenances of the game are a delight. Was there ever such a thing of beauty as the new, unused golf ball, impeccably uniform, immaculately moulded, pristinely painted – ever such a tingling sense of anticipation or perhaps of terror to come, as we unwrap it, in the old days from its individual paper, now from the colourful tube or carton with two of its neighbours? Was ever any artefact so precisely turned as a teepeg? For that matter, has mankind ever fashioned a more seductive surface than the cellulose which contains the head of a new wooden club, standing patiently to attention along the wall of the professional's shop? That same professional's shop is an Aladdin's cave for the golfer, and browsing there is another of the game's more sensuous pleasures – the handling of clubs, the freshness of leather grips, the newness of unbought shoes that will never again know such polish, the inconsequential conversations. The game affords endless if often perverse sensuous pleasures – the final act of lacing the golf shoes in the locker room before going out to face the unknown; the delicious drag of weary legs over the final holes; the damp patch

at the base of the spine on hot summer days; the sudden spring in the step from green to tee after a challenging putt went in, and the battling against the storms, smothered in sweaters, hats, waterproof uniforms, wrestling with umbrellas, wondering why you are there.

The Open Championship of 1987 was played at Muirfield in appalling weather. An intense low pressure system, stabilised just east of the Firth of Forth, deluged the course with walls of rain, driven along by piercing, icy winds. The men of the media, as they had to, made much of it. One American television commentator, with the crispness of his native humour, said, "If this place was an airport, it would be closed." Yet, within days, the columns of Scotland's august *Glasgow Herald* were ringing with damnation of the reporters' attitudes and reactions to the weather. One *Herald* reader claimed that "golf is frequently a game against the elements, and as Muirfield illustrated over four days of golf, no two games are the same. That is the golfing challenge. A seven iron at a particular hole one day may change to a four wood the next. Commentators apologised for it . . . they should have revelled in the typical local conditions. Local golfers loved it . . . as usual, there was only one winner – the Scottish style of golf." It has been said that the Scots, who have always enjoyed inexpensive, and usually undercapitalised, golf, take a hair-shirt approach to the game. Certainly there are pleasures and beauty to be found in putting across an early morning, unswept, dew-drenched green. But the ultimate pleasure of the game, the final essential joy, the ecstasy, lies in the flight of the perfectly struck ball.

The game is difficult. It is the one game in which the player seeks to score the fewest number of points (i.e. strokes). It demands an unnatural physical action. Ben Hogan has said, "There is no such thing as a natural golfer." The game is so difficult, it is so difficult to play well, it is so unconquerable, that striking the ball perfectly and seeing the evidence – the perfect flight of the golf ball – is the ultimate pleasure of this most beautiful game. And it is a pleasure shared, when it happens, by every golfer, regardless of his levels of skill.

The skyscrapers of Singapore; a sharp contrast with the lush fairways of the golf course.

# IN THE BEGINNING

The history of golf as a formalised game such as might be vaguely recognisable today goes back some 200 years. The history of golf as a matter of identifiable record goes back some 400 years. But its ultimate origin, that of a man hitting a stone with a stick, takes us back through all the ages, through the Middle Ages, the Dark Ages to the Romans, perhaps even to the ancient Chinese and Egyptians, may be even to Prehistoric Man.

The simple act of hitting a stone (later a ball) with a stick (later one designed for the purpose) can be accepted as the basis of golf, hurling, shinty, hockey, ice-hockey, perhaps even cricket and baseball. Running, jumping, throwing, striking and kicking are the age-old habits of man. It is known that the Romans had a popular game known as paganica (from *paganicus* meaning a "countryman"). It was played with a ball of leather stuffed with feathers (no doubt the original of golf's "feathery" of later centuries) with a bent stick for a club. Roman soldiers being essentially country boys – Rome was never an industrial empire – we can consider it a country, even cross-country, pastime. And the Romans being Romans, the game would be ordered to some degree, but there is no evidence that it was a contested team game, or played in any enclosure or to a specific target. The Roman Empire in Britain extended to Antonine's Wall across Central Scotland from Forth to Clyde. No doubt the legions made occasional sorties north of that line, by land and sea. They might well have taken paganica clubs and balls to St Andrews and Carnoustie, even if there is no evidence that early caddies were early Christians.

There is recorded evidence that, in the reign of Edward III, a game known as "cambuca", played with a ball and a curved club, rather similar to

paganica not only existed but was proscribed in company with football, handball, cockfighting and other leisurely evils by an edict of 1363 "to the King's Sheriffs". Edward III, poor man, like so many other English kings, found the Scots an irksome lot. If his reign is recalled for victories over the French at Crecy and Poitiers, not to mention the Black Death, it was punctuated by battles and border raids, kidnappings and ransoms with the northern hordes, then, as later, allied with the French.

When one of Scotland's more feckless kings, David II died in 1371, without an heir, the Scottish succession went to his sister's son, Robert Stewart, who ascended as King Robert II. Robert II was the first Stewart king, the first of 14 Stewarts who over three centuries occupied the throne of Scotland, the final six of them monarchs of both England and Scotland. The Stewarts were to become significant in the history of golf.

These were savage times. Scotland was less than a united kingdom. The Highlands and the Highland clans were to remain for many years beyond the control of any central government. In the Lowlands and Borders, land-owning nobles sought to control the Royal succession by any means. Of the early Stewart kings, James I was murdered in Perth in 1437; James II was killed at the siege of Roxburgh Castle against the occupying English in 1460; James III was murdered near Bannockburn in 1488; and James IV, in many ways the greatest of the Stewart kings, was killed at the battle of Flodden in 1513, after 25 years on the throne. It was Scotland v. England with a vengeance. A Spanish ambassador of the time was moved to report "The Scots . . . spend all their time in wars, and when there is no war, they fight one another." The Scottish habit lingers.

This then was the background to the earliest reference extant which uses the word "golf", the edict of the 14th Parliament of James II in Edinburgh,

**Eighteenth century golfers at Blackheath.**

the 6th of March in the year 1457. It was an edict in favour of archery practice, and contained the now famous and much-quoted "And that Fute Ball and Golfe be utterly cryed downe, and not to be used." James II, like his successors, needed all the trained archers he could find. A similar edict in the reign of James III in 1471, and another by James IV in 1491, both specify the banning of football and golf and other "unprofitable" sports, both for the common good and for the defence of the realm. "Fute Ball" seems to have had a hard time – as early as 1424, the first year of the reign of James I, a royal act declared "Item: it is statut and the King forbiddis that no man play at the fut ball under the payne of iiijd."

These proscriptions show that golf was sufficiently established as to provoke royal concern. The game, such as it was in those days, was played on any suitable piece of ground, and what could be more suitable than the *machair* – a stretch of low-lying land adjacent to the sand of the seashore? And what better *machairs* could be found than those at Dornoch, Aberdeen, Montrose, St Andrews, Leith and Musselburgh? The *machair*, or links as it became known, was the open ground between arable land and the seashore, a sundry expanse of bent grass, heather and whins, suitable for not much more than drying clothes, mending fishing nets or whatever recreation was to be found – in our case, hitting a ball with a stick. No doubt such ploys had some appeal to the students of St Andrews University, founded in 1411.

At the end of the 15th century, during a period of relative peace with the English, the royal restrictions on golf were quietly ignored. The new century was to be one of Martin Luther and the Reformation; of Cardinal Beaton, Archbishop of St Andrews, George Wishart and John Knox; Henry VIII and Queen Elizabeth I; of Mary Queen of Scots and the continuing romance of the Scots with the French – against England of course, and finally of the crown of Scotland united with that of England. When James VI went lumbering down to London to become James I of a United Kingdom, it is said that there was a bag of golf clubs in the back of his coach.

With that, golf came to England. The court of James I was at Greenwich, and he exercised at "the gowff" on the adjoining Black Heath, and incidentally embargoed the importation of balls from the Low Countries and gave the monopoly of "home made" balls to one James Melvill. And, in 1603, William Mayne, a bowmaker of Edinburgh, was appointed the first clubmaker royal. Thus if those three early 15th-century Stewarts were "bad" kings, their half-dozen successors were "good" kings – there is acceptable evidence through the 16th century of kings buying clubs and balls, paying golfing debts, appointing ball and clubmakers and indeed playing the game. James V played at Gosforth, East Lothian, and Mary Queen of Scots played at St Andrews certainly, and at Seton all too soon after the murder of Darnley, her husband.

The Stewart kings, or at least those who had come to acknowledge if not to practice golf, and indeed the Catholic Church, were not about to persecute Sunday golfers. But the dour hand of the Reformation touched the game. In 1592 and 1593, the Town Council of Edinburgh forbade Sunday golf and indeed proscribed citizens for "playing of the Gowff on the Links of Leith every Sabbath the time of the sermonses". There were "seats of repentance", often occupied, in "Kirks" at Perth and St Andrews for example. And Scottish Kirk Session records of 1621 (when James VI and I was squabbling with the Scottish clergy) and of 1651 (the year in which Cromwell won the Civil War) report that golfers were ordained to make repentance for the playing of golf on Sundays.

Whatever other claim to immortality he may have, James I of the new United Kingdom clearly inflicted the old Scottish game on the unsuspecting English. The Royal Blackheath Club is generally dated from 1608; Charles I played at Leith and Newcastle; Charles II played at Scone; James II at Leith, Edinburgh's great common in these times. James II, the last of the male Stewart kings, was clearly canny in one of the minor arts of the game: choosing a partner. As Duke of York and Lord High Commissioner at Holyrood, he was challenged by two English courtiers to a match against himself and anyone of his choice. The Duke wisely decided that to be one John Paterstone, who happened to be the local champion. The Duke and Paterstone won handily, and when the Duke gave his partner a sizeable slice of the stake, Paterstone built himself a handsome house in Edinburgh's Canongate (no. 77). Subsequent champions – Bobby Locke, Arnold Palmer and others – were to see the advantages of investing in property. The property became known as Golfers' Land, and, to this day, on a modern building, the ground floor of which is taken up by a pub called "Jenny Ha's Tavern and Ale House (1749)", a bronze plaque records the affair: "On this site stood the tenement known as Golfers' Land. It was built in the 17th century by Baillie Paterstone with, it is

An early and Dutch form of golf, as represented by Aert Van der Neer, a 17th century Dutch painter.

said, his share of the stakes from a golf match when he partnered the Duke of York (after James VI) against two English Noblemen. The bronze coat of arms is a copy of a stone carving, built into Golfers' Land . . ." Paterstone, a cobbler by trade, was also granted a coat of arms which carried the ultimate golfing motto, "Far and Sure".

James I's embargo on the importation of balls from Holland adds a dimension to the saga – the continental connection. Stick and ball games of various kinds were played in various countries. Some were played to a hole in the ground, some cross-country to a mark such as a gate, a post or a door. Some were played on a court, with boundary fences, and these games had become widespread through the Low Countries and France. Holland's great commercial, maritime, empire reached its peak in the 17th century, and there was substantial trade with Scotland, including the embargoed feathery ball, made of a stitched cowhide cover which was stuffed with goose feathers. This operation took skill, strength, special tools, and a good ballmaker would do well to produce three in one day – a labour-intensive operation. Accordingly the balls were expensive, costing more than a golf club itself, and James I, not the last leader to have

such a problem, no doubt had concern over the cost of imports.

The 17th century was to be yet another of endless strife involving wars and rebellions, kings, Church, parliaments, the first and only English Republic under Oliver Cromwell, the last of the Stewart kings, the arrival of William of Orange, and, at the end of it all, the abject "sale" of Scotland to the English when the two parliaments were united in 1707.

Despite all this there is substantial evidence that golf prospered and was widely played in Scotland, and increasingly in England, by kings, courtiers and commoners. Paradoxically, its not-quite-similar counterpart in the Low Countries, *Het Kolven*, declined, perhaps with the decline of the Dutch Empire. With the long tradition of trade between Scotland and the Low Countries, it has been claimed that golf is of Dutch origin, and was exported from there to Scotland (the word *kolbe* is a Teutonic name for club). The probable truth is that two vaguely similar games existed at the same time, and that both had some knowledge of the other. In the first half of the century, Dutch master-painters produced many landscapes showing "golfers", in one

29

instance depicting two players wearing kilts. What is perhaps the most intriguing single item to emerge from the story of the game in this century is the suggestion that golf was played at Fort George (now Albany) in New York State in 1659. Since the Scots have never been disinclined to travel, you can be sure they were trading with and in the North American colonies from the beginning. History was to show that this was an ominous suggestion.

St Andrews was already being considered the metropolis of golf, although the game there was a rough and ready affair, played along what were little more than paths between heather and whin, which the volume of play widened into what we would now think of as fairways.

Edinburgh would no doubt have challenged St Andrews' title. In 1687, one Thomas Kincaid, an Edinburgh golfer and a young buck of the town, felt moved to write what was in effect the first golf instruction manual, the first of a torrent that has flowed to this day, and much of it relevant to this day:

"The ball must be straight before your breast, a little towards the left foot.

". . . and ye must bring back the club by turning yourself about by the right hand, and that as it were upon a centre without moving your body out of the place of it.

"Your arms must move very little; all the motion must be performed with the turning of the body about."

The game remained without much organisation. There were no golf clubs, no clubhouses. It was a catch-up game of individual matches – no medal play, no formalised handicapping system, with the rules made simply by the two or four players before they started. The clubhouse would be the local inn. There were no professionals. There were caddies, often boys, and local artisans who were good players prepared to play with amateurs for a fee which, as often as not, was spent on whisky in the evening. But into the 18th century, things began to change.

In the early part of the 18th century, St Andrews, sustained as it had been for three centuries by its University and the habits of its students, thrived; Edinburgh, abandoned by the Scottish Parliament and now governed like the rest of Scotland from Westminster, withered somewhat. Golf in general

had a dull spell after the Reformation but persisted and flourished for several disparate reasons. There was the beginning of the formation of golf clubs and societies; there was the beginning of the Industrial Revolution; and there was the remarkable Enlightenment in Scotland in the last decades of the century.

Recent research by Donald Stirk, author and golf historian, has indicated that Freemasons were greatly responsible for the formation of the earliest clubs and their organisations and records, and – as a secret society – for the destruction of records if the club be wound up, as some were, for whatever reason. Stirk offers examples:

"The foundation stone of the Company of Gentleman Golfers, later to become the Honourable Company of Edinburgh Golfers, was laid by William St Clair of Roslin, who was Hereditary Grand Master Mason of Scotland. All the committee members save two were Masons and records of the ceremony gave their Masonic ranks.

"The Knuckle Club, a club within the Blackheath Club, drank Masonic toasts, new members went through initiation ceremonies, and membership applications were threatened by the 'black ball' system.

"The captain of the Royal Burgess Golfing Society of Edinburgh could elect three new members each year 'on the shake of a hand', another Masonic ritual."

These early clubs were initially wining and dining clubs in the main, and vast amounts of claret were consumed at their matches and gatherings. Scotland even then had a long-established trade with Bordeaux, happily still continuing, and these dining clubs have left us the legacy of the golf club dinner. Other traditions established were the "Bets Book" and the uniform, the golfer's red coat, maintained in blazers and club crests.

In 1744, the year before Prince Charles Edward Stewart landed in Eriskay in the search for a crown that was to lead him to Culloden and a Roman exile, the Company of Gentleman Golfers, later the Honourable Company as we have seen, was founded at Leith. The Royal Burgess Golfing Society of Edinburgh (1735) disputes to this day the title of the oldest golf club, but, unlike the Honourable Company, does not have the paper to sustain the claim. The founders of these clubs were all prominent men, pillars of the community if not of the Kirk: Duncan Forbes of Culloden, who attained the highest Scottish law offices as Lord Advocate, then President of the Court of Session, was the first president of the Honourable Company. As men of substance, their dining tables bore the best of the silver, crystal and plate. Society golf in this period was for the privileged and influential, and it is reasonable that their old boy network was founded on Freemasonry.

The Honourable Company wrote the first rules of golf, the famous 13 Articles, and when ten years later the Society of St Andrews Golfers, later to become the Royal and Ancient Golf Club of St Andrews, was formed, they adopted these 13 articles almost in entirety. Honourable Company members no doubt had a part in creating the new club at St Andrews – even then many of them had taken to sailing across the Forth to escape from their crowded Leith links and enjoy the altogether better golf in Fife. The Edinburgh men in fact were later forced to move from Leith to Musselburgh, and at the end of the 19th century to their present home at Muirfield.

No doubt, most of these golfers were brother Masons. Indeed, the Masons, in the very nature of their organisation, may have made a major contribution to the spread of the game beyond Britain. Stirk records that in 1743 an order of 96 golf clubs and 432 balls was shipped from the port of Leith to one David Deas, a Leith man, in Charleston, South Carolina. Deas, can you believe, was the first Provincial Grand Master Mason in the United States! Other shipments of balls and clubs went from Glasgow to Virginia in 1750 and 1751, and to Maryland in 1765.

The second half of the 18th century saw Scotland begin to move from being an agricultural to an industrial society. The population of Glasgow, for example, was 17,000 in 1740, 42,000 in 1780 and, by the end of the century, 84,000. Glasgow, before becoming an industrial giant – reaching its peak at the end of Victoria's reign – was a merchant city, vast fortunes being built from the tobacco trade, then cotton, sugar and rum, with the American colonies and the West Indies. The Glasgow merchants had a thriving re-export business with the Continent, and paid for their American tobacco with finished goods (there was already coal-mining and iron manufacture), and turned many a pretty bawbee, building themselves handsome mansions along the downstream shores of the river Clyde.

As Glasgow flourished, Edinburgh revived, and the country strode into one of the most remarkable periods in the history of this small, perplexing but remarkable nation – The Enlightenment. The Enlightenment was more than a Camelot, more than one brief, bright, shining moment – it was an astonishing intellectual explosion that was to make Edinburgh the "Athens of the North". A great outburst of artistic energy seemed to say that the people, the capital, the nation, had had enough of self-pity. The Union of the Parliaments in 1707 had meant "lost king, lost parliament, lost government". All of that had moved to London. So be it. There were empires to build, worlds to conquer, and the Scots still had an abundance to contribute in so many directions.

The Scottish Enlightenment, a cumbrous title, was, more than most intellectual movements, practical. It wanted to know how and why things were, how things worked, how and why they would or could change. In the not-too-distant past, Scotland had been a land of barbarians. Now, in terms of the enquiring mind, it led Europe. The Enlightenment in fact may now be seen as the overture to great Scottish achievements in engineering, science and medicine in the 19th century.

There was David Hume (1711–76), philosopher and historian, whose *Treatise of Human Nature* is still alive and well. There was Adam Smith (1723–90), philosopher and economist, whose *Wealth of Nations* remains a unique work. In painting (an Academy of Fine Arts opened in Glasgow in 1753) there was Allan Ramsey (1713–84) and Henry Raeburn (1756–1824), portraitists with international reputations. In architecture, there was Robert Adam (1728–92), whose work is still to be seen throughout Britain and along the eastern seaboard of the United States. In literature, James Macpherson's *Ossian* signalled a Celtic revival, and there was the blinding genius of Robert Burns (1759–96), leading on to Walter Scott (1771–1832) and Thomas Carlyle (1795–1881). There were the great African explorers and missionaries Mungo Park (1771–1806) and David Livingstone (1813–73).

Of course, it would be simplistic to suppose that golf was part of all this, but golf lived in these times, and towards the end of the century there was a significant spurt in the establishment of golf clubs: in 1761, Bruntsfield Links in Edinburgh; in 1774, Royal Musselburgh; in 1780, Royal Aberdeen; in 1786, the Crail Golfing Society; in 1794, Dunbar. The Glasgow Club, one of the earliest non-links clubs (they played originally on Glasgow Green, the Hyde Park of the city) was formed in 1787. In 1797 came the Burntisland Club, and into the new century there were Royal Albert at Montrose in 1810, Old Manchester, one of the earliest English clubs and established by expatriate Scots came in 1818, and in 1820, the Leven Golfing Society.

Things were stirring elsewhere. Extensive researches by the distinguished American writers Herbert Warren Wind and Charles Price have established the existence of a South Carolina Golf Club in Charleston in 1786, and a Savannah Golf Club some time before 1796. There are records of a Charleston merchant, Andrew Johnston, a Scot, returning from a trip to Glasgow in 1759 with a "quantity of goods" later discovered to have included golf clubs.

An even more remarkable story in the saga of America's golfing evolution is that revealed by Richard Funkhouser, American Consul-General in Scotland in the late 1970s. It concerns Thomas Jefferson, the golfer.

Jefferson (1743–1826) was third President of the United States and the author of the Declaration of Independence, as noble a passage as the English language has to show. It appears that one William Small of Marischal College in Aberdeen was Jefferson's teacher, tutor and mentor at William and Mary College in Virginia, around 1760. Small was a Professor of Nature and Philosophy, and a teacher of ethics, *belles-lettres* and the sciences, yet another Scottish 'lad o' pairts'. As we have seen, this was at a time when the earliest golf clubs were being formed in Scotland, and almost co-incidentally during the Age of the Scottish Enlightenment, and Jefferson's library reflected the intellectual ferment in Scotland. In fact, for Virginian colonists in the matter of mail, news, books and ideas, Glasgow was closer to the colonies than the English ports, often by several days' voyage.

It appears that Dr William Small was a top-flight golfer, and he introduced his young student to the delights of the game on a five-holes course which he laid out along the estuary of the James river. It also served for nature study and field surveying and the like. Jefferson was clearly a strong, healthy youth, a lover of nature and the outdoors, a fine horseman, dancer and fiddle player, if in the beginning none too adept as a golfer. But he improved – the handicapping system whereby Small gave him a stroke at each hole, then in time a stroke each round, or every five holes, intrigued him. Jefferson was a republican, a lawyer and a country squire – he inherited 1900 acres of good Virginia land from his father, but he had no delusions that all men were equal. Small was quoted in later years, referring to his pupil, "He could'na equal Wullie Shakespeare,

Mike Angelo and Moe Zarto."

Funkhouser, from studies in the records of Marischal College and the Universities of William and Mary and Princeton, which each have extensive Jefferson archives, has established (a) that Small and Jefferson played golf virtually every day, and (b) that Jefferson – and this is astonishing – was so impressed with Small's handicapping system that in the original draft to the preamble to the Declaration of Independence he wrote "We hold these truths to be self-evident, that all men are created equal by handicapping". As Jefferson was to complain subsequently, this draft was checked by the inevitable committee and he was forced to delete and alter the text; "by handicapping" was smudged out of the original. Even more startling, Jefferson had written ". . . and are endowed by their Creator with certain inalienable rights, including life, liberty and the pursuit of gouf". *Gouf?* Funkhouser insists that any legible copy of the Declaration will show the word "happiness" written over "gouf". It seems that not all Jefferson's colleagues held the game in such esteem. But it remains a remarkable story, and the presence of Small simply underlines the fact that the Scots were to be found almost everywhere in the known world, and the Freemason connection surely applied – by 1830 there was golf in Calcutta, and by 1842 Bombay and New South Wales had golf clubs.

Golf of one sort or the other may have reached France even earlier, at Bordeaux. On the 30th of June, 1767, the sum of one pound eleven shillings was entered in the accounts of a businessman working in that city, described as being for "the cost of golf balls and clubs". Our man may well have been a Scot, since there was a healthy trade in claret and other things between Bordeaux and Edinburgh's port of Leith. There is early evidence of golf at Pau, in the Basses-Pyrénées, close to the Spanish border, in 1814. Scottish regiments involved in the Peninsular War had been stationed there, and Scottish officers laid out a few holes in that year, on the Plaine de Billère close by the town. Pau became a fashionable resort and a proper golf club was formed in 1856, with the Duke of Hamilton as a prime mover. His Grace gave a trophy, and among the other founding fathers were the Colonels Hutchinson and Anstruther, names perhaps not unknown in St Andrews. By 1869, the club had a professional, one Joe Lloyd from the Holylake area, perhaps the first British pro to venture to work abroad. By 1879, the club had 18 holes and a membership well into three figures, and claims to have the longest continuous history of any club outside Scotland – perhaps not wisely.

Golf was on the move, and the coming of the railway age helped it along. The first half of the 19th century was a virile age of railway barons and speculators as a network of lines was laid throughout the country by private companies in a positive celebration of vintage enterprise and capitalist fervour. The railways reached out to existing golf courses, trailing a string of new courses and clubs behind them. The Glasgow and Ayr line, serving a coastline that threaded together a string of golfing pearls, was opened on the 12th of August, 1840, and touched Troon and Prestwick, noble names in the golfing panoply. In fact, the effects of the spread of the railway systems on the development of the game would make an intriguing subject for any masters thesis. Here they make an interesting aside.

It was the "Glasgow, Paisley, Kilmarnock and Ayr Railway", later the Glasgow and South Western, which reached Ayr in 1840 (The Prestwick Club was formed in 1851). Edinburgh to Glasgow was completed in 1842 at a cost of £1.25 million and the tunnel into Glasgow's Queen St station was considered the greatest engineering feat that Scotland had seen. The line from Leuchars Junction to St Andrews was completed on the 1st of July, 1852, by the then St Andrews Railway Company, operated by the Edinburgh, Perth and Dundee Railway Company, which was later absorbed by the North British Railway Company, the NB. By 1850, the rails had reached North Berwick (the North Berwick Club was formed in 1832, the Tantallon Club in 1853), and in 1855 Inverness connected with Nairn along the Moray Coast, and in 1858 Elgin and Keith were added by the Inverness and Aberdeen Junction Railway. Most of these "local" railway companies in Scotland were amalgamated into two groups: the Caledonian and the North British, the Caley and the NB, which commanded Scotland. They in turn were absorbed by a further amalgamation into the London Midland and Scottish Railway and the London North Eastern Railway, after the First World War, before finally complete nationalisation came following the Second World War. At a time when the fastest coach journey was taking better than 30 hours, the Caley ran a demonstration train from Euston to Glasgow in 1848, in just nine hours 36 minutes.

By 1850, there was a regular steamer service from Glasgow to New York and much of the same was happening in North America. The Canadian Pacific Railway was completed, coast to coast, in 1855, and in 1869, on the 10th of May, at Promontory Point in

Lady Juliet Duff, Cannes, 1913, proving that golf is not just a man's game.

Utah, the American transcontinental railroad became a fact. Coming so soon after the Civil War, it was a stupendous achievement – 1775 miles of track had been laid in three years at an average of one-and-a-half miles a day, over the Rocky Mountains and the High Sierras.

As movement then became easier, so more golf became more available to more people. Yet the sin-

33

gle most important event in the entire history of the game, one which changed the face of golf irrevocably, came in 1848. If it was a year of revolution in Europe, golf had its own revolution with the coming of the "gutty".

*Gutta Percha* is the gum of the percha tree of Malaysia. With Scottish usage, that quickly became "gutty", and St Andrews, as ever, was involved in the revolution which this material brought to golf. The story goes that one Dr Robert Adams Paterson, a reverend gentleman, received a statue of the Hindu god Vishnu, in black marble, wrapped in *gutta percha*, in a package from India. The statue subsequently was to find its way to St Andrews University, but the reverend, finding the packing material malleable, moulded it into the form of a golf ball, and promptly had a Paterson's Patent. Not surprisingly, he sought to make it look like a feathery ball by marking feathery-like seams on it. In play, the ball was found to duck in flight until its cover had been roughed up by play. Indeed, it flew better towards the end of a round when it had been comprehensively hacked. The natural progression, then, was to mark the new balls in advance, which a sharp-eyed saddler in South Street, St Andrews, did with the fine end of a hammer. The gutty was impervious to rain, and, unlike the feathery, maintained its weight in play. A dip in hot water at night would remove any severe cuts on the ball. At first they were rolled by hand on a flat board. Later, moulds were used, giving balls with pimple or bramble patterns, mesh or recessed patterns. By 1850 they were in common use, although the Reverend Paterson's patent was not carried forward to the extent that the man became a millionaire. If only he had had a Mark McCormack.

A good quality feather ball at the time would have cost half a crown, (perhaps 12½p equivalent today, but with vastly greater purchasing power then), and the feathery ball makers, with the Luddite instincts of all hand craftsmen faced with a machine and any degree of mechanisation or mass production, did not like any part of all this. Gutty balls could be made for a few pennies. They were to be decried, resisted. Besides, instead of the two or three featheries a ball maker produced in one day, gutties could be pressed out by the score. The outstanding feathery ball makers of the time were Gourlay of Musselburgh and Robertson of St Andrews, the latter assisted by one Tom Morris ("Old Tom"). Allan Robertson had a healthy business as a ball maker – in 1844, for instance, he turned out almost 2500 balls. Robertson, it is said, was not above collecting gutties from the

links – he sent out small boys to the links to collect them – and burning them, stench or no stench. In an age when man-to-man matches were the norm, Robertson and Morris agreed never to play in a match in which these new balls were used. The inevitable happened when one day Old Tom tolerated a partner who used the new ball. Robertson was incensed, they parted company, and Tom Morris set up in business on his own as a ball and club maker.

The advent of the gutty represented possibly the greatest single revolution in the story of the ancient game. It flew further than the feathery, putted better, was cheaper, and was unaffected by rain. It brought changes in the design of golf clubs and the method of clubmaking; it established a round of golf, indirectly, as being of 18 holes; demanded of golfers a new swing technique; brought masses of a new and growing middle class into the game; and, in the final decades of the 19th century, a rash of newly-formed clubs so that in the 1970s and 1980s golf club centenary celebrations were commonplace. From fewer than 100 in 1875, the national tally of clubs was well past 1000 by 1900. No doubt price was the dominant factor in the influence of the gutty on the game – it came into ever-increasing use as the railway network spread and as the effects of the Industrial Revolution brought more leisure time to a greater number of people in a growing population. No cheap jet flights to Malaga in those days – holidays at home were the thing for most people. But St Andrews, Musselburgh, Montrose and Westward Ho! were holiday towns, and the Lancashire coast, increasingly served by rail, saw the coming of great courses and clubs at Formby and the Royals-to-be at Lytham and Birkdale.

The new ball changed the Old Course at St Andrews, then the only one. Before the gutty, the course had been one of nine holes, the golfers playing out to the "End" hole (using what would now be considered the "back nine"), then turning and playing back in, using the same greens and holes, with priority given to the players playing "out". So crowded and narrow did the links become with extra traffic that separate inward holes had to be used, thus establishing 18 separate holes as the standard golf course, and seeing the birth of St Andrews' famous and huge double greens. The course in those days was played left-handed, that is to say counter-clockwise. Indeed, when the first Amateur Championship at St Andrews was played in 1886,

**The hand forging of clubs, now a rare craft.**

THE BEST OF GOLF

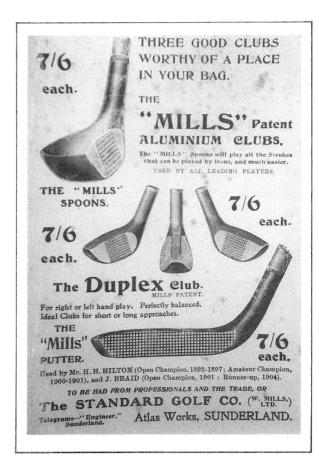

THREE GOOD CLUBS WORTHY OF A PLACE IN YOUR BAG.

7/6 each.

THE "MILLS" Patent ALUMINIUM CLUBS.

The "MILLS" Spoons will play all the Strokes that can be played by Irons, and much easier.

USED BY ALL LEADING PLAYERS.

THE "MILLS" SPOONS.

7/6 each.

7/6 each.

The Duplex Club. MILLS' PATENT.

For right or left hand play. Perfectly balanced. Ideal Clubs for short or long approaches.

THE "Mills" PUTTER.

7/6 each.

Used by Mr. H. H. HILTON (Open Champion, 1892-1897; Amateur Champion, 1900-1901), and J. BRAID (Open Champion, 1901; Runner-up, 1904).

TO BE HAD FROM PROFESSIONALS AND THE TRADE, OR

The STANDARD GOLF CO. (W. MILLS, LTD.)

Telegrams—"Engineer," Sunderland. Atlas Works, SUNDERLAND.

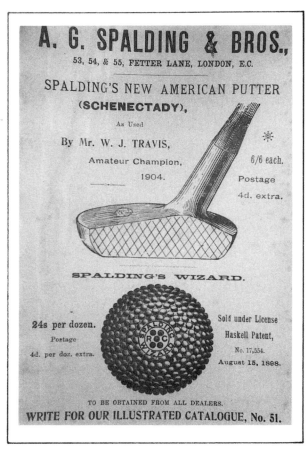

A. G. SPALDING & BROS.,

53, 54, & 55, FETTER LANE, LONDON, E.C.

SPALDING'S NEW AMERICAN PUTTER (SCHENECTADY),

As Used

By Mr. W. J. TRAVIS,

Amateur Champion, 1904.

6/6 each.

Postage 4d. extra.

SPALDING'S WIZARD.

24s per dozen.

Postage 4d. per doz. extra.

Sold under License Haskell Patent, No. 17,554.

August 15, 1898.

TO BE OBTAINED FROM ALL DEALERS.

WRITE FOR OUR ILLUSTRATED CATALOGUE, No. 51.

THE WIMBLEDON GOLF CLUB CARRIER.

Made in Drab Waterproof Cloth, Tan Waterproofed Duck, Scotch Tweed lined with Duck. Strongly made, with Leather Bottom and best Leather Fittings.

To be had from all Indiarubber Depots and Golf Club Makers.

PATENTEES AND SOLE MAKERS,

WILLIAM CURRIE & CO.,

Caledonian Rubber Works, Dalry Road, Edinburgh.

they played the course that way. The gutty was about the same size as the modern 1.68 inch ball, but rather lighter. Although it was claimed that a feathery had been driven 300 yards, 200 yards was an exceptional distance for the feathery ball, even for the best players, but the gutty could handle that comfortably. It needed a strong hit, but paradoxically was liable to fragment when hit too hard, and various substances were added to the rubber to make the ball more sympathetic. It probably demanded more of a hit than the feathery sweep, and it put serious wear and tear on the shallow clubfaces of the time as well as their inserts which were often made of leather.

Until the middle of the 19th century, almost all golf clubs were made entirely of wood, with the shafts several inches longer than present-day clubs, spliced into beautifully-shaped wooden heads, which had a rather swan-like aspect. The splices were bound by glue and whipped with twine. The heads were long, rather narrow, and the faces were shallow, often not much more than one inch deep, all of this designed to sweep away the feathery ball. Even putters, which were used from as far out as 100 yards from the green, were made of wood, as were all the "approaching" clubs.

What has to be remembered is that golf at the time was essentially a running game – there was no question of pitching the ball 50 feet in the air over a greenside bunker and having it plop and stop within a couple of yards. Why, the hole was just that, an unlined hole in the ground from which a golfer's

**Examples of early advertisements for golfing equipment, including Walter Travis' Schenectady putter.**

fist would extract the ball, making the hole a little larger, while golfers teed off for their next stroke only a couple of yards away. Crail Golfing Society claims to have been the first club, in 1874, to use metal liners in the holes. Thorn, apple and pear wood were used for heads, ash for the shafts. Great artistry in shaving and shaping shafts was developed by the clubmakers, many of whom emerged from the carpentry and cabinet-making trades, and two of the more famous in pre-gutty days were Douglas MacEwan of Leith and Musselburgh (1809–86) and Hugh Philp of St Andrews (1782–1856). Philp was also, it seems, a handy player. He became official clubmaker to the R & A, and Philp and MacEwan clubs, when they can be found, are very much collector's items at auction.

Iron heads for golf clubs evolved from the coming of the gutty and the condition of golf courses, most of them on common land scarred by cart tracks. A square, squat, lofted iron head was needed to hack the ball out of tracks and "cuppy" lies, which more often than not meant simply a hole in the ground. Thus the track iron or rut iron came along, the predecessor of the niblick, which in time became the pitching wedge of today. Forged iron heads could handle the gutty better, and the cleek (modern 2 or 3 iron) and the mashie (perhaps the 5 iron of today) led the trend, until, by the end of the century, a leading player would have but two or three wooden clubs in his bag – driver, brassie, spoon. Hickory from Tennessee was found to be both resilient and strong, and for the best part of a century was the preferred wood for shafts. In time, splicing gave way to the simple insertion of the shaft into a hole bored in the iron head, and the craftsmen's days were not over, but numbered.

# PART II

# THE CHAMPIONS

# 3rd Hole
# FATHERS AND SONS

**T**he coming of the gutty in the middle of the 19th century changed the entire social nature of the game. By a quirk of history, 1848, a year of revolutionary fervour throughout Europe, saw the publication of *The Communist Manifesto* by Karl Marx, which in time may have come to be considered to have changed even more the nature of society. In any event, golf was never to be the same again. Until this time, it had been in the main a pursuit of the leisured classes, of farmers and the landed gentry, of retired Army officers, university men and the professions. Now it was to be increasingly the age of the nearly common man and, with that, the age of the champions. In a sense, they may have been the same thing. The early champions emerged from the ranks of caddies, club and ball makers and artisans. Many of them were qualified craftsmen – weavers, carpenters, stonemasons – and in their early days they no doubt played golf simply because it was there. Yet, although they were all of common stock, they all in some strange way seemed aware of an inherent nobility in the game and, with the respect they had for golf, they sustained that nobility.

It could be said that the first "champion" must of necessity be the first Open Champion, Willie Park of Musselburgh, who won the inaugural event at Prestwick in 1860 from a field of eight players, but before then there were powerful personalities leaving their marks on the story of the game. It had been essentially a match play game, played for high stakes, and the first of the great match play champions was surely Allan Robertson (1815–58). Robertson, the St Andrews ball maker, despite being short and stocky, had an easy, graceful style, playing with long, light clubs. He was one of the first players to develop approach shots to the green with iron

clubs, as opposed to the "baffy" spoon, a lofted spoon, and boasted that he had "never been beaten". In this, he was being economical with the truth – Tom Morris certainly could beat him, and did, but Allan had an early appreciation of gamesmanship and the art of knowing when not to accept a challenge, and finding good reasons for it. Robertson lacked the power and therefore the length of many of his rivals, including Tom, and he carefully avoided the temptation of accepting any of the many challenges which Morris's backers offered him. One of these, for £100 a side, Allan simply ignored. For all that, he is described as being a charming partner, of equable temper, and very tolerant of playing partners who were a good deal less skilful than he.

Allan was spry enough to see that in Tom Morris he had a very able partner, and they played many matches against the best of their time, for the most part successfully. The great match of the time came in 1849, when the Dunns of Musselburgh, the twins Willie and Jamie, challenged Robertson and Morris for £400 a side – a huge sum then – over three courses, Musselburgh, St Andrews and North Berwick. The match would be settled, as was the custom, by courses, and not by total holes won and lost. Over their own course, the Dunns overwhelmed the St Andrews pair, 13 and 12. At St Andrews, Robertson and Morris won narrowly. North Berwick would decide. One of the greatest recoveries in golf was at hand. The Dunns – Willie was acknowledged as the longest driver of the day – were four up with eight to play. The St Andrews pairing was 20–1 against. But, despite the fact that Robertson was rather below his best, a remarkable St Andrews sequence followed – won, won, halved, won, halved, won. All square, two to play. The Dunns hooked their second to the next hole, off the course, behind a huge stone, unplayable. Robertson and Morris won on the last green.

In September, 1858, Allan Robertson became the

**Old and Young Tom Morris, c.1872. Between them, father and son won eight of the first twelve Open Championships.**

**Allan Robertson. In 1858 he became the first man to score St Andrews in less than 80 strokes.**

first man to score St Andrews in less than 80 strokes. His 79 included two threes, two sixes. It was a round that stood for 30 years until young Tom Morris scored 77, unlike Robertson in a competitive round. The next year, Allan developed jaundice; he never recovered, and died in September, 1859. Thus he was destined never to play in the Open Championship – it was inaugurated the following year. Tom Morris, his erstwhile apprentice and golfing partner, six years younger than Allan, was to outlive him by no fewer than 50 years, and in such a long life (1821–1908) he was to make a unique contribution to the game, on and off the golf course.

He was born in North Street, St Andrews, and his father, a letter carrier and later a caddie, had decided that the boy should become a carpenter, but a chance remark by old Sandy Herd led to him being apprenticed to Allan Robertson, club and ball maker. After four years as an apprentice, and five as

a journeyman, Allan and Tom parted. As we have seen, the gutty came between them. The boy Tom was playing golf, left hand below right in the beginning, before he was in his teens, and developed into a solid player who in his time could handle Allan Robertson, as well as partner him in many money matches. Occasionally Tom was misguided enough to deputise for Allan when the older man did not much care for a particular challenge.

In the last of a series against Willie Park, on Park's home course of Mùsselburgh, with the match in the balance and a few holes left to play, the home crowd had become so unruly and partisan that Morris and the referee walked off the course, retiring to Foreman's public house. Park promptly sent in a message to the effect that if Morris was not prepared to come out to finish the match, he, Park, would play out the remaining holes and claim the stakes. And he did. They were to clash again, no doubt in more relaxed mood, in the very first Open Championship.

After some three years on his own as a ball and club maker in St Andrews, Tom was approached by one Colonel Fairlie, of the newly-formed (1851) Prestwick Club and was persuaded to go west as "custodian of Prestwick Links". He was to remain there for 14 years, no doubt helping to get the 12 holes course in shape for things to come. As early as 1856, the Prestwick Club had enlisted the support of several Scottish clubs, and Royal Blackheath, for a competition played the following year, each club entering two players (amateurs) and paying an entrance fee of £4 to cover costs and prizes. It was won by Royal Blackheath, and if the R & A and the Honourable Company were perhaps not hugely enthused by it, the fact that they played over public courses may have meant that they felt they might have difficulty in controlling such events. Prestwick went ahead and in 1860 held a competition for "The Belt". Not until 1864 was there prize money, when Tom Morris won £6. In the very first event, Willie Park beat Tom by one stroke, scoring 174 over three rounds, 36 holes, in a field of eight. Park won again in 1863, but over a period of seven years in the 1860s, Tom Morris won four times. By 1865, he had returned to St Andrews to become Custodian of the Links there, to live into a new century, and to become, in his later years, a Moses figure in golf – the great white beard, the clay pipe, the watch chain, the highly polished boots, resolving all disputes, controlling the tee, holding the flagstick on that last green.

**Old Tom Morris, one of golf's earliest champions, lived through an era of major changes in the game.**

He became, in fact, an institution, a simple man of honesty, a very very fine player (at the age of 64 he scored 81 round the Old Course) and in the splendid phrase of the time, "One of Nature's Gentlemen". He was probably also the first professional golfer as we now know it. When he was engaged by Prestwick, for 15 shillings a week, he was charged with maintaining the links, making and selling balls and clubs, playing with members and teaching beginners, most of which is still done by modern club professionals.

Tom Morris was born in the year in which Napoleon died. Lord Liverpool was Prime Minister. James Monroe, of the famous *Monroe Doctrine* was the fifth President of the United States. When Morris died, Asquith was the British Prime Minister, Teddy Roosevelt the American President. In the Badminton book of *Golf*, edited by Horace Hutchinson and first published in 1890, there is a record of a conversation with Tom Morris on New Year's Day in 1886. There is no indication of how, or by whom it was recorded, but Tom says, ". . . an it had na been for gowff, I'm no sure that at this day, sir, I would be a leevin' man . . . I dinna mind [remember] that iver I had an unpleasant ward frae ony o' the many gentlemen I've played wi'. I've aye tried – as ma business was, sir – to mak masel pleesant to them; an' they've aye been awfi pleesant to me."

All told, not a bad way to be remembered, but a greater immortality rests with Tom Morris. Golf had come to terms with the gutty ball, and the railways and the closing decades of the century saw an explosion of new courses throughout these islands. Golf course architecture as we know it today – a sophisticated craft – did not exist, but courses had to be designed somehow. No doubt it was an elemental business, perhaps nothing more than laying down a marker for a tee, a bunker, a green, and clearing some whins or removing a tree, but Tom was in demand. He laid out courses in such far-flung places as Wallasey and Tain, Luffness and Helensburgh, and left us with three gems in particular, modified as they may have been over the following hundred years: Royal North Devon (1864), Macrihanish (1876), and Royal Dornoch (1877). These great courses were laid out by hand and horse power only. They remain monuments to an exceptional man.

Tom Morris lived through an era of very fine players emerging from the two great golfing centres of St Andrews and Musselburgh. There is no doubt that the affluence of the members of the R & A and the Honourable Company, which did not move to its own private course at Muirfield until 1891, sustained

them. The Park brothers, Willie and Mungo from Musselburgh, remain famous, Willie by winning the first championship at Prestwick and four times in all, while Mungo was champion in 1874. Willie had a standing challenge in *Bell's Life*, London, to play "any man in the world for £100 a side".

The Dunn twins, Willie and Jamie, also of Musselburgh, were born in the same year as Tom, 1821, and were such fine players that the wonder was neither of them ever won the championship. Willie was a magnificent driver of the ball and a graceful stylist who later spent many years at the Blackheath Club in London. Jamie Anderson of St Andrews (1842–1912), the son of "Old Daw", a St Andrews caddie and character, was to win the championship in three successive years (1877–79). He was a canny player, once claiming to have played 90 consecutive holes without having hit a bad shot (!), and was an outstanding putter. Bob Ferguson (1848–1912) was his Musselburgh counterpart and contemporary and followed him with three consecutive championships (1880–82). Ferguson, physically stronger than Anderson, might well have made it four in a row. He tied with Willie Fernie in 1883, but lost the play-off, beaten by a birdie on the very last hole when Fernie holed a huge putt. He played little competitive golf after this championship, eventually dying of typhoid, like tuberculosis and jaundice a disease of the times. There were to be many victims, and many golfers died at an early age. Allan Robertson had died at 43. Willie Anderson, like many another at the time, emigrated to the United States, won four US Open Championships, but was dead at 32. Willie Campbell of Musselburgh, one of the most feared match players of the 1880s and at one time professional at Prestwick, went to America and died at 38. David Strath, friend, confidant and opponent of Young Tom Morris, died when scarcely in his 30s and Young Tom, the blazing meteor of golf and surely one of the finest half-dozen players in the history of the game, died at the age of 24.

Young Tom Morris was clearly, by any standard, the first of golf's few supreme champions. But what to write of him, more than a century after his death and when his life is so sketchily documented? Comparisons over generations, even over decades, are treacherous chiels. It would be presumptuous to talk of "genius" in the context of any golfer, any sportsman. When you talk of genius, you talk of Shakespeare, Mozart, Rembrandt. And there is always the "cosmic insignificance of any game". But all things are relevant and relative, and we judge our heroes by their times, their contemporaries and with the hindsight of history. "Tommy" was a prodigy who went on to become a champion. Born at St Andrews in 1851, he grew up and obviously learned his golf at Prestwick, where his father was in command. No doubt he learned something of ball and club making in his father's shop there, but there is no indication that he was "apprenticed to a trade", and the playing of the game surely took up almost all of his time. Thus he was an outstanding boy golfer, and his first public appearance, so to speak, was in a match at Perth, in April, 1864. He was set against Master William Greig, a local juvenile celebrity, even if Perth was considered a Johnny-come-lately among golfing centres. Certainly Master Greig was a fine player, but young Morris prevailed in a match followed by "hundreds of deeply interested and anxious spectators". Tommy probably burst on to the national scene of the time in a big professional tournament at Carnoustie – prize money £20 – in September, 1867, with most of the leading players in the field. Over three rounds, total 30 holes, he tied with Bob Andrew of Perth, and Willie Park, on 140. He won the play-off. Bob Ferguson, Jamie Anderson, Bob Kirk, Willie Dow and his father, Old Tom, competed. In the Open Championship of this same year, he finished fourth, behind his father, in Old Tom's fourth and final win. The next few years of Tommy's life were to be meteoric.

He won the championship in three successive years, and so won The Belt outright. Indeed the Morrises, father and son, won eight of the first 12 such championships. In 1868, Tommy won with a score of 154 (36 holes), three shots better than his father. In 1869, he won with 157, 11 shots better than Bob Kirk. In 1870, he won with the remarkable score of 149, no fewer than 12 strokes better than the next man, his friend Davie Strath. Tommy of course had been weaned on the Prestwick course. He was playing on his own ground, although he now lived in St Andrews. Yet Prestwick, this early, was a leading club, with an outstanding course of the day. The par had been calculated as 49. Tommy scored his three rounds in 1870 – 47, 51, 51 – only two over par for 36 holes. In the conditions of the time, this was exceptional scoring, never beaten, never approached in the 21 years remaining before the championship moved to 72 holes. Tommy, not yet 21, won The Belt outright. It now rests in the Trophy Room of the R & A at St Andrews. The Prestwick club retains a replica, locked safely in a local bank, and in 1985, when the 125th playing of the Open Championship was scheduled, the club had the happy thought of commissioning another replica for presentation to

that year's champion. Even more happily, the winner was the scion of a later Scottish golfing family – Sandy Lyle.

The championship was a modest affair in those early years. In its first decade, it never mustered a field of 20, and it was none too popular with Prestwick members. The club's minutes book records letters from members saying that the whole thing was "frightfully inconvenient". The championship event was usually tucked in, on sufferance, during the September meeting of the club, and was rather casually recorded. Indeed, in this respect, errors have persisted to the present day. Tommy's winning totals of 1868 and 1869 are transposed still in *The Golfer's Handbook* – the *Wisden* of the game – in the R & A's *Open Championship*, published in 1981, in the *Guiness Golf Records 1987*, and in the Prestwick Club's fact book. The Belt itself seems to have the correct inscription. The truth is that Tommy won in 1868 with 154, and in 1869 with 157 (he had a hole in one during the first round of 50 at the "Station" hole, the 8th), and the definitive evidence is in the *Ayr Advertiser*, a weekly, of the 23rd of September, 1869, reporting the championship of the 16th of September.

It had been a busy and interesting week. A lady had been killed on the railway line; there had been a fatal boating accident in Ayr bay; and the Marquis of Bute let it be known that he would celebrate his birthday by undertaking to clear the total debts of Cardiff Infirmary which equalled £1200. There was a meeting of the Incorporation of Weavers of Ayr to elect a new clerk in place of Robert Robertson, solicitor of Ayr, deceased. Robertson had been clerk for 54 years, never missing a meeting, and his father before him had served 50 years in the same office! Under the heading "The Prestwick Golf Club", there is the following (*verbatim*):

The competition for the champion belt of the Prestwick Golf Club came off on the Prestwick Links on Thursday, and was witnessed by a large number of spectators. The weather was very favourable for the game, and great interest was manifested in it. The course for the belt is three rounds of the Links or 36 holes. The match is open to the members of any established golf club as well as to professionals. The trophy, the possession of which is coveted by all golfers is made of a fine red Morocco, richly ornamented, and is a fine piece of workmanship. Seven couples started for the belt on Thursday, viz – Mr G. Mitchell Innes and Doleman, D Strath and Jamie Anderson, Charley Hunter and Tom Dunn, Dr McQuaig and Tom Morris jun., Bob Kirk and Tom Morris snr, Mr C. McArthur and W. Doleman, Mr George McArthur and James S. Imrie. There was some capital play. After the first round, however, it was almost certain that Tom Morris jun., would repeat his last year's performance by carrying off the belt – he having made the first round in 50 strokes. Curiously enough the station hole was made by him in one stroke. The second round he made in 55 strokes, and the third in 52. With this total of 157 strokes he proved himself the champion for the present year. Should he win it next year and thus be the victor three years in succession, he will retain the belt. Bob Kirk was second in 168 strokes and D. Strath third in 169. On Wednesday evening, after the contest for the Eglinton Gold Medal, a foursome match was played betwixt Tom Morris jun., and Jamie Anderson, against Bob Kirk and Strath – the former couple winning by seven holes in two rounds.

The R & A "Open Championship" book has Mr S. Mure Fergusson of St Andrews in third place, but the *Ayr Advertiser* does not list him, and the Prestwick Club does not have a card for him. The reference to the Dolemans is interesting. They were a Musselburgh family of four brothers, and Willie Doleman, above in the sixth couple, was probably the best player. He played in almost all the Amateur Championships up to 1911, and in 1910, at the age of 73, he won his first round match at Hoylake. The eldest brother, John, is credited with starting golf in Nottingham, while A.H. was one of the founders of golf at Lytham and St Annes. Another brother Frank, the youngest, was a golf club maker at Bruntsfield Links in Edinburgh. No doubt he was the Doleman in that first couple in the championship of 1869.

The Prestwick Club remained anxious to extend the event and continued their correspondence with the R & A and the Honourable Company. After a lapse of one year, the three clubs agreed to share a new championship, played in rotation at Prestwick, St Andrews and Musselburgh. This they did for 20 years until the Honourable Company moved from crowded Musselburgh to Muirfield. The 1892 Championship was played on their new course there. A cup in the shape of a claret jug was the prize, and is to this day. Tommy was the first winner of the

Young Tom Morris, a golfing prodigy who had already won three successive Open Championships by the time he was 21. He died prematurely aged only 24.

new trophy in 1872 with the score of 166, 17 shots more than his 1870 total, and surprisingly high even if in poor weather. He never again threatened to win. He did win the first professional tournament played in England, at Hoylake that same year; but, although the evidence is sketchy, there is a certain belief that his health was already failing. It was said of Tom Morris jun. that no one could imagine anyone playing better than he. In the century to come, this was to be said of Harry Vardon, Bobby Jones, Joyce Wethered and Ben Hogan, but certainly over those few years in his late teens Tommy seemed to have been touched by the gods of the game. He was a powerful player, although no giant – he was said to break shafts just below the grip simply by waggling the club in his hands. He poured all his strength into the shot – well back from the ball, well behind the ball at address, a swing slightly shorter than the willowy St Andrews swing of the day, and put so much energy into the shot that he sometimes took a stride forward on the follow through. In our terms, he was surely Arnold Palmer, or Severiano Ballesteros, and, incidentally, like those two great players, he was exceptionally good in a wind.

His great friend and adversary, Davie Strath, more graceful, more elegant, could match Tommy tee to green, but on the greens the young Morris was supreme. He played the ball off his right foot, close to his toes, his left foot withdrawn and turned towards the hole – a common enough technique – and on the short putts he took exceptional care. Putting was a constant topic between Tommy and his father – "Gin the hole was aye a yaird nearer till him, ma faither wid be a fine putter," said Tommy (his "faither" always had problems with the short ones!) And his father was to reminisce "Ah could aye cope wi' Allan [Robertson] masel, but never wi' Tommy."

In September, 1875, Tommy and his father went to North Berwick to tackle Willie and Mungo Park for £25 a side. It was a return match for one played the previous year, which the Parks had won. This time the Morrises won, on the last green. At the end of the match, Tommy was handed a telegram telling him that his wife was dangerously ill. A yacht was put at his disposal and he and his father made off for the Fife shore. They arrived in St Andrews to find that Tommy's wife and newly-born child had died. He never really recovered from this, and he died on Christmas Day, 1875. The romantics would have it that the young man died of a broken heart. The more likely truth is that he died of pneumonia. He was buried in the St Andrews Cathedral graveyard. Clubs throughout the country contributed to a memorial stone, among them four from England: Westward Ho!, Blackheath, Wimbledon and Liverpool. The inscription on it reads:

> Deeply regretted by numerous friends and all golfers, he thrice in succession won the championship belt, and held it without rivalry, and yet without envy, his many amiable qualities being no less acknowledged than his golfing achievements.

When Old Tom Morris died, so many years later, a small memorial stone was put in place for him. To this day, for golfers from all over the world, the grave is a place of pilgrimage. All that we are left with otherwise is a famous photograph, by Cowie of St Andrews, showing Tommy in his best, highly-fashionable attire of winged collar, braided waistcoat and frock coat, striped trousers, watch chain, and wearing The Belt ("fine red Morocco, richly ornamented"). It is a studio portrait of a young man, rather long in the face, with curly hair well arranged, a slim and sleek moustache, and very big hands. And, oddly, wearing an air of complete and confident composure.

| CAREER HIGHLIGHTS | |
|---|---|
| | British Open |
| Willie Park Snr | 1860, 1863, 1866, 1875 |
| Willie Park Jnr | 1887, 1889 |
| Tom Morris Snr | 1861, 1862, 1864, 1867 |
| Tom Morris Jnr | 1868, 1869, 1870, 1872 |

## 4th Hole
# THE GREAT TRIUMVIRATE

The year of 1870, which saw Young Tom Morris at the very summit of his achievement, was to be a seminal year in golf, as in the wider world It was the year of the Franco-Prussian war, of Bismarck's solemn question and answer "What is the decisive fact in the modern world – the fact that North America speaks English". William Ewart Gladstone was Prime Minister of Great Britain, Ulysses Simpson Grant was President of the United States. Cecil John Rhodes, at the age of 17, made the first of his fateful journeys to South Africa. Charles Dickens died. Robert E. Lee died. Lenin was born, and so too was Harry Lauder.

On the 6th of February, 1870, **James Braid** was born, in Elie, Fife. On the 15th of March, 1870, **Harry Vardon** was born in Jersey, Channel Isles. On the 19th of March, 1871, **John Henry Taylor** was born in Northam, North Devon. These three men became a troika which was to dominate the game for the two decades from the middle 1890s until the outbreak of the First World War. All three came to maturity at the height of imperial Britain, and were to make a *belle epoque* in the story of golf. They were given the grandiloquent title "The Great Triumvirate", largely because in the 21 years from 1894, when J.H. Taylor first won, until 1914, only five other men were Open Champions. All in their differing ways were exceptional men. Braid, for example, in the first decade of the new century won the championship five times (the first man to do so) and was second three times. Perhaps the one thing they had in common was a modest, hard-working background.

The place of **Harry Vardon** in the Pantheon of the game is secure, inviolate. His record of six victories in the Open Championship has been approached by Braid, Taylor, Thomson and Watson, all of whom won five times, but never equalled, never surpassed

**Taylor, Braid and Vardon in a painting by Clement Fowler.**

Vardon's achievement. It may never be. He also won the US Open Championship and an abundance of ill-recorded events and in particular challenge matches, still the fashion of his times. But the immortality of Harry Vardon rests not only with his record as a player of the game. He was the first "modern" professional, one to whom we can still relate comfortably. He was the first truly international champion. He changed completely the world's thinking on how the golf club should be swung, on how the golf ball should be struck, and he was responsible in large part for the first major explosion of golf interest in the United States which led that country to become dominant in the game at all levels.

It is now more than 50 years since Vardon died, yet the standards he set, and his influence on golf, persist. No one before Vardon had applied such sheer intellect to the swinging of the golf club, the playing of the game, the handling of the tactical challenges which the golf course poses. From the punchy orthodoxy of the time, he made golf a game of grace and rhythm and beauty.

The bald facts of his life, as with so many others, do little to illuminate the source of the near-genius with which he was touched, for surely he is one of the three or four greatest players in the history of golf. He was born in the village of Grouville on the island of Jersey. He was the fourth of six sons in a family of eight. His father was a gardener and the boy Harry might well have been destined for such a life but for the incidence of golf. When he was seven years old, some English visitors to the island arranged to have a few holes laid out near his home on a piece of common land. Here was the beginning of the Royal Jersey Golf Club. Inevitably, local boys took to caddying, and local boys, again inevitably, began to play the game after their fashion, copying their elders, using sticks shaped from branches as clubs and marbles or taws of suitable pebbles from Jersey's beaches for balls, until they could "find" lost gutties or castoff clubs. The young Vardon was one of such a band. When Harry was 12, he went to work on a nearby dairy farm; two years later he was in the service of a local doctor. Then, as an under-gardener, he was taken on to the staff of a Major Spofford of Beauview, who encouraged his golf and no doubt from time to time supplied unwanted clubs and balls. Of the Vardon boys – George, Philip, Edward, Harry, Tom and Fred – Tom was two years younger than Harry, and clearly a more pushy, outgoing type than his elder brother. At any rate, he was first to break out of an insular world and venture across the water to find himself a job as an assistant professional at St Anne's in Lancashire. Tom Vardon was considered the better golfer. Indeed Vardon later described himself as not much better than 8-handicap at the time, but when Tom reported that there was money to be made at the game in England, and that he was making his share of it, Harry promptly became a professional. He was 20 years old, and in truth had played very little golf. Brother Tom helped Harry to a post as professional and greenkeeper (at that time they amounted to much the same thing) at Studley Royal, long since gone. He moved on to Bury, then to Ganton, that lovely course just inland from Scarborough.

In 1893, he felt ready for a stab at the Open Championship, and played pretty well at Prestwick. It was won by Willie Auchterlonie of St Andrews. In 1894, he finished fifth behind J.H. Taylor in the first championship played in England (Sandwich) and indeed the first won by an English professional. An English amateur, the renowned Harold Hilton, had won at Muirfield in 1892. In 1895, at St Andrews, where Vardon was never very successful, he finished ninth, again behind J.H. Taylor. Taylor was king of the walk, going for a third successive win when the 1896 championship came to Muirfield. Yet he had no illusions about Vardon – earlier that year he had gone up to Ganton for a match with Vardon, and was cuffed 8 and 6, conceding that Vardon was a very fine player. J.H. could be peppery. When a few years later he was beaten 13 and 12 by Vardon in a match at Newcastle, County Down, he said tartly, "I played my game, sir, I played my game." Vardon made a poor start to this Muirfield championship. His opening 83, against the leading and quite exceptional 72 from Sandy Herd, left him plenty to ponder. But Herd collapsed with a second round 84, and at the halfway mark it was Taylor 155, Herd 156, Vardon 161. Herd collapsed even further with a third round 79 and was clearly out of it. Taylor had 81 against Vardon's 78. He was catching up. Taylor

had finished when Vardon came to the very last hole, needing four to win, five to tie John Henry Taylor, reigning champion. The 18th hole at Muirfield, then as now, was a stiff par-4 to a raised green, protected by cross bunkers. Vardon hit out a useful drive, in the fairway, but was left with a second shot of better than 200 yards if it was to carry past the bunkers and reach the green.

Our man, then, was faced with the timeless challenge of the game, the challenge that has faced every golfer, however modest, at least once in every round of golf ever played – the challenge of the critical decision. If Vardon's second shot was snared, as well it might be by those gulping bunkers, he would be hard pressed to score six on the hole. Not good enough. He played short of the hazards, pitched on to the green, took two putts and tied with the Open Champion. Over the 36 holes play-off, he won with strokes to spare. Harry Vardon had arrived.

After a hiatus in 1897, when the championship was won by a remarkable Hoylake amateur, Harold Hilton – who won two Opens, four Amateur Championships, and a US Amateur Championship by the age of 40 – it was Vardon again in 1898 and 1899.

In 1900, at a time when golf was beginning to take a grip in the great republic – the United States Golf Association had been formed in 1893 – Vardon undertook the first of three extensive tours there. He played dozens of exhibition matches and challenges, for months on end, from New England to Florida, rattling up and down the eastern seaboard, in trains of course. He gave demonstrations in department stores, and at Wheaton, Chicago (Chicago was considered "the West" in those days) he won the US Open Championship by no less than nine clear strokes. Vast galleries by the standards of the time followed him and marvelled at his skill and accuracy. Yet many friends of Vardon came to believe that this gruelling caravanserai took a heavy toll of his health. In the first decade of the new century, he won the Open at Prestwick, but came close to being unable to finish the championship because of ill health. In the same year he moved to the South Herts Club at Totteridge in North London, where he was to remain until his death in 1937, but several times in his 30s he required hospital treatment for the tuberculosis which plagued him to the end. Indeed, whilst playing a 72 holes challenge match with Taylor against the Scots Braid and Herd in 1905, scheduled over two Scottish, two English, courses, for the sum of £400, Vardon on the eve of the last match at Deal

**Harry Vardon, in 1905.**

was extremely ill. He insisted on playing. He and Taylor won, 13 and 12, yet those early years of the 20th century were to become the decade of Braid, who won five championships in the ten years. Vardon was to win again in 1911 and finally in 1914 – six times Open Champion. Taylor won in 1900 at St Andrews, in 1909 at Deal and in 1913 at Hoylake.

**John Henry Taylor**, the youngest of the three by a few months (born 19th of March 1871) was born in the village of Northam, near Bideford, in Devon. His father died when he was four years old, a fact that surely helped fashion the character of the man-to-be. He had a rudimentary education at Northam village school, which he left when he was 11, and worked at many things, among others as a mason's labourer and of course as a caddie on the neighbouring links of the North Devon club. He became a capable player at the Northam working men's golf club, perhaps the first artisan club, and was given a job on the greenkeeping staff, which made him a professional. At the age of 21 he went to the Burnham club as professional and greenkeeper to help contain the rabbits and the sandblow on that Atlantic coast, and by 1883 he was ready for the Open Championship.

Taylor went up to Prestwick and opened with a record score of 75, which gave him a three stroke lead, but a rainstorm swept him away to a second round 89, and another young man, Willie Auchterlonie of St Andrews, won with the rather high score of 322. Taylor was a quick learner – he came back the next year with an even higher score over Sandwich, the first English championship course, and a new, raw, rough tract of a golf course. Thus Taylor was the first non-Scottish Open Champion. He won again in 1895 at St Andrews, a favoured place, despite a crippling opening round of 86, but shrugged off another rainstorm during the last round to win by four strokes. A brilliant career was surely launched. He was to finish with five Opens, the French and German Open Championships, and a brace of national match play titles.

Given the miserable start to life he endured, Taylor was a remarkable man. Even this early, he had a keen appreciation of the value of the champion's title and the need to hold on to it. The game was becoming more and more publicised, champions were becoming something of national figures. From the Winchester Club, he was to design Royal Mid Surrey, a busy London club, and by 1900 he had become the professional there. In association with George Cann, a boyhood friend, he created a

thriving clubmaking business. Courses galore were now being built, and Taylor had a designing hand on many of them – Royal Mid Surrey, Royal Birkdale, Queen's Park in Bournemouth, Selsdon Park Hotel in London, and many others.

John Henry Taylor had a burning desire to "better" himself. In a modern context, one thinks of Gary Player or Ian Woosnam. By hard study and concentration, he made himself a lucid writer and speaker. He had a keen awareness of the shortcomings of many of his professional colleagues, and with the respect, but certainly not the subservience, which he himself showed to everyone, he was anxious to promote the status of the professional, and he became a critical figure in the creation of the Professional Golfers' Association. He lived to within a few months of his 93rd birthday, and never lost his interest in the affairs of the PGA. Taylor, at five foot eight inches, was the shortest of our three champions, and did not have the length of the other two. This, and the winds of the Burnham shore, no doubt influenced his action. His swing was solidly planted – "flat-footed golf, sir, flat-footed golf" – and he punched at the ball rather than swung through it, with an odd little grunt at impact. He used an open stance, and a short follow-through. The action was compact, not too much body turn, elbows close to the body. His personality was pugnacious, tenacious, often wilful, and the swing, a powerful swing, reflected that. He attacked the flag with every club and, again in character, often had problems with an over-heating temperament.

**James Braid** was a very different animal. At better than six foot one, with the muscles to match, he was nevertheless more benign, less feisty, than Taylor, as big men often are, and it was said of him that "No one could be as wise as James Braid looked". That might have been expressed more aptly as "No one could have been as wise as James Braid was", for he was to reign like a benevolent cardinal over the lovely courses at Walton Heath for more than 40 years, investing his money shrewdly all the while. He was born at Earlsferry, close to Elie on that Fife coast which is stiff with fine links courses and he was a scratch player at the age of 16. Golf was the thing for the young Braid, but his parents put him to a trade. As a joiner, he moved around the area and was soon winning local amateur events as far afield as Edinburgh. In 1893, a friend, C.R. Smith, who was a clubmaker with the Army and Navy Stores in London, offered Braid a job there. He had never made a golf club in his life, but he was

John Henry Taylor in 1908.

a quick learner and woodworking tools were his friends. Before long, the word was out in London golfing circles about the new, young Scot, and when he held J.H. Taylor, the reigning Open Champion, to a halved exhibition match at West Drayton, with birdies on the two closing holes to do it, Braid was established. The year was 1895. It was the Vardon experience at Ganton repeated. Braid had played in the Sandwich Open of 1894, finishing ninth. When the Romford club was formed in 1896, he became professional there – he had been precocious enough to design the course. He was second to Harold Hilton in the Open of 1897, at Hoylake, and won the first of his five in 1901, at Muirfield, the last championship won with the gutty ball.

Braid was tall, wiry, resolute, reserved, patient, imperturbable, canny – he talked little, listened a lot, and carefully. As a player he was rather the opposite. He walked the fairways with a measured, almost sleepy, stride, but attacked the ball, in Horace Hutchinson's phrase, with a "divine fury". He was a tremendous driver. He was said to have gone to bed one night a short driver, and woke up the next morning a long driver. It can happen. He was a marvellously accurate iron player, like many a Fifer before and since, and was a master of the running shot and the push shot – a strong, dashing player. The power of his game – he had a rather strong left hand grip – sometimes rewarded him with a big hook when he was giving the shot a bit extra. Alas, like many another player before and since, he had problems with putting – "It's aye the putting." He may well have coined the deathless phrase, "Putted like an auld sweetie wife". But he

53

**James Braid, a powerful and dashing player.**

improved with practice, and of course there never has been a great golf champion who was not a fine putter.

Like J.H. Taylor before him, Braid was much in demand as a designer of courses (Vardon was much less prolific, perhaps because of his health, in the new century). In this, Braid's achievement was staggering. He designed scores, probably hundreds, of golf courses from Brora and Boat of Garten in the north of Scotland to Perranporth in Cornwall; from Dundalk to Limerick and Waterford in Ireland. His bunkering was often severe. Of a Braid bunker at Prestwick, Taylor is said to have suggested that the man who made it should be buried there "with a niblick through his heart". The jewel in his crown is no doubt the King's Course at Gleneagles Hotel, surviving in majesty to this day, which we discuss elsewhere.

This then, in their order of birth, was the triumvirate of Braid, Vardon, Taylor. How to separate men who won 16 championships in 20 years is a task not worthy of much consideration. Rubies are rubies, pearls are pearls, diamonds are diamonds. But surely only the impact of a truly great player and his achievements can bring changes in the conception of how a game should be played, and the impact of Harry Vardon and his achievements did that. He brought grace, rhythm, intellect, the power of rational thought to the simple business of swinging a golf club, and to the management and organisation of a round of golf, or of a complete championship. Before Vardon, there had developed essentially two methods of swinging the club, with a wide range of variations between these extremes. There was the St Andrews swing, which featured a two-handed grip and an open stance. The club was swung miles beyond the head, with the left knee buckling in to the right, the left arm bent, the club at the top of the swing almost falling out of the fingers and the clubhead down behind the waist, with a huge body sway and turn. How the golfer got the clubhead back to the ball with a re-established grip passeth all understanding. The ball was smashed away with a sway and a lurch, with the weight finally back on the right foot. The other extreme, only just being developed, was what might be called the Taylor swing – short, compact, flat-footed, short backswing and a positive smash at the ball, again.

Vardon changed all that. He concluded that there were two absolute basics in the teaching of golf (he often said he preferred teaching to playing!), and these were simply to keep the head still, and to maintain a uniform grip of the club from the beginning to the end of the swing. There are few people still alive who saw Vardon play, but it is clear that he evolved a swing which allied rhythmic beauty with a stunning efficiency. In his early days, he lifted the club quite noticeably on the backswing, with his right elbow floating rather freely. Taylor when he first saw it, remarked on how upright Vardon's swing was. In Vardon's maturity, the right elbow was under control, tucked in, even if there was still a suggestion that his very first action was to start his hands back slightly before the clubhead moved. At the top of his swing, his left arm was slightly bent. He never did believe in a straight left arm, although what he probably meant was a "rigid" left arm. "I am firmly convinced that there is no such thing as a straight left arm at the position where so many golfers have been informed there is," he wrote (i.e. the top of the backswing. "A straight left arm at the top of the backswing is impossible in anything approaching a correct movement. This fact must be apparent to anyone who gives it a moment's thought." Vardon was a gentle, modest, quiet man, but, as that last sentence shows, he could be acerbic. Bobby Jones recalled being paired with Vardon in a qualifying round for the US Open of 1920, and topping an easy pitch into a bunker. Hoping to ease his embarrassment, the teenaged Jones said, "Mr Vardon, did you ever see a worse shot in your life?" Vardon replied, "No." His stance narrowed, became less open, although he always had his left foot turned towards the hole. Leading slightly with the hands, he took the club away rather slowly, his left heel only just rising from the ground. He seemed to grip the club quite lightly, swing very easily, as though he had decided that there was no point in smashing the ball away, one actually swept it away. Vardon was much taken with the hands, and the clubhead, and with centrifugal force.

His power seemed to come from the first few feet of the downswing, until his hands were at perhaps hip height, as though that was some kind of optimum point. From there on, there was no more power to be found and it was simply a question of "releasing" the wrists and therefore the clubhead, and swishing the ball away. Vardon was not a divot taker. At the end of all this, there was a high, balanced finish, with all the weight nicely on the left foot.

With elegant swingers, one often thinks, "if only he had gripped it a little more tightly, given it a bit more at impact, it would go further." NOT SO. IT CAN'T BE DONE. The speed of the clubhead at impact governs how far the ball will travel. Speed at impact is the result of the entire swing movement. It isn't possible to give it an extra squirt. And there is no need to clutch at the club – there is an involuntary tightening of the grip at impact. Every player, given that his swing is *under control*, generates an optimum speed, and swinging faster, trying to hit harder, panting for maximum speed, will work only if the entire action is *under control*. Sam Snead and Gene Littler, for example, gave the ball a good crack, but their swings were smooth, elegant, and above all under control.

This then was Harry Vardon – the polished brogues, the plus fours, the shallow starched or celluloid collar, always with a tie, of course, the jacket, the cap, often with a pipe in his mouth, relaxed and comfortable with that immaculate swing. His name is immortalised by the Vardon Trophy, awarded in the US to the professional with the lowest stroke average for the year, and in the UK to the professional who is the leading money winner on the European Tour. And he is remembered above all for the "Vardon Grip", the one in which the small finger of the right hand rides over the index finger of the left hand. Ironically, he did not invent the grip. It had been used by Johnny Laidlay, Amateur Champion of 1889 and 1891, and a stuffy Lothians golfer. It was taken up by other professionals, Taylor included. In his book, *How to Play Golf*, published in 1912, Vardon records that it took him "a year of constant experimentation to satisfy myself as to the superiority of this grip over all others . . . it did not come naturally to me . . . it seems to create just the right fusion between the hands . ." (Vardon had very large hands.)

He won three of his championships with the gutty ball, three with the so-called Haskell ball, which was to bring, like the gutty in its time, a revolution to the game, albeit one of slightly less wide-ranging effect. In 1898, Coburn Haskell, a Cleveland golfer, was visiting a friend at the Goodrich Rubber Company in Ohio when he noticed a pile of thin rubber strips laying around, and speculated that by wrapping these strips around a rubber core, and encasing this in a *gutta percha* cover, he might have a much-improved golf ball. He and his friend went to work on such a ball, and it swept the gutty into the limbo of history and into museums. The new ball was livelier – one version of it was dubbed "The Bounding Billy" – and it did not require a perfect hit, as did the gutty. The average player could mis-hit the thing quite success-fully, and it went further! Vardon felt that through the air the new ball did not go appreciably further than the gutty, but on landing it ran much further, as much as 20 yards or more. Vardon did not much care for the new ball, perhaps since it reduced the advantage he had with his perfect striking, control and placement of the gutty, but like the rest of the golf world, he was converted.

Vardon won the US Open of 1900 with the new ball. J.H. Taylor, who had travelled to Chicago for the event, was invited to use it, suspiciously resisted the temptation, and regretted it – Vardon beat him by two strokes. At the Hoylake Open of 1902, Taylor was still not fully convinced, but he surely became so when Sandy Herd, the St Andrews man who was always a handful for the triumvirate, used the new ball and won. His victory meant that the gutty, mainstay of the game for half a century, passed into total oblivion.

When Vardon won his sixth and last championship in 1914, the era of Braid, Vardon and Taylor came to a close. Never again was a championship to fall to any of them. They had enjoyed golden years. They had immense regard, respect, possibly even love for each other and each other's integrity, and they had brought to golf many new dimensions. Yet before that terminal year, there was to be a remarkable overture, and after it a remarkable coda, to Harry Vardon's long romance with America.

In 1913, during Vardon's second tour of America, the championship was scheduled for The Country Club, at Brookline, near Boston, Massachusetts. He posted 147 for the opening 36 holes and seemed to have things nicely in control, two ahead of Ted Ray, four ahead of Walter Hagen, at 21 making a first appearance in the Open, and four ahead of Francis Ouimet, aged 20, a local amateur. Ted Ray, like Vardon, was a Jerseyman, a giant who smashed the ball vast distances and played invariably in a jacket,

as was the fashion, with a hat clamped on his head and a pipe clenched in his teeth. He had already proved himself with his win in the British Open at Muirfield the year before. Hagen, from Rochester, was at the beginning of what may well be the most astonishing career in all of professional golf, and which brought him two US Opens, four British Open titles, a host of other titles and a vast fortune, some of which he may have kept. Ouimet turned out to be Huckleberry Finn. Of modest family, he lived in a house across the street from the Country Club, and probably entered the championship simply because it was there. He had learned his golf hustling around his own back yard, or back garden, and by sneaking a few holes on the big course across the street, at quiet times. He was nothing more, they said, than a good local amateur, but he was to have plenty of raucous friends on the sidelines during this Open. Ouimet could play. He was the Massachusetts State Champion and had gone all the way to the semi-finals of the US National Amateur at Garden City, New Jersey, before losing to the eventual winner, Jerome Travers. Ouimet could play – his halfway placing should not have surprised anyone.

On the third round, on the morning of the second day, he had caught the two English cracks Vardon and Ray with a solid 74. All three were tied on 225. On the final round, over a long, muddy, rain-soaked course, the Englishmen could make little of the conditions and each scored 79 for 304 totals. Ouimet, too, struggled. He was 43 on the outward half, then scored five at the short 10th hole. To catch the English pair and tie, he would have to score two under fours for the final seven holes, surely an impossibility under the conditions. Ouimet did it. He picked up a birdie at the 13th, then another at the 17th – with a 20 foot putt! Score 79, total 304, a three-way tie. (When the USGA, seeking to commemorate the 50th anniversary of Ouimet's championship, staged the 1963 event at The Country Club, again there was a three-way tie, with Julius Boros, the eventual winner, Jackie Cupit, and Arnold Palmer.) Ouimet's play over these closing holes of the championship represents a stretch of the finest, bravest play the American Championship has known. And when young Ouimet on the play-off next day played an ice-cool round of 72 against the par of 71, he had overwhelmed the Englishmen. Vardon scored 77, Ray 78. Ouimet was an unknown. He had beaten two of the three or four best golfers in the world and he was the first amateur to win the US Open Championship. It was a fairy tale. And since American newspaper editors never have been able to resist a fairy tale, Ouimet and the story of the 1913 US Open Championship was on every front page. The effect on American golf was incalculable, since the game had previously been one taken from the Social Register. It was said that Ouimet's win took America from the country club to the golf club. Francis Ouimet went on to win two US National Amateur Championships, play on and captain Walker Cup teams galore and become the first American, the first "non-Brit", to become Captain of the Royal and Ancient Golf Club of St Andrews. He also went on to have a worthwhile career in a Boston stockbroking house. With suitable modesty, he was later to write that he always considered his win in 1913 "to be in the nature of a fluke". The records of the event do not confirm that.

America was not yet finished with Vardon. In 1920, at the age of 50, he felt able to tackle a third and last American tour, a third US Open Championship. This one was to be played at the Inverness Club on Lake Erie, near Toledo, Ohio, and yet again he was accompanied by his fellow islander, Ted Ray. They faced a new generation of Americans. The young Walter Hagen, who had finished fourth in the rains of Brookline – he had been level with half a dozen holes to play on that last round – had won the championships of 1914 and 1919 and was very much on hand again. Appearing in a US Open for the first time were such starry names as Bobby Jones, Gene Sarazen and Tommy Armour. August weather in the Mid West can be insufferably hot, but at the end of the first day, after 36 holes of golf, Vardon was coolly in touch with the leaders. With rounds of 74 and 73, his 147 total put him two shots behind the leader, the expatriate Scot Jock Hutchison, one behind Leo Diegel and level with Hagen and Ray. The cream had come to the top. A quite brilliant 71 on the morning of the second day put Vardon in command, and when he reached the turn of the last round in 36 the championship was his. With seven holes to play, he was five strokes ahead of the field. But, as he came to the 12th tee, an immense thunderstorm swept in from the lake (are there always storms at US Opens?) Vardon was undone. Straight into this gale, he dropped a stroke on the 12th, then missed a very short putt on the 13th. In his later years, Vardon was prone to this. He was not alone. From Old Tom Morris to Ben Hogan to Arnold Palmer and beyond, great golfers, particularly in their more mature years, have been ravaged by short putts. Vardon three-putted each of the next three greens. His second shot to the 17th only just fell, short, into a burn in front of the green. He had taken 42 strokes for the inward nine holes of the round for a 78 and a total of 296. He eventually finished tied in second place with Billy Burke, Diegel and Hutchison, one miserable stroke behind Ted Ray. Ray's closing 75, none too distinguished, let him join Vardon as the only British player to win the championships of both countries until Tony Jacklin did it, half a century on.

| CAREER HIGHLIGHTS | | |
|---|---|---|
| | British Open | US Open |
| J H Taylor | 1894, 1895, 1900, 1909, 1913 | |
| Harry Vardon | 1896, 1898, 1899, 1903, 1911, 1914 | 1900 |
| James Braid | 1901, 1905, 1906, 1908, 1910 | |

## 5th Hole

# THE AMATEURS

In golf, as in so many other human activities, the select few of the professionals, the apex, is sustained by the vast, toiling mass of the amateurs, the broad base. The early professionals, as we have seen, emerged from the ranks of artisan caddies, club and ball makers, but it was "the amateurs" who gave the game its form. In establishing the golf club or society, with its habits, customs, uniforms and insignia; in buying land for the design of courses and the building of often handsome clubhouses; in creating and administering championships; in codifying the rules of play and indeed administering the entire game, it was the amateur, the club member, who took the game along, onwards and upwards. The coming of the gutty and the huge expansion of the game which it brought meant that increasingly the amateurs were able to influence golf on the course as well as off, and by the closing decades of the 19th century the standards of the amateur game at its best were approaching and occasionally equalling those of the professionals. The game was in good health. It attracted more and more coverage in newspapers, and there came the beginnings of what seems an endless flood of golf books over the past 100 years: *The Golfer's Manual* was published in 1857; *Golf, an Ancient and Royal Game* was published by Chambers in Edinburgh in 1875; Horace Hutchinson produced *Hints on Golf* in 1886; and 1887 was a vintage year – *Golfing* by Chambers, *The Art of Golf* by Sir Walter Simpson, and *The Golfing Annual*; the famous Badminton Library produced *Golf* in 1890.

The strength of the game remained centred on St Andrews (R & A), Musselburgh (The Honourable Company) and North Berwick, with Prestwick becoming increasingly important, and Blackheath the one distant outpost before the rise of the Royal North Devon club at Westward Ho! (1864) and Royal Liverpool at Hoylake (1869). One George Glennie scored the Old Course in 88, in 1855, an amateur record that stood until Horace Hutchinson did 87 in 1884. Glennie was for many years honorary secretary to the Blackheath club and in 1881 he presented to the R & A the Glennie Medal, still awarded, for "the lowest aggregate score at Spring and Autumn meetings". Then there was Colonel J.O. Fairlie of Coodham, the man who had taken Old Tom Morris to the new Prestwick club – he held medals at Prestwick, St Andrews and North Berwick all in the same year, 1866.

Just as the Prestwick club played a critical part in the creation of the Open Championship, so Royal Liverpool, at Hoylake, was to be instrumental in launching the Amateur Championship. Such was the spread of the game, the abilities of the leading players now emerging from all corners of the kingdom, and their appetite for competition, a national amateur championship was inevitable. In 1884, Thomas Owen Potter, who became a quite famous secretary of Royal Liverpool, suggested that an open amateur tournament should be held in the spring of 1885. It was. But one of the first problems the tournament committee had to face was that of amateur status, a vexed problem which faces the game, as it does almost all sports, to this day, and still requiring its own code of regulation. It seems that Douglas Rolland, a stonemason from Earlsferry in Fife and a mentor of the young James Braid (he was ten years older), entered the tournament. He was as tall as Braid, and even more powerful. He could drive with a cleek as far as most others could with a driver, and, straight as a Guardsman, was a handful for any of his contemporaries. Although he had not formally declared himself a professional, he had tied for second behind Jack Simpson in the 1894 Open and pocketed the prize money, such as it was. Also entered for the event was a young local boy, **John Ball**. A few years earlier (1876) he had finished sixth in an Open in Scotland and retained under advice the massive prize of ten shillings. The Hoylake committee in its wisdom deemed Rolland a professional and refused his entry, but allowed young Ball to call himself an amateur and allowed him to play. The fact that Ball was a local man did not escape the attentions of Rolland's supporters, but in hindsight the decision was both wise and correct. Rolland made a perfectly good professional career for himself, while John Ball went on to become the outstanding champion of the half dozen or so who were to dominate the amateur game into the next century.

The first championship in 1885 was won by Allan Fullarton McFie, an Edinburgh man who learned his golf at North Berwick. He is to be remembered as a fine, if wristy, putter who often had the ball spotted behind his right foot, an easy swinger with his left arm straighter than most, accurate and serene. McFie went on to win competitions and medals at St Andrews, Westward Ho! and various Lancashire clubs, but he never again figured prominently in this, the major amateur event. His opponent in that first final, however, was a very different animal.

**Horatio Gordon Hutchinson** in action, by the standards of today, was a freak, nothing less. Any modern golf teacher would be appalled to see him swing. He held the club in the palms of his hands, thumbs round rather than down the shaft. On the backswing, his right knee sagged, his left buckled in towards it. At the top of his swing, his left arm was completely bent, the club slipping round in his fingers, and the clubhead would be all the way round his back, almost above the ball. How he got the clubhead back square to the ball, with any kind of control in his hands, is a blinding mystery. But he did. This swing may not have been considered unusual in the times – it was a version similar to that of several of his contemporaries – but even in terms of the current willowy St Andrews swing, this was a caricature. Hutchinson clearly made it work for him – he won the championship in the two following years, 1886 and 1887, and was a finalist as late as 1903. Hutchinson was born in London and played much of his golf at Wimbledon, but he had learned the game at Westward Ho! and was later much involved in the development of the game at Eastbourne. He wrote extensively about the game in an often eccentric, often flamboyant style - like his golf swing, you might say.

In the final of 1887, Hutchinson beat John Ball by one hole, on his own ground of Hoylake. He might have come to see it as his greatest achievement, because Ball went on to become one of the outstand-

ing players in the history of the amateur game. Hoylake and the Royal Liverpool Club had been born some 20 years earlier when Robert Chambers of Edinburgh and George Morris, brother of Old Tom, went down to lay out nine holes on the existing racecourse. George's son Jack stayed to become professional to the club. John Ball senior owned the Royal Hotel, across the street from the present 17th green, and his son, John Ball junior, born in 1861, made a boyish playground of the new links. When he won the championship of 1888, he started a remarkable sequence of eight wins in 24 years – 1888, 1890, 1892, 1894, 1899, 1907, 1910 and 1912. He was beaten finalist again in 1895, and in 1890 he was both Amateur and Open Champion, the first amateur to win the Open. He won six of these championships with the gutty ball, three with the new rubber-wound ball. These plain facts establish the man as one of the greatest champions, considering that his record was achieved in what must be seen as a vintage time in amateur golf.

Great contemporaries included Hutchinson, of course, but also J.E. Laidlay, Leslie Balfour Melville, Mure Fergusson, Harold Hilton and Freddie Tait. John Ball can be considered a "modern" golfer in terms of the swing, and in some respects he was a precursor of J.H. Taylor, nine years his junior. Like Taylor, he was firmly planted with a rather wide stance. He had rather a two-handed grip, with the right hand somewhat under the club. He teed the ball back towards his right foot and with the minimum of leg movement contrived a full shoulder turn with the left arm nicely firm. It was a controlled, repetitive, beautiful swing, even if he was up on his toes at impact. And even before Taylor, Ball was renowned for hitting full fairway shots not just to the green but to the flag. Ball was a fine driver, deadly accurate in his iron play, a good putter, and had the coldest of temperaments. Could a championship golfer want more?

The golfing lives of Ball and Freddie Tait were irrevocably intertwined. **Frederick Guthrie Tait** was born in 1870 in Edinburgh, the son of a professor of mathematics and philosophy at Edinburgh University. Father was a card who spent the entire summer vacation in St Andrews for the best part of 30 years, and was obsessed with the game of golf. He found that by starting at 6 am he could get in five rounds a day in the long Scottish summer light, provided

John Ball, from Hoylake, one of the outstanding amateur players of golfing history.

the supply of caddies held up. He tried night golf, with phosphorescent-coated balls, which succeeded for only one hole and a bit – the phosphorescence wore off. He made intensive studies of trajectory, centre of gravity and initial velocity of the golf ball, and eventually concluded in 1892 that a golf ball could be hit a maximum distance of around 190 yards. He was somewhat miffed when his son, that same year, belted out a record drive of 341 yards on the 13th hole of the Old Course. The ball was reckoned to have carried 250 yards. Freddie, his son, was Young Lochinvar. He was the ultimate Scottish golfer, idolised by an entire nation, for whom the centre of the universe was St Andrews and match play the life blood of golf. He dismissed stroke play as mere "rifle shooting". He was a gay gallant of a golfer, brave, confident, magnetic for the galleries, much as Walter Hagen and Arnold Palmer were to be in the days ahead. He could be a prodigious driver, yet with an easy, controlled swing. The more flippant of the enthusiasts of golfing lore remember Freddie for having been the cause of one of the game's most repeated quotations. He went to North Berwick and beat wee Ben Sayers, cock of the local walk, by eight holes. Sayers said, contemplating such a defeat by an amateur, ". . . it's no' possible, but it's a fact."

He first won the championship at Sandwich in 1896, beating Harold Hilton 8 and 7 (Hilton could never really handle him), and in reaching that final, in successive rounds, he beat such fine players as G.C. Broadwood, Charles Hutchings, J.E. Laidlay, John Ball, Harold Hutchinson and finally Hilton – these men were to amass 17 Amateur Championships among them. One of the greatest of all finals was that of 1899 at Prestwick, when Ball, five down at one point early in the match, finally beat Tait, the defending champion at the 37th hole. Within months, they were both in South Africa in the Boer War, Ball with the Cheshire Yeomanry, Tait with the Black Watch. Ball returned. Tait did not. Freddie, the cavalier of Scottish golf, died in action at Koodoosberg Drift on the 7th of February, 1900. In the memory we have of Freddie Tait, there is surely a piece of Young Tom Morris there. Andrew Lang, Scottish man of letters, wrote of him:

I never heard a word said against him except a solitary complaint that, in the lightness of his heart, he had played pibrochs around the drowsy town at the midnight hour. What would we not give to hear his pipes again.

In this last decade of the 19th century, another

of golf's early citadels, Muirfield, to which the Honourable Company moved in 1892, was powerfully represented by two exceptional members of the club, J.E. Laidlay and Leslie Balfour-Melville. Arthur Balfour, later to become Prime Minister, was an enthusiastic golfer, a well-publicised enthusiasm which further spread the popularity of the game. He played frequently at North Berwick but also teamed with Laidlay for matches at Muirfield, and eventually became a member of the club. John Ernest Laidlay went to Loretto School, close by the Honourable Company's Musselburgh course (Fettes College is the other famous public school in Edinburgh, provoking the cry, "Fettes for culture, Loretto for corporal punishment"), and was an early starter, helped along nicely by Bob Ferguson and later Jack White, Open Champions both, so much so that at the age of 16 he got round Musselburgh's nine holes in 36 strokes, four scored at each hole. Laidlay was also by way of being a gymnast in his youth, then a naturalist, photographer and cricketer – he played for Scotland against Yorkshire. Over four years in amateur finals, he lost to John Ball (1888), beat Melville (1889), lost to Ball again (1890), then beat Harold Hilton (1891). Two years later he was a finalist again, but lost to Peter Anderson, a St Andrews man who vanished to Australia and helped the game along there. Laidlay's technique had an oddity of the times in that he had the ball spotted well in front of his left foot. More important than that, he is the first golfer of note to have used and established the overlapping grip, the one that came to be known as the "Vardon Grip".

One other Muirfield man was to have a positive effect on the development of the game as the First World War approached, even if his influence off the course was the greater. **Robert Maxwell** won both of his championships (1903 and 1909) significantly at Muirfield. He never seemed wholly at ease away from the place, but "at home" was well-nigh unbeatable. He was leading amateur in the Opens of 1902 and 1903, an immensely strong player with a wide stance, a short backswing, and, with right hand under the shaft, gave the ball an immense smash. He was captain at Muirfield in 1912 and 1913, and was much involved in the purchase of additional land in modernising the design of the course. After winning the Military Cross with the Royal Scots during the war, he helped persuade the R & A to take over the administration of the national championships in 1919.

In the decades up to the First World War, the dominant champions in the amateur game,

**Francis Ouimet in 1913.**

paralleling in an intriguing way the professional Triumvirate were John Ball and Harold Hilton, Hoylake men. Had Freddie Tait survived the South African war, he would have stood shoulder to shoulder with them. Ball, the first amateur, the first Englishman, to win the Open Championship, won eight Amateur championships over 24 years. In addition he was twice a finalist who lost by only one hole. Ball was clearly the game's finest amateur going into the new century, but there were critics to claim that Hilton surpassed him.

**Harold Horsfall Hilton** was born at West Kirby, a few miles from Hoylake, in January 1869, and like Ball grew up with the new golf course. He won two Open Championships, four Amateur Championships and the US Amateur Championship, in some ways the most significant of all. He won the first Open played at 72 holes – in 1892 at Muirfield – and second at Hoylake in 1897. In fact he had two Open trophies on his mantelpiece before he won

an Amateur Championship, despite having reached three finals. In 1891 he had lost to Laidlay at the 20th at St Andrews, in 1892 to Ball at Sandwich by 3 and 1, then was swept away by Tait in 1896, again at Sandwich, by 8 and 7.

The First World War changed the face of Europe and began the disintegration of the great colonial empires and came to be seen as a watershed in history. So it was in golf, and in particular during the year 1914.

In 1913, **Francis Ouimet** had stunned the world of golf on both sides of the ocean by defeating Vardon and Ray in the American championship, and he confirmed his place in the game by winning the American Amateur in 1919. In 1914, Vardon won his last Open, and the young Walter Hagen won his first US Open. And in those early 20th century years, there were three or four events of lasting significance in the story of the game. John Low, a handy golfer who had taken Hilton to the last

The remarkable amateur, Walter Travis.

green in his 1901 win at St Andrews, and had reached a couple of semi-finals, was in addition a prominent legislator, for several years an influential chairman of the Rules of Golf Committee. He helped found the Oxford and Cambridge Golfing Society, and in 1903 he took a team to America, where the young gentlemen played matches against clubs and colleges along the eastern seaboard. The quality of American golf astonished him and he came home to preach of a coming American invasion, to all who would listen, in the thundering, testamental phrase, "I can hear the hooting of their steamers in the Mersey". The invasion began the very next year in the considerable person of Walter J. Travis.

**Walter J. Travis** may just be the most remarkable golfer in the history of the game. He won the first tournament he ever entered, within a few weeks of first hitting a golf ball, at the age of 35. He won the last tournament he entered, and beat Jerome

Travers, the 1915 US Open Champion, in doing it. The event was the Metropolitan of 1915. Travis was 54 years old. Within four years of starting the game, he had won the American Amateur Championship, and from 1900, when he was 39, until 1904, he was amateur champion of the US three times and of Britain once. He was of slight physique, with small hands and never did weigh more than ten stones. These are the bald facts of Travis the golfer. He was born in Maldon, in Victoria, Australia, but moved to the USA with his family when still a boy. Unlike all the great champions, without exception, Travis had no early background in the game, no particular youthful interest in it. On a trip to London in 1896, he bought some clubs to take back with him – some of his friends were planning to start a golf club, and he thought he should support them. Travis was never a man for half measures. If he was going to play golf, he would be as good as he could be. That winter of 1896–97 he devoured all the golf books he could lay his hands on. The following summer, he played very little golf. Instead, he practised his swing, and the perfecting of it, relentlessly, hour after hour, day after day. The intensity of the little man had, that early, intimations of the later Ben Hogan. He came to realise that, since putting could account for 50 per cent of the shots in a round of golf, it should get most of his attention. He practised putting into holes two inches across, only marginally larger than the ball, for hours on end. He concluded that putting was essentially a right-handed game. The left hand was a guide, the right hand, palm towards the hole, should drive a nail into the centre of the back of the ball and go right through it, towards the hole. In the winter of 1900–1901, his health failed him and he made a trip to the UK to rest and attempt to recover. During his visit – he was American Amateur Champion – he played many of the leading players and lost to most of them. Back home, his health restored, he finished third in the US Open, led the qualifiers in the Amateur, and successfully retained his US title. After he won it for the third time, in 1903, he resolved on an assault, the next year, on the British championship, still considered the premier amateur event in the world.

Travis was in Britain three weeks in advance, planning to play St Andrews and North Berwick for a week, then to spend the rest of the time practising at Sandwich, the championship venue. In Scotland, he played "atrociously". He had completely lost form, perhaps because of the voyage. He bought new clubs, laboured at his game, fiddled with his technique, and still everything was wrong. In the end, he got

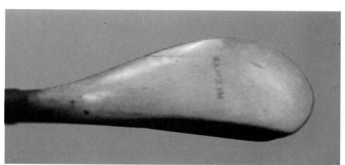

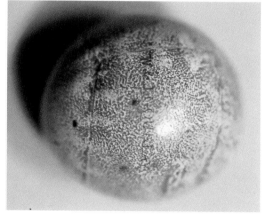

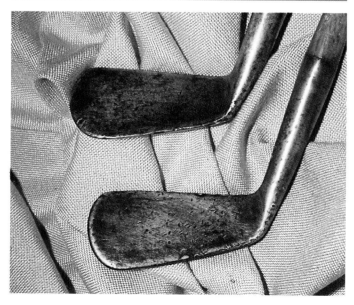

Golf through the ages.
*Top left:* As seen in a 14th century stained glass window in Gloucester Cathedral.
*Middle left:* A McEwan wood c1860.
*Left:* Smooth-faced irons c1890.
*Top right:* Box of rubber core balls.
*Middle right:* Feathery ball c1845.
*Above:* Gutty ball c1900.

*Opposite:* Gary Player in distinctive action. *Above:* Arnold Palmer.
*Below:* St Andrews clubhouse from the 18th green.

*Left:* Sandy Lyle, the first Briton to win the US Masters,
seen here holing his winning putt in 1988.

*Above:* Lee Trevino, one of the most colourful golfers of the
post-war era.

*Left:* Greg Norman, the great Australian, hitting one of his powerful drives.

*Above:* Tom Watson, twice winner of the US Masters, here seen playing at Augusta.

*Right:* The talented and charismatic Spaniard, Severiano Ballesteros.

*Overleaf:* Jack Nicklaus.

to Sandwich with only a week to prepare, and in a rather sullen mood. But rather than tackle the unknown course, he took out a cleek he had bought in North Berwick, and a few balls, and walked out a few holes of the course. When he did try a shot, it was the Road to Damascus. The light shone on Walter J. Travis. He was later to write "The first ball I struck I knew I was on the road to recovery. For the first time in two weeks, I could "feel" the ball. The necessary 'touch' and 'timing' were there." Putting remained a problem. Travis tried a variety of stances, strokes and putters and eventually borrowed a putter, a Schenectady putter, so-called because it was made in that city, from one of his fellow-travelling Americans. The Schenectady featured a shaft inserted into the *centre* of a mallet-blade, for the British an unprecedented design.

All told, from Travis's point of view, it was to prove a championship of bitter experience. He was to write about it in a simple, direct, forceful way, leaving no doubts about his feelings, in *The American Golfer*, a magazine which he helped found in 1908, and which he edited with distinction until 1919. Travis and his half dozen or so compatriots entered for the championship were not able for some reason to practise with the leading British players. Travis was not allotted a locker – he had to change in a corridor in the club, and had to store his clubs overnight in the professional's shop. He also had caddie problems. He wrote, "I had had, ever since I had been at Sandwich, one of the worst caddies it had ever been my misfortune to be saddled with. This young man, about 26 years old, was a natural-born idiot, and cross-eyed at that. He was too nervous to think of performing the customary duty of teeing a ball, and rarely knew where it went." Somehow, despite his efforts, Travis was never able to persuade the caddie master to find him another caddie.

In his first round match, he beat one H. Holden from Hoylake by 4 and 3 in less than two hours, and in a rainstorm. With half an hour before his second round match, he was not given enough "time to get into dry togs". He went out in the afternoon against James Robb and had a "ding-dong match", which he only just won by one hole. By this time, Travis had become increasingly aware that around the clubhouse and in the local Bell Hotel there were several members of the Oxford and Cambridge Golfing Society team which had been in America the previous year and had enjoyed that lavish hospitality which is traditionally American. He was even more aware that precious little effort was being made to reciprocate this kindness to the small band of Americans

in Sandwich. All of this simply made Travis more determined, more bloody-minded, about doing well. Perhaps his Aussie blood was rising. What the locals had not then realised – they soon would – was that Travis was a quite exceptional golfer. No one, not even Harry Vardon, had studied golf more intensely, more broadly, than Travis. Probably no one alive at that time *knew* as much as Travis about the business of playing the game. He was not long off the tee, but he was unerringly accurate, an astonishing judge of distance, and he was a demon putter. He paced along, taciturn and deliberate and in a cocoon of concentration, usually wearing a hat, and wearing a black cigar. One contemporary photograph taken at the top of his backswing could be a golfer of the 1960s – nicely balanced on the right foot, left heel comfortably raised, left arm straight, left wrist in line with his forearm, clubface closed, shaft parallel to the ground, head perfectly placed over the ball.

In the third round, he beat A.M. Murry 3 and 1, and in the fourth he ran into his toughest match against H.E. Reade, a former Irish champion. Reade was two up after four holes, and Travis was never in front in the match. Two down with four to play, Travis finished the round relentlessly in 15 strokes for those final four holes to win. Next up, in round five, was Harold Hilton, champion of 1900 and 1901. Travis won the first three holes with the tightest of par figures – he was out in 36 – and it finished 5 and 4. He was in the semi-final, facing another giant – Harold Hutchinson. Hutchinson had been losing finalist to Robert Maxwell of the Honourable Company the year before, and had taken his revenge in this championship. But he was 45 years old – since Travis was 42, it might have been dubbed a middle-aged affair – and Travis had the bit between his teeth now. He was out in 34, two under par, three up and finished the match 4 and 2. The little man was in the final. The world, at last, began to notice him. *The Times* report on the Hutchinson match said:

All doubts that may have existed as to the quality of Mr Travis' golf were set at rest by the game in the afternoon, when he beat Mr Hutchinson. He has played better golf each day, seeming to play well within himself, and to bring out a game just sufficient to beat each successive opponent. His short game is certainly marvellous, almost every long putt quite dead, if not in the hole. Mr Travis is quite imperturbable, having apparently no nerves . . .

Travis was set against Ted Blackwell in the final over 36 holes. Blackwell, of a St Andrews golfing family, was a bull of a man, big and strong, forbidding. He had spent several years farming in California, and now, aged 38, was no doubt at the peak of his strength. A prodigious driver, he was said to have driven a gutty ball to the steps of the R & A clubhouse from the 18th tee at St Andrews. Travis was always going to be 30 or 40 yards behind Blackwell, given each their very best shots. The final was not distinguished. Travis won the first hole with a five to a six, then holed a putt better than 30 feet to win the second in three. This early, it was an ominous thrust. The American was out in 38, and three up, round in a rather moderate 78 to Blackwell's 82. The power of Blackwell's hitting was not matched by any kind of accuracy and Travis, imperturbable, simply ground the big man down. On the third hole of the morning round, Travis, seeking to be sociable, had mentioned to Blackwell that his driving was "wonderfully long". Blackwell, already two down, replied with a mumble. There was no further conversation. And the Travis win at the 36th hole was received in a stunned silence by the gallery.

It would be true to say that Travis was not exactly overwhelmed by congratulations at the St George's club, save of course from the small American contingent present, or treated with the respect that any American champion deserves. All of it may not have been one-sided – Travis could be a forthright, argumentative little man. Over this long stretch of years, it is difficult, impossible, to establish the truth. Royal St George's, then and now, is a fairly exclusive club. With the British Empire still at its height, perhaps Americans were considered to be still "colonials". (It was easy for the British to ignore the fact that in 1899, the year of Queen Victoria's jubilee, the gross national product of the United States, and indeed that of Germany, had passed that of Great Britain.) And while the Americans have always and rightly taken the view that the letter of the law is to be followed absolutely, and the British had persuaded themselves that the spirit of the law is at least as important, perhaps an incident in the Travis first round match against Holden of Hoylake compounded his problems at Sandwich. One of the local rules of the time was that there was no permanent grass in a hazard. At the seventh hole, Holden's tee shot went into a bunker with grass growing in it, the ball finishing on the grass. Holden grounded his club on the grass, breaking the rule. When Travis called him on it, Holden, bursting with rage, said he'd never heard of such a thing, and it was a damned silly rule. He prattled on throughout the rest of the round about it, and no doubt in the clubhouse later. Travis was always a stickler for the rules. He would tolerate no deviation from them. Holden was clearly wrong, but these differences in attitudes and approaches to the rules were to be well expressed by Jack Nicklaus when he insisted that the Rules of Golf are for the player's protection and that they are a Bill of Rights, and not a Penal Code.

Walter J. Travis was the first "foreigner", the first non-British golfer, to win the Amateur Championship. There were sad footnotes to the saga of Travis at Sandwich. When the trophy was mailed on to him, it had been insecurely packed, was dented and there was excess carriage to pay. Travis never did defend the championship. And a few years later, the R & A banned the Schenectady putter, as though it was the putter, and not Walter Travis, which had won the championship. The absolute essence of Travis came in his remark, "I never hit a careless shot in my life . . . I play each shot as if it were for a championship."

Finally, in those pre-war days spiced by the coming universality of the motor car, 1911 was to become a memorable year. Then, Harold Hilton won the American Amateur Championship, the first, last and only British player to do it, and Johnny McDermott won the US Open Championship, the first native-born American to do it. Although Hilton's achievement was seen by many at the time as a revenge for Travis at Sandwich, it was no more than Travis in reverse. The men had much in common. Hilton, like Travis, was small – five foot six. Hilton, like Travis, and like his Hoylake clubmate John Ball, was a most intense student of the game. Where Travis chomped on his black cigars, Hilton was seldom seen without a cigarette in his mouth, a 50-a-day man, a total equalled and occasionally surpassed by Bobby Jones, challenged for a spell by Arnold Palmer. If not as spiky as Travis in temperament, he was self-possessed, with a good opinion of his abilities, although, as a basically quiet man, he seldom expressed them. From tee to green, Hilton was probably a better player than Travis. On the green, he was not – no one was. Hilton was a deep thinker, a great experimenter. He could draw or fade the ball as he pleased with fairway wood shots, in that respect inviting comparison even with Harry Vardon. His grip was loose, in the old 19th

**Harold Hilton, American Amateur Champion at 42 years old.**

century manner, his swing a rather quick, flashing up-on-the-toes affair but perfectly controlled, and in fact ball control was perhaps the outstanding feature of his game. Hilton was a friendly if quiet chap, with a quick, logical mind, but he was highly strung. He always insisted that he preferred stroke to match play, but he could fight his corner when he had to, as four Amateur Championships confirm. Two Open Championships in the era of Braid–Taylor–Vardon and two near-misses support his preference, but an early round match in the Amateur of 1913 at St Andrews, which he won, demonstrated his nerve, and guts. Against Heinrich Schmidt, a young American who came and went in one season, he was all square playing the 17th. Hilton had played two good shots just short of the green, and ran up his third with his putter – and ran it into the Road Bunker, the evil canyon which screens the left front of the green. This is not too difficult to do. Many an honourable man has done it since. Hilton splashed the ball out, got his half and won the match with a long putt on the 19th hole.

At Apawamis for the 1911 American Amateur Championship, Hilton declared his intent immediately with rounds of 76, 74 for 150, to lead the stroke play qualifying competition by two strokes. He eased through two rounds comfortably, then came face to face with Jerome Dunstan Travers in the third. Jerry Travers was an outstanding American amateur of the time (he fought many dogged battles with the older Walter Travis) and was to win the American championship four times (in 1907, 1908, 1912, and 1913) and the US Open of 1915. The son of a wealthy father, he started to play on the family estate on Long Island and was later taught by Carnoustie's Alex Smith at the Nassau Country Club. Travers had rather a long backswing and was inclined to be quick, but he had fast hands and above all an ice-cold temperament. He was a talented scrambler and was a match player as tough as they come. Fortunately for Hilton, he played poorly on their morning round to be four down after the first 18. In the afternoon, Travers recovered his rhythm, stormed back to be only one down with nine to play, but Hilton rallied to win 3 and 2. He then walked all over C.W. Inslee in the semi-final, and found himself set against Fred Herreshof in the final. Herreshof was a big fellow who could belt the ball past the best of them from the tee, and who depended on his driving as much as anything. Hilton played him conservatively, as he did with most of his opponents, keeping his own ball carefully in play and letting the other man take the chances and make the mistakes. On the

morning round, Fred made many and at the lunch break, Hilton was four up. In the afternoon, Fred squandered the first and third and was six down, 15 to play. The party, surely, was over. But one of the great recoveries in man-to-man golf was at hand. The American won the 6th, 8th and 9th. Hilton faltered. He lost 11 and 12, the 29th and 30th holes. With four to play, Hilton was still one up, but when Herreshof won the 34th to square the match, the gallery, numbered in thousands, went wild. The American missed short birdie putts on both 35 and 36 and the match went to the 37th. Both men drove in the fairway, Herreshof's ball well past Hilton's. The Englishman played first, but his spoon shot drifted off line to the right. The ground to the right of the green rose up to a mound, however, and Hilton's ball, pitching on it, broke neatly to the left, and rolled on to the green. It was a fantastic stroke of luck for Hilton, when he needed it, and Herreshof was unnerved. He left his approach short of the green and needed five to get down. Hilton two-putted formally and was American Amateur Champion.

Hilton was 42 years old when he won. His victory was a chastening reminder to the Young Turks of American golf, such as Travers and Herreshof and the rest of them, that the Old Country was not yet ready to surrender all of the glory in the old game. Yet that very same year came an event of surely equal importance. Jerry McDermott, a bantamcock from Atlantic City, won the US Open. He was the first native-born American to do so. From its very beginnings in 1894, the championship had been in the gift of the immigrants from North Berwick, St Andrews, Carnoustie and Musselburgh who had flooded to a new and promising land of golfing riches. McDermott in 1910 had tied with two of them, the Smith brothers from Carnoustie, Alex and Macdonald, before losing the play-off to Alex, mentor of Jerry Travers. But he won at Wheaton in Chicago in 1911, repeated in Buffalo in 1912. McDermott had only a few bright shining moments at the top. His health broke down, and in 1915 he suffered a nervous breakdown. By then, the world was at war.

If the World War of 1914–18 is clearly a massive watershed in the story of mankind, so it proved in golf, one of mankind's simpler pastimes and pleasures. In spite of Vardon's heroics in the 1920 US Open, the war spelled the end of the Great Triumvirate. Never again, on either side of the ocean, would they win an open championship. The years of their lives had seen massive changes. In 1871, when Braid, Taylor and Vardon were in their very first year, Charles Darwin published *The Descent of Man*. In the 1870s and 80s, Alexander Graham Bell was at work on the telephone, Thomas Alva Edison produced the first electric light bulb and the gramophone. In 1893 came the first motor car. In 1898 radium was discovered by the Curies. In 1898 London had its first motor bus. By the turn of the century, electricity and central heating were no longer considered miracles. In 1901, Marconi sent a radio signal across the Atlantic, and in 1903 the Ford Motor Company was launched and the Wright brothers flew, at Kitty Hawk in North Carolina. And perhaps, most momentous of all, in 1905 came Einstein's *Special Theory of Relativity*.

When Harry Vardon was winning the 1914 Open at Prestwick – his last – Walter Hagen was winning the US Open at Midlothian, Chicago. One year earlier, in Atlanta, Georgia, over the man-sized East Lake course, a boy named Jones had scored 80 – at the age of ten. In 1916, he won the Georgia State Amateur Championship, against men. In 1917, he won the Southern Amateur Championship against golfers from all the southern states, and in 1919, the year of Hagen's second US Open Championship, he was runner-up in the Southern Open and the Canadian Open (in each case against leading professionals) and was a finalist in the US Amateur Championship – all this at the age of 17. This boy Jones was clearly a prodigy. Walter Hagen and Robert Tyre Jones jun were totally contrasted in background, education and personality, yet they were to dominate international golf throughout the 1920s, making it a golden decade in which golf reached a pinnacle in the annals of sport, even in the affairs of man.

| CAREER HIGHLIGHTS | | | | |
|---|---|---|---|---|
| | British Open | US Open | British Amateur | US Amateur |
| John Ball | 1890 | | 1888, 1890, 1892, 1894, 1899, 1907, 1910, 1912 | |
| Harold Hilton | 1892, 1897 | | 1900, 1901, 1911, 1913 | 1911 |
| Francis Ouimet | | 1913 | | 1914, 1931 |
| Walter Travis | | | 1904 | 1900, 1901, 1903 |

# THE HAIG

**W**alter Hagen was born on the 2nd of December, 1892, in Rochester, New York the only son in a family that featured four daughters. His parents were of German stock, his father being a blacksmith in the local railroad repair shops. The Country Club of Rochester was within handy reach of the family home, and, by the time he was eight, young Hagen was lugging golf bags around for a few cents. At that time, a golfer's bag would include no more than a half-dozen hickory-shafted clubs. Although the Hagens were working class people, they were never really impoverished, yet Walter, who had little to do with school after the age of 12, hustled through his early teens with a variety of jobs in the true American tradition. But always he caddied through the summer, this allied to learning how to play the game and collecting clubs and balls discarded by the members. Young Walter had an abundance of physical energy, which emerged from good health, and he caddied for all the captains of local industry who were members of the club. He was impressed with their elegant outfits and by the ease with which they discussed business deals and the affairs of the world. By the time he was 14, he had pinned down a job in the professional's shop, where he was to stay for five years, in that time learning the business of clubmaking, becoming a pretty good player and incidentally stretching to close on six feet at better than 12 stones. When the club professional, Andrew Christy, moved on, Hagen got the Rochester job at the age of 19 – $1200 for eight months of the year, $2 an hour for lessons, and the sales in the pro shop, a treasure trove for a young man. This left him four winter months to spare. He quickly latched on to the fact that there were professional tournaments listed in Florida during the winter, and that was the place for him. In the years ahead, Florida was

**Walter Hagen a stylish and seminal figure in golf.**

to become Shangri-la for Walter Hagen. By the time the 1913 US Open came round, the famous Ouimet–Vardon–Ray Open, Walter had saved up enough to make a cheap rail trip to Boston and played a pretty good championship, being very much in the action with half a dozen holes of the last round left. Hagen was also a pretty good baseball player and had ideas of making a professional career in that sport when, in the summer of 1914, a club member, impressed with his efforts in the 1913 (it was the first time a Rochester professional had even qualified for the Open), offered to pay his expenses for the championship coming up in Chicago. Hagen had not planned to go, but with that he was on a train as quickly as you could say "Merion", and promptly won the US Open! His first round of 68 was a record and he led the championship all the way.

The world of Walter Hagen changed completely. He was invited to play in tournaments, to give exhibitions, to endorse products. He found that he loved the glamour of tournaments, the gasps of the galleries, the attentions of the Press, and particularly the thrill of competition; but almost as much as anything he could see the commercial value of having a "title", the accolade of being a champion. And for the next 20 years he was seldom without a title of one kind or the other. The war years were a round of charity exhibitions which took him the length and breadth of his vast country, opening his eyes even further. His world was expanding, and Walter was a quick study. He realised that golf could take him into the highest and richest levels of American society. And he realised that American crowds, the galleries at golf events, wanted a show, that professional tournament golf was show business. If they wanted a show, Walter Hagen was the man to give it to them. He embraced the life as to the manner born. At one time he had a Cadillac car that was as long as a street and returned four miles to the gallon from its 16 cylinders. When Walter arrived, the whole town knew about it. In 1918, he was invited to become head professional at the new, huge Oakland Hills club in automobile-rich Detroit. It was a plum job which any other professional would have given his right arm to get, but after he won the US Open of 1919, he quit. He had decided that he could not combine the duties of resident pro. at a busy club and play in all the exhibitions and tournaments and championships that were on hand. So Walter Hagen became the first full-time playing professional, or "business man pro." as he called it. It was the sensation of the hour, but Hagen had done his sums – he was sure he could earn enough to keep his car in petrol and sustain a regal lifestyle. Never again did he take a "club" job. The sky was to be the limit for Walter Hagen, but he could be perceptive. He had the good sense to turn down an offer of $1500 a week for 40 weeks (!) to appear in variety theatres across the country, on the grounds that his stage was a golf course, and not a theatre. In this same year of 1919, Hagen also won the Metropolitan, the Western, the North and South and the West Coast of Florida Opens – all major tournaments at the time. He had also found time to marry, in January 1917, and to welcome the arrival of Walter junior in 1918; but by 1921 the marriage, under the strain of Walter's, shall we say, travels, was dissolved. By 1920 Walter was ready for his first tilt at the "British" Open, still considered by the world of golf as the game's greatest single event.

He set off with a journalist friend, Dickie Martin, crossed the Atlantic on the *Mauretania* and installed himself in the Carlton Hotel, London, in some comfort. Hagen hired a Daimler with a chauffeur and footman and set off for Deal and his first Open. His presence in England, as the US Open Champion, had attracted massive newspaper coverage.No American had ever won the Open, and the British galleries could hardly wait to see this American superman. When they did, it was well worth it. Hagen had been stunned by the fact that, as a professional, he was not allowed to enter the clubhouse – he would have to change "in the pro shop". Since the pro shop was little more than a shack, this was not good enough for Walter – he would change in the local inn, have his limousine parked prominently, even ostentatiously at the clubhouse, and change his shoes in the car. When he did emerge from the car for his first round, he was something to see – black sleeveless pullover, white silk shirt with dark tie, white flannel "knickers", black and white golf shoes and grey stockings. It was one of a dozen matching outfits he had packed. For the British, the two-toned shoes in particular were

a shocking novelty. His play in the championship was not so startling. Out in 37, he was caught in a gale of wind on the inward half and took 48 more for a round of 75. He was out of the championship before he started, and finished 53rd in a field of 54! But Hagen knew how to lose in style – he lost with a smile. It was to be one of his characteristics. He had not got the knack of playing a links course, but he was intrigued by the operation, and, like General MacArthur after him, declared "I shall return". He did – with a vengeance. But before he sailed back across the ocean, he had recovered sufficiently to taste most of the delights of Paris and to win the French Open, at La Boulie.

Hagen returned to play the Open of 1921, finishing sixth behind Jock Hutchison at St Andrews, but this year was to see the beginning of a run of success scarcely equalled in professional golf. He won the American PGA Championship (match play), beating Jim Barnes 3 and 2 in the final. He did not enter in 1922. He lost in the final of 1923 against Gene Sarazen, at the 38th hole. In 1924, he started a run of four successive years of victories in this championship, a total of 20 consecutive matches. He played in six PGA Championships from 1921 to 1927, and lost only one match out of 30, when Sarazen had beaten him in the 1923 final.

He won the Open Championships of 1922, 1924, 1928 and 1929. In 1924, at Hoylake, he arrived late for a qualifying round, had to talk the committee into letting him play and only just qualified. He holed a difficult putt of five feet at the 72nd hole to win. With a new wife, Edna Strauss, Walter took off for a few weeks on the Continent, finished three strokes behind Cyril Tolley in the French Open, won the Belgian Open, took in the Olympic Games and generally enjoyed himself. Hagen's Open win in 1924, his second, opened the gates to an American domination of the championship – Jones, Armour, Sarazen, Shute – for eleven years until Henry Cotton won in 1934. Beginning in 1927, Hagen captained six US Ryder Cup teams, and also the 1939 team, selected for a match that was never played because of the war.

Walter Hagen, "The Haig" or "Sir Walter" as he became known, is a seminal figure in golf. He was a big fellow, with a powerful body perched on rather slender legs, his strong face permanently tanned, black hair always perfectly sleeked down. He had an abundance of charm (he'd keep kings and presidents waiting but dissolve their irritation with one smile) which he used mercilessly not only on a long succession of ladies but on the most hardened of his fellow

**Hagen and his wife celebrate his win at the Open at Hoylake in 1924.**

pros. Most of the time, it worked. Walter was lucky, or perhaps blessed with some instinctive cunning, in that he had recognised early in life a few basics. One was that tournament golf, exhibition golf, was show business, and he would give the people a show. (In his prime, he'd often play exhibition matches for the gate money, and Bob Harlow, his manager, later founder of *Golf World* magazine, would carry the loot off in a suitcase!) He would hand his winner's cheque to his caddie. He'd order champagne for the whole room. He would arrive at the golf course like a potentate, flashing the smile, descending from a limousine or from behind the wheel of an immense, preposterous roadster, with a quip on his lips – "Who's gonna be second?" Hagen was for the grand gesture. His shirts were of silk, his sweaters of cashmere, his coat of camel hair, his shoes impeccable. On his trips to England, he took to commanding a suite at the Savoy Hotel (£5 a day!), and London's best shirtmakers and shoemakers would come to him with their wares. His prime decade was the 1920s, the Roaring Twenties, a jazz age following a war

from which America had emerged hugely strengthened economically, in which the entire country was booming, in which everything seemed possible, and was. Hagen well knew the value of a smile, a word to the gallery, a touch of gallantry in what so many people took to be a serious business.

He had also observed that people, in the last resort, are concerned only with their own problems, and not the other man's. Oh, they listen and make sympathetic noises, but they are not really concerned. Walter, by and large, was on his own. If anyone did him a favour, he knew there would be something in it for them and that was fine by Walter, provided they paid. And he knew that the whole world was fascinated by money, and by the other man's earnings. His annual trips to Europe cost him around $10,000 each time, and often he had to hustle to make it. In the other direction he never sought to correct stories about the vast amounts he was pulling in for his labours. He knew that money, riches, true or false, were a compelling source of public interest. In a period when America had prodigious sporting heroes like Ruth, Dempsey, Tilden and Weissmuller, The Haig was right up there with them. And although his creed was "I never wanted to be a millionaire, I just wanted to live like one" (which he did), if the public thought he was a millionaire, that was fine by Walter. He knew very well that the one thing Americans love above all else is – success. His image as a roisterer, a Casanova, a big drinker, someone generous to a fault scattering money in his trail, was over-embroidered. At a party, he would never say no to a drink. The resulting hassle was more trouble than it was worth. He said yes to every offer, but most of the time the Martinis would disappear into potted plants, or into the bathroom, and Walter would get through the entire evening on a "couple of hoots", as he would have said.

If he was a man for the grand gesture, he worked hard at life and certainly got through a vast amount of money. But most of the time it was there for the taking. In 1920 Dr William Lowell, a New Jersey dentist, whittled a piece of wood into the modern teepeg, and by 1922 was marketing the Reddy Tee. The days of a pinch of sand from the sand box on each tee were over. Hagen and Joe Kirkwood, the Australian trick shot artists, played 125 exhibition matches in America in 1922 and left, religiously, a trail of Reddy Tees across the land. Fee? $1500. Walter dabbled in the Stock Market, and once set up as a broker for a few weeks. In 1923, he signed a contract with the Pasadena Golf and Country Club, on the West Coast of Florida (at the height of a Florida building boom). It required him to publicise the development through the tournament season, and live at the club from December to March. He was given a building plot, and he was to have an additional plot for each exhibition he played (he finished with ten plots), plus a fee of $30,000! The club opened in January, 1925, and Sir Walter lorded it in Florida each winter until 1928, when the bubble burst, shortly before the Wall Street crash. Walter dabbled with Hollywood, too, and made a coupld of short films. He set up The Walter Hagen Golf Products Corporation to make golf clubs, with mixed success it should be said. It was taken over in the 1940s by the Wilson Company, and to this day Haig Ultra clubs are on sale in the pro shops.

With Joe Kirkwood, Hagen played exhibitions galore. Kirkwood was the complete antithesis of Hagen – he didn't drink or smoke, was on the quiet side with little to say to the newspapermen, and kept a close eye on the accounts. They made an odd couple. But Kirkwood, Australian and New Zealand Open Champion of 1920, was a whizz at trick shots. He'd hit a full drive off the face of a watch, hit balls straight up in the air, swing with a shaft of rubber, hit one-legged, hit balls without looking at them, play left-handed, right-handed, and so on. They went on tour once for six months; another time they went clear round the world. They toured Australia, New Zealand, the islands of the Pacific, Japan. They were in India, East, West and South Africa. Hagen the hunter pursued tiger, antelope, lion, like a Hemingway. All of this was possible because, unlike today when the entire year is taken up with professional tournaments, there were plenty of blank weeks in the year, which the other players filled back at their clubs. Hagen changed that too, as the first full-time playing professional. After Oakland Hills, he never held down a club job. He took the professionals out of the professional's shop and into the clubhouse, on both sides of the Atlantic, and eventually into boardrooms. He set the professional game on the way to becoming the great spectator sport it is today. If only there had been television in the Hagen days!

As a swinger of the golf club, Walter was less than elegant. His swing was described as "starting with a sway, ending with a lunge". From a wide stance, he took an equally wide backswing, then a tremendously long follow-through which often saw him spinning around on his left heel. His concern was simply to get the ball out there, down the fairway whence he'd attack the green, and if it slid off into the rough, why, he'd just knock it out of there. On one occasion, when just that happened, Hagen arrived at the ball and a spectator standing close by said, "That was terrible luck, Walter, terrible luck." With his philosophical smile, Hagen said, "Yes, but that's where it is, my friend, that's where it is." He simply stepped up and whacked it out of there. His mental approach to the game was perhaps his greatest asset. He had long decided that, in any single round of golf, he was likely to hit a few bad shots. When he did, they were dismissed from his mind. He got on with the next one. He was without nerves. Nothing that happened on the course, nothing that an opponent did, troubled him. And he was never much interested in finishing second – first was the place for Walter, and, if he couldn't finish first, he would go out with all guns blazing. In these respects, the coming of Arnold Palmer, 30 years on, seemed like Hagen incarnate. He was something of a genius on recovery shots, often prowling around the situation, making it seem very dramatic, then bringing off an apparently miraculous recovery with a flourish on what was in fact a simple shot. Above all, Hagen always knew that three bad ones and one good counted four, just as four good ones did.

In Hagen's time, the conditioning of courses was less than sophisticated. Bunkers were not often raked, and, with the heavy-flanged sand wedge still to come, recovery from bunkers had to be made with a thin-bladed niblick. Hagen was a master of this shot, nipping the ball cleanly away and stopping it close to the flagstick. The green was Hagen's greatest arena. He was quite simply a superb putter, with stunning feel and touch and judgment. Bobby Locke, the best putter of *his* time, wrote "Hagen in his day was probably the world's greatest putter and I was happy to learn from him." Walter perpetuated the myth that he didn't practise much, that he would roister the night away and turn up on the tee next morning in dinner suit and dancing shoes and go out and score 68. That was good for the image and it probably happened once or twice, but he practised, especially putting, more than anyone realised. He believed you had to find the "sweet spot" on the putter blade and hit there every time, and he would sometimes chalk the face of his putter and putt and putt until the chalk was worn off. The man, incidentally, had the most beautiful, elegant, lucid handwriting.

This then was Walter Hagen, a giant in the game, a handsome devil of cheeky charm and flashing smile, the world's sweetheart, no doubt a child of his times, above all of America's time (he lived through Prohibition!), which is long gone. But he remained in character to the end. Even in his 60s, Walter Hagen's kerchief was of finest silk, his suit of mohair, his topcoat of cashmere. If you ever wanted someone to play for your life, it would be Walter Hagen. You would, of course, make it worth his while.

It would be difficult to imagine two more contrasting characters than Sir Walter and Bobby Jones – Bob to his friends. Hagen was from the industrial North, Jones from a Deep South which, at the turn of the century, was still largely pastoral. Hagen's background was blue collar, Jones's was middle class. Hagen came from the world of caddies, while Jones had been a "country club" member since childhood. Hagen left school at 12, Jones was highly educated at no fewer than three prominent universities. Walter Hagen was an extrovert, larger than life, preposterous, a character of dazzling wardrobes, luxurious cars and outrageous demands on life, of expansive statements and gestures, of two marriages and no doubt of many idylls. Jones was modest, shy in his early years, perhaps a touch introverted then, a conservative dresser, precise in his language with both the written and spoken word, and a family man who married a good Catholic girl called Mary Malone, and raised a family of two girls and a boy. Yet both had charm in abundance, if of a different kind, and their careers over-lapped and coincided through a decade and more of the most thrilling sports achievements imaginable.

| CAREER HIGHLIGHTS | | | |
|---|---|---|---|
| | British Open | US Open | USPGA |
| Walter Hagen | 1922, 1924, 1928 1929 | 1914, 1919 | 1921, 1924, 1925 1926, 1927 |

# THE IMMORTAL BOBBY

**R**obert Tyre Jones, junior, named after his paternal grandfather, was born in Atlanta, Georgia, on the 17th of March, St Patrick's Day, 1902, the year of the gutty ball. He was the only son of Robert P. Jones, a successful Atlanta attorney, known as "Big Bob" or "The Colonel". Young Jones was a sickly child with an overlarge head and a digestive ailment that prevented him from taking much solid food in his early years. His father was a member of the Atlanta Athletic Club, with its golf course out at East Lake, a neighbouring town since swallowed by the spread of the city, and when the child was five the Colonel took a summer cottage out at East Lake "across the street" from the golf club, hoping that the cleaner country air would help build up his son. It did, and while his parents played golf the little fellow would follow along with a cutdown club, batting an old ball, trying to keep up. When Steward Maiden from Carnoustie followed his brother Jimmy as the East Lake club professional, the boy Jones took to following him. Maiden was a taciturn man, and paid the boy little attention – contrary to belief, Jones never had a lesson as such from Maiden. In later years, when Jones was in competitive golf, he might ask Maiden to check one point or another in his action. The child had the gift of impersonation and much of Maiden's rational style surely rubbed off on him. The years went along. By the time he was seven the young Jones was allowed to play the course, Mondays to Fridays. Like all schoolboys, he tackled any sport that came along, in particular baseball, until he read about Francis Ouimet's exploits in the 1913 US Open, then saw Vardon and Ray play an exhibition match in Atlanta. From then on, golf was to be the game for him, and later that year, aged 11 and triumphantly, he scored 80 round the East Lake course for the first time.

**Bobby Jones' triumphant return to New York.**

Even before this, at the age of nine, he had won the East Lake junior championship, beating a boy of 16 in the final. A couple of years after his first round of 80, he was winning the club championship with a round of 73, and it was clear that the Southland had a prodigy in the young Jones. By the time he was 14, he could drive a ball 250 yards, and he was allowed to travel beyond Atlanta and tackle other tournaments in the South with his friend Perry Adair, a good player a few years older. Perry's father George, a friend of the Jones family and very prominent in golf in the South, kept an eye on them, and, when young Jones beat Perry in the final of the first Georgia State Amateur Championship, the boys were rewarded with a trip to Philadelphia, with father Adair as chaperone, to tackle their first US Amateur Championship, the National Amateur. The year was 1916, the course that of the Merion Cricket Club, as it was then called. The name "Merion" was to be a marker in the Jones career. Bobby Jones was now 14½ years old, five feet four inches tall and almost 12 stones in weight, a chunky, solid character on strong legs, with a very healthy appetite and a very good conceit of himself.

This was reflected in a perfectionist strain that saw him with a neat lexicon of grown-up language and a strong right arm for the throwing of golf clubs, traits in which he indulged. The lad had a temper, directed of course at himself and his, by his own lights, occasional imperfections as a golfer. Merion was Jones's first major trip away from home. He qualified for the match play rounds and was drawn against one Eben Byers, champion ten years earlier. They played atrociously and scattered clubs all over the course. Jones reckoned that he won eventually (3 and 1) only because Byers ran out of golf clubs before he did. At the 12th hole, Byers threw an iron clear out of bounds and insisted his caddie leave it there. One spectator called the whole thing a juggling match. Jones, as the boy wonder playing in his first national event, had exceptional attention from the media, and his temper got more attention than his golf – he was severely lectured in print. He got past Frank Dyer by 4 and 2 in the next round and met Bob Gardner, the defending champion, in the third. It was to prove educational for the young Atlantan. In the afternoon round, Gardner time and time after time got down in a pitch and a putt, or holed a long one, to save himself until at last Jones's nerve cracked and Gardner ran out 5 and 3. Gardner was a first-class, seasoned player – he went all the way to the final that year, losing to Chick Evans – but it was a hard lesson for the youngster. He was later to reflect that he learned more from defeats than from victories. For all that, the Georgia schoolboy was famous, or at least nationally known. In the gallery at Merion had been the audacious, pugnacious Walter J. Travis, three times winner of the championship and controversially of the British Amateur at Sandwich in 1904. Intrigued by the boy, Travis had declared that Jones could not improve on his shot-making, but he still had to learn when to play this or that shot and "his putting method is faulty". A few years later, Travis saw Jones putt poorly at an exhibition in Augusta, talked with him after the round, and, before anyone knew it, Jones had become one of the best and most consistent putters in the game, perhaps even better than Hagen.

After Merion, it was back home. By the next spring, America was at war and championship golf was out for a couple of years. Jones did win the 1917 Southern Amateur at Birmingham, the youngest player ever to do it. With Perry Adair and Alexa Stirling, yet another outstanding young Atlanta golfer, he was engaged when free from school in an extensive round of Red Cross matches and War Relief exhibitions. Alexa Stirling's achievements, with those of Jones and Adair, had America wondering about Atlanta, this proving ground of champions.

Alexa Stirling, five years older than Jones, won quickly and early a secure place in the story of American women's golf. She first played in the National Championship at the age of 17, in 1914, losing in the first round. In 1915, she was a semi-finalist, losing at the 22nd hole. In 1916, she won the championship, the first of three in succession. In 1921 and 1923, she was a finalist, and indeed had been a finalist in five out of six successive championships.

For Jones, although still a boy, these exhibition matches were a critical phase in the making of a champion, a phase that has been all but overlooked.

He travelled widely during summer vacations. He experienced a variety of grasses on the greens, from the fine, subtlely-breaking bent grass of the northern courses such as he had to handle at Merion, to the heavy, broad-bladed Bermuda of the South, a grass which is grainy, which puts excessive and progressive turns on the ball, and which demands firm striking. He learned to play before larger and larger galleries, even if they never reached Merion proportions, and no doubt he learned some of the ways of the world. He also learned to rein in – most of the time – his temper.

In 1919, Bobby Jones came out of his first year at Georgia Tech, where he studied mechanical engineering, taller at five feet seven and slimmer by a good 15 lbs than he had been at Merion. It was to be a year which saw his first real jousting with the best professionals, the first of 11 such years. He played four events, two regional, two national. In the Southern Amateur, at New Orleans, which he was defending after the break for the war years, he was beaten in the semi-final. In the Southern Open, played at East Lake, he was runner-up, one stroke behind Jim Barnes. In the Canadian Open, played at Hamilton, Ontario, he and Jim Barnes were joint runners up behind J. Douglas Edgar, the English professional who had come to the Druid Hills club in Atlanta that same year – but 16 shots behind! Edgar's rounds were 72–71–69–66 for 278, a total that stood for years in any Open Championship, and, finally, in the US Amateur, Jones was taken out in the final 5 and 4 by Davidson Herron, playing on his home course, the fearsome Oakmont, near Pittsburgh. Jones in truth had not played particularly well that week. One incident in the final gives us some clue as to the boy/man that Jones was then, and of the man he was to become in terms of his temperament. Playing the long 12th hole, Jones, three down with seven to play and by no means beaten, had started to swing into a fairway wood shot when a marshall with a megaphone bellowed at the gallery. Jones skulled the ball. The incident so unnerved him that he never again looked like saving the match – half a dozen years later, he might well have shrugged it off. The incident was to have its bizarre counter in his Walker Cup match with Cyril Tolley at St Andrews 11 years later, although Tolley then was the victim.

After all these near misses in 1919, surely 1920 would be a better year. Surely this would be the year in which the young, blazing star of Dixie, comfortably into his studies at Georgia Tech, would break through at national level. His first event was the Southern Amateur at Chattanooga, which he won in style. Next came the Western Amateur at Memphis, where Chick Evans was installed as favourite. Jones qualified with a record 69–70, and went to the semi-final of the match play, where Evans stopped him, but only just, one up after 36 holes. Oddly enough, in major championship play, no leading player ever beat Jones more than once. Evans, Bob Gardner and Francis Ouimet beat him, but he had his revenge, twice against Evans and Gardner, three times against Ouimet. Unabashed, Jones set out for the National Open, due at the Inverness Club, near Toledo.

The 1920 Open was one of the most dramatic of all the long series of American championships. As we have seen, it was Harry Vardon's final championship fling, and would perhaps have been his final triumph, but for the storm that swept him away on the final round. And this championship was significant for something else – it saw the beginning of the end of the generations of British-born golfers which had dominated, or influenced, the event since it began. In the 1920 championship, Ted Ray and Harry Vardon topped the bill. Walter Hagen defended his championship, but the entry was stiff with such names as Hutchison, Barnes, Macfarlane, Macdonald, McLeod, Ayton, Hunter, Sargent, Cunningham and Robertson. It also saw the first appearance of Gene Sarazen, aged 18, a fledgling professional; Mr Tommy Armour, still an amateur, the black Scot from Edinburgh who was to become the "Silver Scot" and win all the game's glittering prizes as a professional; and Bobby Jones. In the qualifying rounds, Jones, 18, was paired happily with the grand old man, Vardon, aged 51. Jones called him "Mr Vardon", Vardon called him "Master Bobby". In the first round of the championship, Jones dropped a stroke at five of the first six holes and played quite poorly for a 78. His second round 74 left him seven strokes behind the halfway leader, Jock Hutchison. A splendid third round 70 saw him four strokes behind Vardon who was now in front. The young college boy was ready for another lesson on how to handle the pressures of championship golf and how, above all else, what is required is a certain kind of resolute calm. He decided that, to have any chance of catching the majestic Englishman, he would have to score 70 or better. He would have to go for all the shots. He did – and missed most of them with a 77. In the event, what with the storm that swept Vardon off course, a total of 72 would have won him the championship, the first he had entered. Years later he was to reflect "It was as fine a thing as ever happened to me. If I had won that first Open, I might have got the idea that it was an easy thing to do." Fifty-six years later, Johnny Miller, in winning the Open Championship at Birkdale to add to his earlier US Open, counselled Severiano Ballesteros, the young Spaniard still in his teens, who had come blazing out of nowhere to finish second, that "your time will come". It did, three years later, at Lytham. And for Bobby Jones, his time came, three years later, at Inwood.

The leading British amateurs Cyril Tolley, Roger Wethered, Lord Charles Hope and Armour had come over for the 1920 US Amateur at the Engineers Club on Long Island. Only Armour qualified and he went out in the third round to Francis Ouimet. But the visit gave them the chance to discuss with their American friends the business of rationalising their golfing relationships, and it was decided that a team of Americans would make a trip to the old country in the following year for an informal match. It was to be the forerunner of the Walker Cup series between the amateurs of both countries. Bobby Jones again found the US Amateur beyond his reach – he went out in the semi-final by 6 and 5 to Ouimet. The American team which crossed to Hoylake in 1921 was powerful and included Ouimet, Evans, Guilford and Jones. They won the warm-up match against the British 9–3, then tackled the British Amateur over a treeless Hoylake course baked brown, hard and fast by a drought. Jones went out in the fourth round. The last Americans, Paul Hunter and Freddy Wright, went out in the fifth and sixth rounds, respectively, each to Bernard Darwin. Next on their schedule was the Open Championship at St Andrews, as dramatic as any, and one which was to bring to young Jones an incident as fateful as any he had experienced and one which took him a huge step closer to maturity. In the first round, Bobby was paired with Jock Hutchison and Jones had the pleasure of seeing him make a hole in one at the 8th hole, 142 yards, then almost repeat it at the 9th, where he smashed an immense drive the best part of 300 yards onto the green. The ball touched the rim of the hole and stopped inches away. Hutchison, a native of St Andrews, played one of the great rounds of golf in this championship. As he went to the first tee of the final round, he heard that Wethered had completed his last round in the lead. Hutchison would need a 70 to tie. He did just that to force the play-off, much to Wethered's dismay – he had promised to attend a local cricket match in London on the next day, an obligation which in the true amateur spirit he considered more important than merely playing-off for the Open Championship. However, he did stay over, and was routed by Hutchison. Jones had a rather

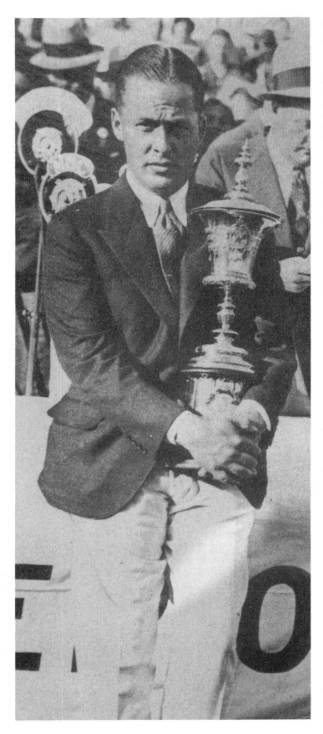

Bobby Jones after winning the US Amateur Championship in 1930, his last major title.

different experience during this, his first visit to St Andrews. In the third round, after using 46 strokes on the outward half, then taking six at the 10th hole, he picked up his ball, and quit. This action haunted him the rest of his days. It was the only time in major competition that he did such a thing, but it remains the one thing the golfer does *not* do – he plays until he is beaten, or until the competition is finished, even if he scores 100 on the round. Not even being 19 years old excuses it.

The 1921 US Open, played at the Columbia Club, near Washington D.C., was a romp for Jim Barnes, the big Cornishman. He opened with a 69, and won the Open by nine clear strokes from Walter Hagen and Fred McLeod, the home pro, with a 289. Jones was to have another odd experience in this championship. Going into the final round nine strokes behind, he had nothing but hope – the hope that Barnes would disintegrate and that he, Jones, would put together a phenomenal round. He set about it. He made three threes in the first four holes. At the long 5th, 560 yards, after a big drive, he launched into a fairway wood shot intended for the green, perhaps 280 yards away, intended for a birdie, intended even for an eagle. He pulled the ball wildly out of bounds. He dropped another ball, and did exactly the same thing. He dropped yet another ball, advanced it up the fairway, pitched on the green, took two putts, scored nine on the hole. But this time there was no club throwing, no explosion of temper. He came in with a hard-salvaged 77, in fifth place. The four players ahead of him, Barnes, Hagen, McLeod and Evans, were all Open Champions in their time. After it was all over, Walter Hagen said to O.B. Keeler, "He's got everything he needs to win any championship except experience and perhaps philosophy. He will win the Open before he wins the Amateur." Hagen was to be proved a wise, observant prophet.

O.B. Keeler? Oscar Baun Keeler, known always as "O.B.", was an Atlanta journalist, and if the life and achievement of Bobby Jones is probably unique in the history of sport, the coming of Keeler as its chronicler was the happiest, if the most bewildering, complement to it. Born in Marietta, Georgia, he laboured as a cashier in an insurance office before talking himself into a few weeks' trial at the *Atlanta Georgian* in 1909 – "no pay, and bring your own typewriter". Keeler was lucky – his first story made the front page and he was hired. He wrote about everything and anything. In the spring he took to writing about baseball. He had become intrigued by golf, still an esoteric pastime in America, by reading magazine articles, and from having seen a golf course and golfers in action on family vacations in the North. He soon became aware that out at East Lake were young Perry Adair, little Bobby Jones, and Alexa Stirling, three exceptional "golf-playing children". O.B. became a golf writer and Jones came back from the Amateur Championship at Merion in 1916 only 14 years old, but a national figure. From then on, Keeler reported every championship, every single event of consequence in which Bobby Jones took part, at the same time contributing to the fame of one of America's leading newpapers, the *Atlanta Journal*, with the quality of his writings. He attended 45 major championships, seven with Alexa Stirling, 27 with Bobby Jones. He travelled some 120,000 miles with Jones, most of it by train, to California, New England, and eventually to Great Britain. He saw him win all his major titles. They travelled together, shared rooms together save when one or other's wife was travelling, and ate together, in a relationship surely unique in sport. But Keeler was more than just a Boswell to Jones's Dr Johnson. He was a father confessor who suffered as much anguish in defeat and as much ecstasy in victory as ever Jones did. He was tall and kindly, with a kind of Henry Fonda, country good looks behind his rimless glasses. He had read, it seemed, everything and could spout verse by the hour, knew when to be on hand, when to leave Jones on his own. It was a remarkable association.

In 1922, Bobby Jones had surgery on the veins of his legs, no doubt required after years of clumping across golf courses; graduated from Georgia Tech; finished second by one stroke to Gene Sarazen and his blazing final round of 68 in the Open at Skokie; and was swamped in the semi-final of the Amateur by Jess Sweetser, 8 and 7, at The Country Club. Sweetser stormed through the championship, beating defending champion Guilford, Chick Evans and Willie Hunter en route. In the autumn, Bobby Jones entered Harvard University. It was the year which Keeler recalled as the last of the "seven lean years", which, since Jones was still only 20, seemed harsh. In Open Championship play, he had finished successively eighth, fifth and second, an impressive progression. In Amateur Championship play, he had gone to the third, final, semi-final, third and semi-final rounds, in five tries. The seven fat years, again Keeler's phrase, would start in 1923, when Hagen's prophecy came true, and ensured the immortality of Robert Tyre Jones jun.

The next "seven years" (in reality it was eight) were not so much fat as obese. Over these years,

from 1923 to 1930, Jones the amateur dominated golf as no man had done before, and no man has done since. He won the US Open four times, in 1923, 1926, 1929 and 1930; the US Amateur in 1924, 1925, 1927, 1928 and 1930; the Open Championship three times, in 1926, 1927 and 1930; and the Amateur Championship in 1930. In addition to his four US Open wins, he lost twice in play-offs, and finished first or second in every year save one. In his eight final attempts at the US Amateur, he won five times. After his humbling experience in his first Open Championship in 1921, he won three times in three appearances, and, at last, won the Amateur Championship, with its hurly-burly of 18 holes matches in 1930, the year in which he won all four championships – the Open Championships of Britain and America and the Amateur Championships of both countries – the "Impregnable Quadrilateral". Of the 27 major international championships in which he appeared, he won 13. And he won every Walker Cup match, foursome or single, in which he played. The whole thing was stunning, and looking back at it from the 1980s it seems close to incredible. But, in the words of Keeler, "as long as the records of golf championships endure, the world will never forget". If one contemplates the enduring names in sport, the Olympians Jesse Owens, Carl Lewis, Emil Zatopek, Jean-Claude Killy; the likes of Babe Ruth, Jack Dempsey, Fangio, Joe Louis, Mohammed Ali; Willie Shoemaker and Lester Piggott; Stanley Matthews and Pele; the Bobby Jones of 1930 must be in the forefront. There is no ultimate means of judgement and comparison, but the Jones career is beyond the slightest doubt unique. He must have been the greatest competitive sportsman in history.

Moreover, championship golf itself is perhaps unique in sport in that, with practice and preparation, it makes demands on a man for the best part of a week. Arnold Palmer has said, "A round of golf takes a long time – a championship seems endless." Perhaps the only immediate comparison is a Test match in cricket. Jones, once he had his temperament under control, came to realise (with the help of Keeler, it should be said) that a championship would come to a man who made a relentless pursuit of par, par, par, and let the birdies fall where they may, and when the disasters came, defy them! Jones learned to remove himself from the world and to remove himself to some extent from his opponent, and concentrate on the shot in hand and the golf course itself. It is a good philosophy for anyone who has ever played the game at whatever level. But there were brilliant shots, compelling shots, critical shots, even if, by 1923, Jones was beginning to feel that perhaps fate had laid a clammy hand on him. Going into the last round of that championship, his "breakthrough" championship of 1923, he had a lead of three strokes. With three holes to play, he needed a par finish of 4, 4, 4 for a 72 and certain victory. He finished 5, 5, 6. Bobby Cruikshank tied him with an implausible birdie on the very last hole. Over the 18 holes play-off, they won and lost holes in turn and came to the 18th all square (it was of course medal play). Jones had a long drive which dribbled off the right side of the fairway into a bare lie. Cruickshank skulled his drive, pulling into the left rough. This last green at Inwood was closely defended by bunkers and above all a lake which demanded a long carry. Cruickshank could not reach the green. He played out short of the water – he would be hard-pressed to make four, with a single putt. The challenge was with Jones. He didn't hesitate. Taking his mid-iron – probably a 4-iron in today's terminology – he picked the ball cleanly off the dirt and hit an immense shot, all of 190 yards, which stopped six feet from the hole. Bobby Jones had won a national championship at last. As he waited for the presentation ceremony, Jones said wistfully, "I don't care what happens now." Perhaps, at last, he was master of that fate with the clammy hands.

In the Jones portfolio, there is another shot of note, not less significant. For the 1926 Open Championship, scheduled for Royal Lytham, he was a late entry, deciding at the last moment to stay over from the Walker Cup matches at St Andrews. In the 36 holes qualifying at Sunningdale, he scored 66 and 68, and his round of 66 is considered to be one of the most perfect ever played. He had 33 shots, 33 putts. He was never off the fairway, never missed a green save marginally at the short, downhill 13th, where he chipped close for a par-3. There was no five on the card. He was out in 33, back in 33. He was putting for birdies on 13 holes, putting for eagles on four, and missed no more than one putt from around six feet. It is a round beyond comment. In the championship proper, he came to the 71st hole tied with Al Watrous, professional, fellow-countryman. The hole is a dog-leg to the left with a bunker and heavy rough set in the angle, and better than 400 yards long. Jones hooked his drive into the bunker. Watrous was straight down the fairway, and played his second easily to the front edge of the green. He probably thought that the bunker would end Jones's championship hopes. But Jones had a clean lie. He had 175 yards to the pin, over rough and broken ground all the way to the putting surface. He would have to catch the ball perfectly on the clubface if he had any hope of bringing off the shot – a few grains of sand either way would smother the shot – and the ball would have to fly all the way to the putting surface. Jones took his mashie, the modern 5-iron, and hit one of golf's historic shots, perfect contact sending the ball soaring beautifully to the green, stopping closer to the flag than that of Watrous. The shot broke Al Watrous – he three-putted, and Jones was champion. Some comparison might be made between the Jones shot and that of Sandy Lyle from the bunker at the 72nd hole of the 1988 Masters tournament, which set up his winning birdie, but the Jones shot was much the more difficult. On reflection, and after his career was long over, Jones declared that the Royal Lytham shot, under the circumstances, was the single best shot he had ever made. In an emotional speech at the prize-giving, the old master, J.H. Taylor, who in the third round, at the age of 56, had scored 71, said plainly, "Bobby Jones is the greatest golfer who ever lived". To this day, a plaque in that bunker commemorates the shot. Three weeks later, Jones was also US Open Champion, the first man ever to win both championships in the same year.

Looking back to the age of Jones and Hagen means looking back over 60 years, a healthy span. Although automobiles were there in abundance and the universality of the car was approaching, travel over the vast distances of the United States meant the train. The aeroplane age had not quite arrived. The 1920s were a decade of the train, marvelous monsters whose whistles set a mournful, haunting wail across thousands of miles, across river and deserts, through and over enormous mountain ranges, with their Pullman cars, sleeping cars, restaurant and club cars. When Jones, and Keeler of course, travelled from Atlanta to Pebble Beach near San Francisco for the Amateur of 1929, they spent days and nights in trains, only for Jones to lose in the first round, by one hole, to Johnny Goodman. Indeed, Goodman had made his way from Omaha to Pebble Beach, 100 or so miles south of San Francisco on a cattle train – not all the champions were privileged people. Like Ouimet, Evans and Jones, Goodman was to win an Open (in 1933) before he won an Amateur (in 1937). He remains the last amateur to win a US Open Championship. It was a time when courses were primitive in comparison to the highly- and scientifically-manicured designs of the 1980s. Steel shafts did not really become the norm until Jones had retired (they were legalised by the USGA in 1926, by the laggard R & A in November 1929).

82

The galleries in the days of Jones and Hagan were huge, rowdy, not always well marshalled, seldom roped off. Yet it was a decade of very great players, and for most of Jones's fat years the best of the amateurs could still match, most of the time, the best of the pros. One of the most intriguing of the amateurs was one Chick Evans, whose career was a prelude to that of Jones in that he had seven years of "failure" before he broke through. When he did, he did with a vengeance. Evans from Chicago came through the caddie ranks, and by the age of 16 he had a simple uncomplicated swing that saw him qualify for the Western Amateur. Somewhere along the way, he also put together a temperament that ranged from the depths to the heights of emotion. From tee to green, Evans was an immaculate player – Harry Vardon had claimed, Ouimet not withstanding, that Evans was the best amateur he had seen in America – but his putting was less than reliable.

In 1909 at the age of 19, in 1910 and again in 1911, Evans was a beaten semi-finalist in the US Amateur. In 1912 he made the final against Jerry Travers, squandered a three-up lead and went out 7 and 6. In 1913, he was again a semi-finalist, but in the next two years he went out first round to lesser players. As Ouimet had done, as Jones and Goodman were to do, Evans won the Open before he won the Amateur. In 1914 he had finished second to Walter Hagen, his chip shot to tie at the very last hole finishing inches from the cup. In 1915 at Baltusrol, he finished ten strokes behind the winner Jerry Travers, for Evans, one suspects, a *bête-noir*. But in June, 1916, at Minneapolis, Chick won the championship, two strokes in front of Hutchison, four ahead of the next man, Barnes, with a 286 which lowered the record by four strokes and stood for 20 years. In September at Merion, in Bobby Jones's first championship, he raced through the Amateur field and took Bob Gardner, defending champion and the Yale man who was to play Cyril Tolley in an epic British Amateur final at Muirfield in 1920, by a useful 4 and 3 in the final. Chick Evans was the first man to win both Open and Amateur titles in the same year. In 1914, for him a lean year, Evans had a chastening experience in the British Amateur at St George's. In the first round, his opponent Charles Macfarlane played the opening nine holes in 31 strokes. Macfarlane was something of a protege of Lord Northcliffe, the British press lord, who had promised to take him to America. They were virtually on their way to the ship when war was declared in August. Macfarlane went on to become a golf writer, covering the tournaments for

a London newspaper on an aged motor-cycle which he insisted on calling "The Bentley". Evans played in his 50th Amateur Championship in 1962 at the age of 72 – even then he was still writing crotchety letters to his friends. He repeated his Amateur win in 1920, taking particular pleasure no doubt in beating Ouimet in the final. Evans, the Chicago man, one suspects had a certain dislike of "Easterners" and of men of substance. Few were men of more substance than Jerome Dunstan Travers, who surpassed him in achievement with four Amateur, two Open titles, and was the man who had beaten him in the final of 1912.

Jerry Travers first swung a club on his father's estate(!) at Oyster Bay on Long Island. He had instruction from Alex Smith of Carnoustie – the 1910 champion. Jerry never had any problems in paying for a caddie, but his outstanding quality was a temperament that let him divorce himself from opponents and galleries and everything but the playing of the game and the winning of the match. Evans was the last of the amateur Open Champions before the coming of Jones, but the amateur game was stiff with very fine players – Jesse Guilford, Jess Sweetser, Watts Gunn, and of course Ouimet and Evans himself, who soldiered on for so long. And back in the old country there were fine upstanding amateurs – Cyril Tolley, twice champion, Sir Ernest Holderness, also twice champion, Roger Wethered, who tied for an Open, and Eustace Storey. The professional game had an abundance of stars, the preposterous Walter Hagen apart, in the likes of Tommy Armour, Jock Hutchison, Leo Diegel, Bill Melhorn, and the young Gene Sarazen. And in the old country, too, there were characters and players of high ability – George Duncan, Arthur Havers, Abe Mitchell, Archie Compston, Percy Alliss. But the world was changing, and as early as 1923, the first of the great Jones years, Harold Hilton was announcing "to put the matter in the very plainest of language, American players of the present day are better golfers than their British cousins". By the end of the 1920s, the immigrant pros who had flocked to the US at the end of the 19th and the turn of the 20th centuries had all but passed from the scene. Walter Hagen after 1930 never won any of the bigger prizes. Tommy Armour, who had come to America after the First Wold War, took the Open Championship of 1931, but by and large, from 1930 onwards, home-bred Americans were in control of American golf, and one of the most intriguing was the son of an immigrant Italian carpenter.

Eugene Saraceni, born in Harrison, New York,

in February 1902, the same year as Bobby Jones, from his earliest days knew the value of a dollar and how to turn it into ten. His childhood would be deemed under-privileged today. By the time he was eight years old, much like the young Hagen, he was caddying, first at the Larchmont Country Club, a few years later at the Apawamis Club in neighbouring Rye, a much busier club. The family was a good deal less than rich, and Gene was quickly into any odd job. He left school at 15, the family moved to Bridgeport, Connecticut, and the boy was quickly doomed to a factory job. An attack of pneumonia led to the medical opinion that he should find an outdoors job. He began to spend time at a local public course, then, when he was 16, he found work at the Brooklawn Country Club, helping in the professional's shop as a general dogsbody, but also learning something of the business of clubmaking, and playing as much golf as he could. By the age of 17 he decided he would be known as Gene Sarazen – Saraceni sounded too much like an opera singer – and, calling himself an assistant professional, he made for the winter matches and events in Florida and the other Southern states. Gene was never bashful. He contrived to cover the overheads, and a whole new world was opening for the cocky young Sarazen. He was aiming high. In 1920, he was "head pro" at a small club in Indiana. He entered the US Open and finished 30th. The next year he advanced to 17th place. In 1922, he won the Southern Open in New Orleans by eight shots from Leo Diegel, his first major success, and he promptly won the US Open that year with a birdie on the 72nd hole – two blows with a driver on the par-5 hole – a closing round of 68 and a record total of 288. He had made up four strokes on the round and finished one ahead of Mr Robert T. Jones, if you please. Sarazen thus beat Jones, his direct contemporary, to the US title by one year. He had arrived at the Open at Skokie a country pro, a complete unknown. He left a national figure, like Ouimet after Brookline, Jones after Merion. He won the PGA championship the same year, defended it successfully against Hagen in 1923, and despite a disastrous try at the Open Championship at Troon, where he was swept away by a storm and failed to qualify, his career was off and sprinting.

As the US Champion, Sarazen endorsed clubs, balls, a correspondence course in golf, anything you pleased. Few golfers have made more of their talents than did Sarazen. He launched into a profitable series of exhibition matches with Hagen among others – Sir Walter irritated Sarazen by calling him "Kid" or "Eugene" and they milked, for all it was worth

commercially, a certain public animosity, although in private they were good friends with a healthy respect for one another. The precocious Sarazen strangely lost his form for the next half dozen years in terms of major championships, but he came to life again in the 1930s, proving himself the bravest of golfers when the requirement was the devastating shot, the devastating round, the devastating burst of scoring. He was a finalist in the PGA Championship of 1930, losing by only one hole to Tommy Armour. He beat Willie Cogan in the final of 1933. In the US Open of 1932, he produced a final round of 66, played the final 28 holes in 100 strokes and set a new record of 286. In the Open Championship of 1932 at Princes, he won by five strokes with a record aggregate of 283 and became one of the few men to win the Open of both countries in the same year (Jones, Hogan, Trevino and Watson are the others).

In 1935, in the second playing of the US Masters, Sarazen hit one of the historic shots of golf. As he walked after his drive on the 15th hole of the last round, a hole of 485 yards since lengthened, he learned that Craig Wood had birdied the last hole and finished on 282. To win, Sarazen would need four birdies over the four closing holes. This 15th hole features a wide fairway rising to a crest in driving range, then downhill to a shallow green. But covering the entire front of the green is a wide pond which makes the second shot the ultimate challenge of the hole. Always depending on the wind, the modern player can handle the second shot comfortably – the longest of hitters have been known to reach it with a 7-iron second shot – but in Sarazen's day it needed a 4-wood, a club then in its infancy but of which he was already a master. With better than 200 yards to go, all carry, Sarazen let fly – and holed the shot. The ball pitched on the green and ran into the hole. Score two on a par-5 hole, a "double eagle" as the Americans call it, and if it had to be a lucky shot, it was certainly a brave shot. With one flashing blow, Sarazen had picked up three strokes. He made careful pars at the three closing holes, tied with Craig Wood, and next day won the play-off by five strokes. Thus Gene Sarazen became the first player to win the modern Grand Slam of the professionals – the Masters, the US Open, the Open Championship and the US PGA Championship. Only Ben Hogan, Gary Player and Jack Nicklaus have achieved it since. Poor Craig Wood! He was third in the US Open of 1933, tied

**Eugene Saraceni, known as Gene Sarazen, was the first golfer to win the modern Grand Slam.**

and lost a play-off in the Open Championship that same year, tied and lost in the Masters of 1935 – he had been second in the Masters the year before Sarazen stole it from him – and tied and lost the US Open of 1939, to Byron Nelson. But the man persisted – in 1941, at last, he won the US Open and Masters.

Sarazen was as tough as old boots – he tied Lawson Little in yet another US Open, in 1940. And surely no champion, by accident or design, has been more adroit in maintaining himself in front of the public, in fashioning a quietly comfortable lifestyle for himself, than has Gene Sarazen. Through the 1960s, he was host to the television series *Shell's Wonderful World of Golf*, in which leading professionals of the day played matches in all the capital cities and luxurious resorts of the world. The series ran for seven years and was broadcast throughout the world.

In 1947, at the age of 45, Sarazen beat Sam Snead in the second round of the PGA Championship, 25 years after he had first won it. And the next year, he took Ben Hogan to the 36th hole – Hogan went on to win the title. In the 1958 Open Championship at Lytham, aged 56, he scored 288, the same total as the defending champion Bobby Locke. In the late 1960s, he was appointed Director of Golf at the Marco Island development, near Naples on the west coast of Florida, where he spent his subsequent winters, and in 1973 he made an evocative visit to Troon, 50 years after his initial disaster in his first Open. Playing an opening round with Arthur Havers, the 1923 champion, and Fred Daly, the champion of 1947, he promptly holed his teeshot at the impish and famous Postage Stamp hole, the 123 yards 8th.

As a swinger of the golf club, Sarazen may have been somewhat overrated. He was a solid, chunky, little bull of a man, had an unprepossessing grip and swing, rather flat-footed and considered by some to be downright ugly in action. Gene was not too concerned with style, but he played briskly, even quickly, giving the ball a lusty smash that often saw him topple over or take a stride or two forward after impact. He spent many of his mature summers on his farm in Germantown up the Hudson River valley, where he rejoiced in the title "The Squire of Germantown". Into his 80s, he was teaming with Byron Nelson to play an honorary nine holes as the overture to the Masters each year, following in the footsteps of Jock Hutchison and Freddie Macleod. Off the course, he was funny, puckish, informed, a good companion, warm and friendly, enthusiastic in

reminiscence and conversation about the game and its champions, reminding the young bloods that there had been some pretty good players in the best years of Gene Sarazen.

And there were, too. Leo Diegel was a magnificent player, another of the best who never won an Open Championship. He finished second, third and, three times, seventh in the US championship and won the PGA title in successive years, at match play of course. He was a player with all the shots, but also with a putting neurosis, not only in the stroke, but in the implement. He'd file and scrape and hammer and add bits to putter heads without ever finding the magic mean. Bill Melhorn was another fine player, whom Hogan described as the best man he had seen from tee to green. Then there was Thomas Dixon Armour of Edinburgh, who fought in the Great War and lost the sight of an eye in doing so, played for the British amateurs against the Americans, the American professionals against the British, and won the Open Championships of Britain, America and Canada, the US PGA Championship and many another. The game was not a game for Tommy unless there was money riding on each round, each nine holes, every single hole if he could make the bets. Armour lost a fortune in the Stock Market crash, but recouped it at his summer club, the Congressional in Washington D.C. and, in winter, commanding vast fees for his instructional talents, sitting under a huge sunshade at the luxurious Boca Raton club in Florida. Herein lay one of the great advantages American professionals had over their British counterparts. They had an all-year season. When the north-eastern states, the north and the middle west were smothered in snow for long weeks, hundreds flocked south in search of the sun and the action. The action was not hard to find, particularly in the 1920s before the Depression, since thousands of Americans who could afford it spent at least part of each winter in the warmth of Florida. The pros followed them – to teach, to partner, to play Florida tournaments and promotional exhibitions at the burgeoning golf courses, hotel and property developments, as Hagen did for the Pasadena club. After the Second World War, the south west had its turn, with hundreds of such developments blossoming in the sun states of Arizona and New Mexico, and in Southern California. All this while, the British professionals were no lions in winter. They'd spend their time making do and mending, or more likely shivering around a coal fire in the back shop. For all that, even if the strength of the game, both amateur and professional, was firmly in the grasp of the Americans, in the Old Country outstanding players emerged.

The first Open Championship after the 1914–18 war brought into stark relief the contrasting personalities of two outstanding British golfers, and the quixotic, crucifying nature of the competitive game. When the war started, George Duncan (1884–1964) from Aberdeen was 30, Abe Mitchell (1887–1947) from Forest Row in Sussex was 27. Clearly the war had cost them valuable years, but both men had been established after a fashion before the war. Duncan had finished fourth to J.H. Taylor in the 1913 Open, and Mitchell had taken the great John Ball to the 38th hole of a memorable Amateur Championship final at Westward Ho! in 1912, the last of Ball's eight championships. Duncan had had a part in forming the "Niblick Brigade", a grouping of professional golfers who served in the Army. They were a long way below brigade strength, but they served in the 2nd Company, the Rifle Brigade. The first post-war Open was scheduled for Deal in 1920. Mitchell opened with impressive rounds of 74 and 73 and led by six shots from Jim Barnes and Sandy Herd. Duncan was down the field, 13 strokes away in fact with 160. Mitchell never did like championships. He thought they "took too long". He never slept well during a championship week, and on the final day he made the mistake of going to the course too early, in time to see Duncan finish with a cracking third round 71. The result was – when Mitchell started his third round, a booming hook off the tee, three putts on the first green and a round of 84 – all 13 strokes wiped out in 18 holes. A solid 72 from Duncan in the final round saw him win by two strokes from Herd. Mitchell finished fourth. He never again did better than that in an Open, whereas Duncan by contrast was hard at it in 1922, chasing Walter Hagen all the way to the very last hole at Sandwich. He came to it seeking a par-4 to tie with a round of 68, but missed by one stroke.

George Duncan, one of a large family, made his way through the caddie and assistant professional undergrowth to a club job at Hanger Hill, in North London, and in time to plum jobs at Wentworth and Mere. He was brisk, temperamental in argument, quick in discussion, dogmatic at times and an inveterate theorist. Yet no man ever took up a stance and fell into a perfect grip more naturally than did George Duncan; no one got the ball away, or played the game, more quickly than he. His book *Golf at the Gallop* was aptly named.

He bubbled over with confidence, was liable to rip off either the most dazzling play, or just plain rubbish. Like Armour, he was never afraid of Hagen, and captained the Ryder Cup team against him in 1929. George probably liked to talk as much as he liked to play golf. He and Mitchell toured the US in 1921, 1922 and 1924, sponsored by the Silvertown Company, makers of the Silver King golf ball; Duncan incidentally finished eighth in the US Open of 1921 and sixth in Sarazen's Open of 1922. Of their tours, George said, "Abe played, I talked". It was an exact illustration of the two personalities.

Abe Mitchell came from a family of gardeners and foresters in rural Sussex – he was a product of the Cantelupe Artisans, one of the oldest of artisan clubs – and developed wrists and arms of steel from such work. No one ever hit the ball harder or in those days further than did Abe Mitchell, but he was a quiet, reserved, reticent, perhaps bucolic, perhaps introverted, man. He never did have a club job, being first private professional to Lord Northcliffe at his course at North Foreland, and, when Northcliffe died in 1922, private professional to Samuel Ryder, the man who presented the Ryder Cup, at the Verulam course near St Albans. Mitchell was said to have an annual retainer from Ryder of £1000 – a very substantial sum in the 1920s. He held the club with an odd, baseball grip, left thumb outside the shaft and behind his right hand, had a long, flowing backswing, but not much of a follow-through. A fierce and crisp puncher you could call Abe Mitchell. He was a quite marvellous spoon player (fairway wood, that is) as was Duncan, and a beautiful putter. He didn't practise much, didn't care for steel shafts, and, all told, quite a few of his contemporaries felt he might have been in the wrong business. On and off the course, he always wore matching plus-four suits, carried a cane, and suffered the soubriquet "Best player never to have won an Open". He once lost to Walter Hagen 2 and 1 over 72 holes for £1000, when Hagen kept him waiting 30 minutes on the first tee – Hagen would never have done that to George Duncan.

Both of these men were leading figures through the 1920s and into the early 30s – Mitchell died of ulcers at the age of 60, Duncan talked on until he was 80. The champion of 1923, Arthur Havers, at Troon, was to be the last British champion in the Open for eleven years, years dominated by the Americans and in particular by Jones and Hagen until the coming of Henry Cotton in 1934. Characteristically, Hagen, defending his championship in 1923, came to the last hole at Troon needing a birdie to tie. He had chased

Havers hard over the closing nine holes. He cut his second to the 72nd hole and it faded into a bunker. Hagen very nearly holed the bunker shot. Arthur Havers was a player all right – he had qualified for the Open in 1914 at the age of 16. He was something of a gentle giant, perhaps lacking fire, and with the mien of a bishop, but physically strong with a very good long game, if not quite so good on short approach shots. Arthur made the most of this single win. As 1923 Champion, he teamed with Jimmy Ockenden, the 1923 French Open Champion, in a tour of America which was so successful that Arthur came back with £8000 in his pocket. He confided in George Gibson that he could afford a new car, and rather fancied an Austin. He and George went to see Chris Buckley, sales manager of Austin in Birmingham, whom they both knew. Buckley asked Havers about his American trip, and Arthur, without quite telling him how much he had, said he had done fairly well. Buckley said "Whatever you have, put it into Austin shares – you'll never regret it!" Havers did, and never did regret it. Austin paid a 100% dividend the following year.

For the best part of 50 years, George Gibson was highly influential in the professional game, off the course. A shrewd, delightful, soft-voiced Scot with a sharp business brain, George was the son of William Gibson of Kinghorn, clubmaker. The young Gibson went into banking and was at the Royal Bank of Canada in Montreal when he had to return home on the death of his father in 1921. He was persuaded to stay and get into the golf business by Jimmy Thomson, then managing director of the Professional Golfers' Co-operative Association. The idea of a co-operative trading association for the professionals had first been mooted in 1907, and was eventually formed in 1921. The PGCA was what it said it was, a co-operative for the pros, who were the shareholders. It held huge stocks of all the manufacturers' products and distributed them to the pros. Instead of having a myriad of accounts with a myriad of manufacturers, the club professional had one comprehensive monthly account with the PGCA. George Gibson started in the golf trade as a traveller with A.G. Spalding and Bros, and, when Jimmy Thomson died in 1934, George succeeded him as managing director. By 1960, Gibson was reporting a £1 million turnover, and when he retired in 1970 the PGCA had passed the £2 million sales mark, with warehouses in London, Birmingham, Manchester and Glasgow. By his management skills, in his advice, by judiciously extending credits to professionals who might have been having a lean time, and in very many other ways, George Gibson was an outstanding friend to all the British and European professionals.

Prominent in British golf through the 1920s and 30s in tournaments and Ryder Cup matches, and eventually for collecting into the family one Open Championship success, were the Whitcombe brothers, Charles, Ernest and Reginald, the last of these the Open Champion of 1938, won in a gale at Sandwich. They all had their start in the game at the Came Down club in Dorchester, where their mother was clubmistress. Charles, considered the best golfer of the three, became greenkeeper–pro at Marlborough, then at Landsdown in the hills above Bath, where things were quiet during the week and he had lots of time for practice. One day he went home and said to his wife, "How much money do we have?" She said, "Why?" Charles said, "The *Daily Mail* tournament is coming up at Deal. I think I can hit this ball as well as Duncan or Mitchell or any of them – I'd like to have a crack at it." His wife said, "We have £40." Charles said, "Can I have £20 to go to Deal?" "If you have that much faith in yourself, you'd better take the lot," said Mrs Whitcombe, clearly a very proper wife. He went, and won the tournament, holing three full iron shots in doing it. He later reflected that this win had altered his life. "I'd have to scrimp and save to buy a suit. Now that I am well known, and can easily afford a suit, I find that people are anxious to give them to me."

Archie Compston from the Midlands, tall, handsome, unfathomable, was something of a rough diamond, a phrase surely invented for him. Less than highly educated, he was a hungry reader and torrential talker on any subject. Archie seemed to know a little about everything. At the Coombe Hill club in London, Archie would play anyone off handicap, giving a two-hole start, for £50. He was eventually nailed by the revenue for £6000 in a case which went to the House of Lords. Never a diplomat, Archie could swear like an Irish trooper and often did, regardless of people, place or circumstance. He tackled Walter Hagen in a 72-holes match at Moor Park in 1928 and ran all over him, winning 18 and 17. For Hagen, this was the first of an exhibition series, and perhaps he had not found his land legs, but in his limousine driving away from the course, he said to his distraught manager, Bob Harlow, "I can beat that son of a bitch the best day he ever had." A few weeks later at the Open Championship at Sandwich, Hagen was first, Compston third. Archie reigned for a good 20 years as overlord of the Mid Ocean Club in Bermuda, no doubt issuing his instructions and commands to all and sundry with his feet on the table.

British professionals up to the 1939–45 war and beyond were very much golf club professionals, inhibited and compromised by money or the lack of it and by the lingering class structure in British society. They were "servants" of their clubs and as such had to know their "proper place". Throughout the 1920s, and well into the 30s, there might be no more than half a dozen professional tournaments to play for, in addition to the Open Championship, and the Match Play Championship, which was considered an important event, so it was necessary, economically, for professionals to have a club job, a retainer often modest enough, and sales from the shop to sustain them. The pro shop could be appalling – in many cases little more than a shed, built as an afterthought to the clubhouse, heated by a coke stove at which bread on the end of a three-pronged fork would be toasted, tea gulped from a cracked mug. This is not too much of an exaggeration. With courses closed for perhaps several weeks in winter, professionals often found life hard. This was a time for making clubs. Eddie le Seuer, a Channel Islander who worked for Reggie Whitcombe for a spell, made the most beautiful woods for which he probably got a couple of pounds and not much thanks. And the pro shop inventory would consist of clubs, balls and a few chocolate bars, not much else. Fashion had not then discovered golf as it has today. The pros were a tweedy lot. The Vardon influence seemed to linger certainly into the 1920s – it was all plus-four suits in brown or oatmeal colours, woollen stockings, polished brogues, ties, shirts with cuff links – almost a regalia. Many of them were smokers – pipes, 30 cigarettes a day, nicotine-stained fingers. They lived rather modest lifestyles. No one went out to dinner then, and holidays would be two weeks in the year at a town on the coast such as Brighton, Scarborough or Blackpool. But the family unit was strong. There were few divorces. Homes were modest. The old boys of the Vardon era were even more modest. Ted Ray lived in a terrace at Oxhey; J.H. Taylor, when at Mid Surrey, lived in a two-up, two-down terrace at Richmond; Sandy Herd lived above stables, and Vardon himself lived in a little corner house within walking distance of South Herts. The grass on his tiny front lawn was said to be the "finest in the world". Ted Ray was reckoned the richest man in golf when he left £29,000 during the war. Harry Vardon left £13,000 when he died in 1937. Most of them would walk to work, as Vardon did. Even much later, John Burton at Hillside cycled to the course – he didn't want the members to know he owned a car. Things were slightly better in the

1930s. By 1938, Percy Alliss at Ferndown, a fairly affluent club, had a four-bedroomed house, with garage, worth then perhaps £1000. But, save at certain clubs, it was not the thing for the professional to have a car that was in any way grander than the average member's and it was certainly not the thing for the professional to cross the portals of the clubhouse save when invited, and that was seldom. Even at a club like Ferndown, the same Percy Alliss might go in perhaps only on Christmas Morning, have a couple of whiskies with the captain, then be home for Christmas lunch – very much a question of knowing one's place! Yet it was not wholly a bad thing, since professionals galore have ruined careers by too much sipping at the club bar, by not being able to handle the "privilege".

Life ·for the American professional was entirely different. American golf clubs were spacious, well-equipped. The British way would have appalled him, as it did Walter Hagen. He could rejoice in a year-round season, with jobs, exhibitions, competitions in Florida, the South and South West in winter, when the northern courses were smothered in snow. But there were deeper differences of wealth, affluence, economics and economic philosophies. The American people then, as they do now, demanded first-class service in all things, for which they are quite prepared to pay. The British then, and to this day, do not. The great wealth of the British Empire was built, certainly in part, on an abundance of cheap raw materials from the colonies, with a cheap, low-wage, manufacturing labour force at home. The United States too had an abundance of cheap raw materials from its own "empire", contained within the boundaries of one continent, but this was processed by an industrious, energetic, ambitious high-wage labour force, and an adventurous banking system. The American philosophy has always been to keep that dollar bill moving, circulating fast and their banking systems and financial philosophies have encouraged this. British banks by contrast have been conservative, short-term, not too attracted by risk – the philosophy lingers to this day. But then almost everything changes to a greater or lesser degree. Hagen had shown the future to professionals in America and to some extent in Britain. The Hagen torch was to be carried along in the Old Country by an exceptional man, and exceptional champion – Henry Cotton – whose greatest single stroke of fortune was that his time came after the time of Walter Hagen and Bobby Jones.

\*    \*    \*

89

Thus Bobby Jones in his time had tackled many great players, amateurs and professionals, American and British. His achievements are all the more bewildering, and more than half a century on it is difficult to appreciate fully the status of the man as the ultimate American champion, the ultimate American sporting hero. As a child, he was, inescapably, a prodigy, as much as Yehudi Menuhin was. As a youth, he suffered the conflict of his talent with his temperament and emerged in control and finally became something of a Rennaissance Man, a Leonardo of golf. He played little tournament golf in fact between championships and virtually none through the winter months while in college. Here too he was exceptional. After a degree in mechanical engineering at Georgia College of Technology, there was a degree in English at Harvard, then qualification as a lawyer at Emory College in only two years of a four year course, all this done while he was amassing a golf championship record that astonished the world, and also raising a family of three children. The man was a perfect gentleman, modest in victory, noble in defeat. He was always gracious without exception to his opponents. He always played to the rules, more than once calling penalties on himself for infringements no one else had seen. One of these came in the US Open Championship of 1925. His ball moved as he addressed it in the rough. No one but Jones could have seen it. He reported the fact and insisted that he be penalised the regulation two shots. In the event, these two shots cost him the championship – he tied with Willie Macfarlane and lost the play-off. "There is only one way to play this game," was the Jones philosophy. And in the second round of the 1926 US Open at Scioto, his ball moved slightly as he addressed it on the 15th green. Again no one else could have realised it. Jones insisted he be penalised. He did win that championship.

The Jones swing was long, rhythmic, almost, it seemed, lazy. In contrast to Hagen, for example, he had a narrow stance which became progressively narrower as he worked through to the shorter clubs, until on short pitches his feet were almost touching. Like Vardon, he took his hands away fractionally before the clubhead moved, then brought it slightly inside the line. He had a very big shoulder turn which generated great power and speed at impact – Jones was a beautiful and very long driver – and the hands and arms went through and up to a high finish. It was a drowsy, poetic swing since Jones believed

**Bobby Jones at St Andrews in 1927. He won the Open Championship three times in all.**

91

that "you can never swing a golf club too slowly", and featured precise and controlled weight transference which made it very much a one-piece swing. Jones swept the ball away. As his career developed, he became an excellent putter. And he also came to believe that golf was a game of character, of intellect, so that he schooled himself to play against par, against the golf course, against himself, rather than against human opposition, so that in Open championship play he seldom produced a succession of brilliant rounds which scattered the field. Rather it was the relentless nature of his play that brought him from behind to win, or to hold off the others by a stroke or two. An exception to this was the Open Championship of 1927 at St Andrews, when his first round of 68, including 28 putts, scattered the field and let him win by six strokes with a record total of 285. In this respect, it is intriguing to look more closely at that climactic, stupendous year of 1930, when Jones won all four championships, and, more than once, simply survived. In the first of these, the Amateur Championship at St Andrews, one would have to claim that the Jones victory was, simply, pre-ordained. In the sixth round, against Harrison "Jimmie" Johnston, the US Amateur Champion, Jones was comfortably four up with five to play. He won, only just, on the 18th green. In the semi-final against his countryman George Voigt, Jones was one down with three to play and holed a frightening putt of 12 feet on the 17th to stay one up and win again on the closing hole. The greatest match of this championship was Jones v. Tolley. Jones certainly had to dispose of some of the best amateurs in the world to take the title. Before a vast crowd, estimated finally at 15,000, there was never more than one hole in it. Again St Andrews's dread 17th hole played a critical role in the drama. Tolley outdrove Jones, who had to play his second shot to the green first. He decided to play to the *left* of the Road Hole bunker, and had the huge crowd moved back. He then hit a beautiful shot which bounced up, struck into the gallery and left him an open chip along the length of the green. Tolley's second shot stopped short of the bunker, leaving him a fiendish pitch over the trap and a challenge to stop the ball on the narrow green, much less get it close to the flag. Tolley played an exquisite little pitch, and stopped it two feet from the hole. He later called it the finest shot he ever made. The Jones chip was left eight feet short, but once more the ball went truly into the centre of the hole. They played the 18th nervously, and halved – on to the 19th. Tolley's approach putt there left him stymied, and once again Jones had survived. It had been a

monumental match between two very hardened competitors, and there is a famous photograph of Jones, looking totally drained and quite exhausted, being escorted back to the clubhouse by two large policemen. In the Open Championship which followed at Hoylake, Jones went into the last round leading by a stroke and was touched by some unseen spirit on the second hole. His drive was cut out to the right, bonked on the head of a steward, and broke back across the fairway into a bunker. From there, Jones pitched to the green, and holed from 20 feet for a preposterous birdie. He then took seven at the next hole, but prevailed and survived yet again to win the championship by two strokes. He had been in Britain for six weeks, what with the Walker Cup matches, the Amateur and the Open, and his form in that last event was perhaps as poor as anything in any of his victories. On the boat train from London to Southampton, Cyril Tolley, who was going over for the US Open, said to him, "Do you think you have ever played so badly for so long before?" Jones answered "No!" For all that, when the *Europa* arrived in New York, there was a tremendous welcome. His friends from Atlanta were there in a ferryboat to take the hero off. Fireboats sent fountains into the sky and there was another Broadway ticker-tape reception.

Bobby Jones went directly from there to Minneapolis for the US Open at Interlachen and what was to be a gruelling championship. The heat, in the shade, exceeded 100°F and the humidity was fearsome. After one round, he had to have his sodden necktie cut off. Tolley lost nine pounds in one three-hour round. In the second round came another famous Jones shot, the "lily-pad" shot. He half-topped a spoon shot from a tight lie at the ninth hole. Like a flat stone propelled across the waves by a small boy, the ball skipped twice and reached the far bank. It never did skip off a lily-pad. Typically, Jones chipped to the green and made a birdie. His third round 68 was the best he had ever played in a US Open and gave him a six stroke lead. He eventually won the championship by two strokes from poor Macdonald Smith, the stylist who never could win a championship. For Jones, that was three out of three, and, as he waited in the clubhouse for the last of the players to come in, he decided that, come what may in the last of the big four, the US Amateur, 1930, this would be his last year of championships.

Bobby Jones had won two Open Championships in three weeks, 4000 miles apart. Now he was to go back to Merion, where he had played his first championship 14 years earlier, where he had won his first championship eight years earlier, where he was to win the fourth of the four in one year. He stormed through the championship, beating such players as Ross Somerville of Canada and Jess Sweetster, winning all five of his matches by 5 and 4 or better. In the space of four months, Bobby Jones had won the Grand Slam of the Open and Amateur Championships of Britain and the United States. It is said that 2,000,000 words were transmitted by the journalists covering the event at Merion. In the middle of November, 1930, Jones announced his retirement from competitive golf.

Robert Tyre Jones jun., was perhaps ultimately a Southern gentleman. Had he been an old-time plantation owner, one would imagine him to have been a benevolent "massa". His heritage was "Dixie". It lingers on, in American culture, bringing up short the unsuspecting foreign traveller arriving for the first time at, say, Atlanta airport. The entire place is awash in Confederate blue – flags, banners, souvenir mugs, teeshirts, car number plates, ashtrays, every conceivable object. Chided once with all of this, implanted in the Southern ethos more than a century after a ferocious civil war had left the States united, Jones said with a smile, but archly, "Isn't it much the same as the English and the Scots, who go back much further than we do?" This cultural background, plus his legal training and practice, gave Jones the ability to make particularly gracious public statements. He had enchanted a St Andrews crowd in 1927, when having won the Open Championship he asked that the trophy be held for the next year in the safe-keeping of the Royal and Ancient Club. The public statement which he issued after his Grand Slam makes the same point, tinged with the language of the law, and produced a strange, perhaps sad, perhaps controversial aftermath to a glittering championship career. Offers worth hundreds of thousands of dollars for commercial enterprises poured in on him, the amateur who had beaten all the professionals (Walter Hagen for example never won a championship in which Jones competed). Acceptance of any of these offers would, of course, have totally compromised his cherished amateur status.

Jones wrote:

Upon the close of the 1930 golfing season I determined immediately that I would withdraw entirely from golfing competition of a serious nature. Fourteen years of intensive tournament play in this country and abroad had given me about all I wanted in the way of hard work in the game. I had reached a point where I felt that my profession required more of my time

and effort, leaving golf in its proper place, a means of obtaining recreation and enjoyment. My intention at the time was to make no announcement of retirement, but merely to drop out quietly by neglecting to send in my entry to the Open Championship next spring. There was at that time no reason to make a definite statement of any kind; but since then, after careful consideration, I have decided upon a step which I think ought to be explained to the golfers of this country, in order that they may have a clear understanding of what the thing is and why it is being done.

On November 13, 1930, I signed a contract with Warner Bros. Pictures to make a series of twelve one-reel motion pictures, devoted to exhibiting and explaining the methods which I employ in playing the shots ordinarily required in playing a round of golf. These pictures are to be purely educational in character, and it is the ardent hope of both parties that they will be of some value, first by improving the play and thereby increasing the enjoyment of the vast number of people already interested in the game, and second, by creating an interest where none exists now among the many who may find enjoyment and beneficial exercise on the golf course.

The talking picture, with its combination of visual presentation and demonstration, with the possibility of detailed explanation, appeals to me as the ideal vehicle for an undertaking of this nature.

Of course, the matter of monetary compensation enters into the discussion at this point, and it is for numerous reasons that I wish to be perfectly understood on this score. The amateur status problem is one of the most serious with which the United States Golf Association has to deal for the good of the game as a whole. I am not certain that the step I am taking is in a strict sense a violation of the amateur rule. I think a lot might be said on either side. But I am so far convinced that it is contrary to the spirit of amateurism that I am prepared to accept and even endorse a ruling that it is an infringement.

I have chosen to play as an amateur not because I have regarded an honest professionalism as discreditable, but because I have had other ambitions in life. So long as I played as an amateur, there could be no question of subterfuge or concealment. The rules of the game, whatever they were, I have respected, sometimes even beyond the letter. I certainly shall never become a professional golfer. But, since I am no longer a competitor, I feel able to act entirely outside the amateur rule, as my judgement and conscience may decide. When these pictures have been made, I expect to return to the practice of my profession, unhampered by the necessity of keeping my golf up to championship requirements.

The Jones films, a series of twelve of about ten minutes each, were very successful – they were shown in some 6000 cinemas, were followed by a second series and produced for Jones the sum of $600,000, a vast fortune at the time, with which Jones set up a trust fund for his family. He then contracted with the A.G. Spalding Company with whom he helped design woods and iron clubs, producing what was perhaps the first matched set of steel-shafted clubs on the market. This too was successful. He wrote, doing all the writing himself, a weekly syndicated newspaper column, and with O.B. Keeler presented a weekly half hour radio programme. All in all, in the first few years of his retirement, at the age of 28, Jones probably collected more money from golf than any half dozen of his professional opponents might have dreamt of.

Thus Jones's status in the game which his statement, combining dissembling and legalese at the same time, claimed was now irrelevant, left some disquiet in the halls of the United States Golf Association, charged, as was the R & A, with administering the Laws of the Game and the Rules of Amateur Status, in short, of the propriety of golf, the governance of the game. Significantly, when the R & A decided that, at last, the club might elect an American to the captaincy of the club, they passed by Robert Tyre Jones jun., who would otherwise have been the most compelling choice, and decided on Francis Ouimet, in 1951. Even with such a championship career behind him, Jones was not yet finished with the game, although he had buckled down to an Atlanta law practice. Inspired by the energy and calculation of Clifford Roberts, a friend and Wall Street merchant banker, he created the Augusta National Golf Club and its beautiful course, which we discuss elsewhere. And he was not yet finished with St Andrews, where this odd aftermath to his career meant little to the natives, who persisted in idolising the man. In 1936, Jones and Grantland Rice, the famous American sports journalist, with their wives, set out to attend the Olympic Games

in Berlin. On the ship, some friends announced that they were planning to have a few days at Gleneagles en route. The Jones party joined them, and Bobby decided that he could not be that close to St Andrews without paying the town a final visit, for one last round.

Gordon Lockhart of Gleneagles Hotel and Willie Auchterlonie of the R & A were to play with him. When Jones arrived at the first tee for an informal, friendly game, some 2000 people were assembled. By the time they had played three holes, the crowd was 4000 strong. And by the time they finished the round, it seemed that the entire population of the old town was around the last green. Jones had played the first nine holes in 33 strokes, the complete round in 72. He was to return to St Andrews once more. When the World Amateur Team Championship for the Eisenhower Trophy was inaugurated in October, 1958, Jones, by then crippled and in a wheelchair, was elected captain of the US team. At the same time, St Andrews invited him to accept the Freedom of the City, the first American to be so honoured since Benjamin Franklin, 199 years before. The ceremony was held in the Younger Graduation Hall, a handsome room, into which were packed more than 1500 people, including all the Eisenhower teams and officials and citizens of the town. The ceremony was at once one of great dignity and friendly warmth. Jones spoke brilliantly in his soft Georgia accent, and at the end, when he made his painful way from the stage to join the Provost and drive out down the central aisle in an electric golf cart, draped with the flag of the State of Georgia, the entire audience, quite spontaneously, broke into that old Scottish air which is at once an anthem and a love song, "Will ye' no' come back again?" The emotion of the moment was perfectly caught by Herbert Warren Wind, writing in the American magazine *Sports Illustrated* with perceptive care: "So honestly heartfelt was this reunion for Bobby Jones and the people of St Andrews (and for everyone else) that it was ten minutes before many who attended were able to speak again with a tranquil voice."

In his middle 40s, Bobby Jones had been stricken with a rare disease, syringomyelia. It is described as "the dilution of the central canal of the spinal chord, or the formation of abnormal tubular cavities in its substance". It is a progressively crippling disease which led Jones in time to a wheelchair and endless suffering. This was little discussed outside his immediate family, and each year, when legions of friends made the pilgrimage to greet him at the Masters championship in his cabin near Augusta

National's 10th tee, they knew well not to mention his illness. His hands had become deformed, and since he remained an enthusiastic cigarette smoker in his middle years he took to having a cigarette lighter strung round his neck to help him with business. Lighting the cigarette was slow and complicated, but, although one longed to help with the procedure, at the same time one knew it would certainly not be the thing to do.

Jones died on the 18th of December, 1971, at the age of 69. It seems that a few days earlier, when he knew it was coming, he said to his family, "If this is all there is to it, it sure is peaceful." That seemed very much in character with the way in which the man had lived his life. And later, Ben Hogan, in considering how Jones had borne a crippling illness for more than 20 years, said: "I think we have finally discovered the secret of Jones's success. It was in the strength of his mind."

| CAREER HIGHLIGHTS | | |
|---|---|---|
| | British Open | US Open |
| Bobby T Jones | 1926, 1927, 1930 | 1923, 1926, 1929 1930 |

# CYRIL JAMES HASTINGS...

**C**yril James Hastings Tolley, MC, born in 1895, was an outstanding golfer during what is now seen to have been a golden age in the game. He was Amateur Champion in 1920 and 1929, and won the French Open Championship in 1924 and again in 1928, each time against the cream of the professionals of the day, including strong contingents of Americans. He played in half a dozen Walker Cup matches, captained the team, and was Captain of the Royal and Ancient Golf Club in 1948. His lifestyle permitted him to make golfing trips to Scotland and the Continent, and more than once to the United States.

But it is as a symbol of his times, as much as a golf champion, that we can consider C. J. H. Tolley. He would seem to represent perfectly another age which is almost, not entirely, but almost, gone. That is, an age of privilege, an age when young men of the proper background and family went to Eton College and Winchester, then Oxford or Cambridge University as a matter of course. They were not required to be aristocrats, nor enormously wealthy, but simply 'proper chaps', the products of proper, 'well-to-do' families.

Tolley played the game in the grand manner, flamboyantly, an amateur Walter Hagen. He discovered croquet late in life and declared 'My dear fellow, had I known what a wonderful game it is, I'd never have spent so much time on golf.' Such a cavalier, amateur spirit was typical of his times and of his contemporaries. His close friend, the amateur Roger Wethered, was irked that tying for the Open Championship of 1921 meant he would have to stay over in St Andrews to play-off on the Saturday, when he had promised to attend a local cricket match that day in the South. These fellows, of course, like millions of others, had come through a

fearful war. This is not to suggest that Tolley and his fellows were without merit. Many of them were highly talented and made impressive careers in the wider world, but his time was a time of privilege for the few.

Tolley's own words, recorded verbatim in 1965 in the bungalow at Eastbourne where he spent his closing years, and the attitudes which emerge from his words, seem to us to be illustrative of how things were in his times, for a section of society, with meritocracy still to come.

I was born in London, and had my 70th birthday the other day. We came down here in 1905 because, as a small boy, I used to get bronchitis quite often. We went to various places in the summer, and one particular summer we came to Eastbourne, and father thought it suited me and so we moved down here in 1905. At that time I had gone to prep school, and I played various games, you know, like cricket and Association football and I was more or less free of this bronchitis, but father was very anxious for me to play football, although he was a very good rugger player – played for Kent clubs like West Kent Wanderers and the Eagles and various clubs like that. He was a stand-off half. It came to going to Eastbourne College; they wanted me to go there and I said I'd rather not go to Eastbourne College if you're not going to let me play rugger, because it's going to be perfectly stupid going there, so I finally didn't go, and I had tutors. He was anxious for me to go into work in the Bank of England in London.

My father was a coffee merchant in London, in a firm called Phipps and Company, and they had houses in New York and Costa Rica, and dealt in cotton and other things. It was a wealthy firm, but he was not especially a wealthy man and I remember when I was quite young he came back one afternoon and was very worried. Mother said what had happened and he said he had lost £100,000

Cyril Tolley, symbol of a bygone age.

97

that afternoon. Then I went up to London and got an interview to go to the Bank of England which was a thing I wasn't looking forward to, but father was very keen that I should always have, for the future and when I got to retirement age, I should have a pension and everything from the Bank of England. Well, then the war came along in 1914, and I said, well, I'm going to go to fight and father was very much against it because he said I'd got this bronchitis and I mustn't go and so we had rather a lot of trouble for about eight or nine months. Finally I said I can't go on like this; people were sending white feathers because I was big and strong to look at. I did get a white feather, and it was very worrying, and so I said to father "I can't go on like this – it's too ridiculous," so I joined the Inns of Court OTC. We trained at Berkhamstead and played a certain amount of golf and things, then I was to have a commission in the K.R.R., with a great friend of mine, Freddy Taylor. We went off to cadet school at Letchworth, the Wickendon Barracks, and it was fiendish, absolute hell. They asked for volunteers for some sort of secret thing, we didn't know what it was, and I said to Freddy Taylor, "Freddy, I can't stick this infantry any longer . . . will you come?" He said, "No, I think I'll stay." He stayed, went into the K.R.R., and in due course was killed.

As I say, I was put down for this secret thing, which turned out to be tanks. We went down to Bovingdon in Dorset, not very far from Bourne-mouth, for training, and in due course we went to France in '17. The tanks had already been in action, and there were a lot of weaknesses in their particular design, and, when we went over, we went with the Mark V and did a certain amount of recce at Arras, because they thought they would put us in there then they came to the conclusion that the ground wasn't suitable. Then in July, the 31st, we went into the third battle of Ypres, in the mud – you couldn't imagine anything worse than the mud and we had a hell of a time there – we put in the whole of the battalion, that is three companies. I would think there were 36 tanks, and of those 36 tanks only three got to their objective, and of those three, only one got back and that was mine – so that was pretty lucky. For days we were working in the mud to try and dig out all these poor tanks stuck in the mud. It rained like mad, they got us back for re-fitting, and they said we would not have many more battles for tanks, and that in due course – which I believed – we would go back to England. I was just a tank commander, Second Lieutenant. Suddenly we were warned we'd got to go down to the Cambrai area to make some kind of a feint attack, because the people up north at Ypres were having a bad time and I think the French were not having a good time in the South. It was to be a feint to get the Germans to draw away some of their reserves. Well, it turned out to be the most wonderful attack because the country in which we operated was beautiful terrain, just like the South Downs, and we went through at terrific speed. This was the 20th of November, and by the end of November we'd penetrated quite a long way up towards Cambrai. We had been warned that the Bosch was massing troops to the south. We said, "You don't think he'll counter-attack?" "Oh, no, he won't counter-attack," they said. Of course he did, swept round behind us, and I was captured and spent 13 months in Germany, where I played no golf at all. I was at Karlsuhe for four weeks, then Heidelberg, then to Furstenburg and Mecklenburg, north of Berlin, lovely country, lakes and forests. We had a lot of mercantile marine officers there and they used to build these little model yachts and race them and they used to bet, of course. All the time I was in Germany I did nothing but gamble. I was slightly wounded in the hand, tiny bullet splinters they couldn't do anything about. Sometimes they hurt – when the Second World War looked like starting, they started to hurt again, little hard lumps!

Anyhow, I came back and I said to my father "I'm going to stay in the Army, I like it very much" and he said, "Well, you've had your ration of being in the Army." I was missing for a whole month, and they didn't know what had happened to me and the first message they got was a telegram I'd sent them from Germany. The War Office had said that I was missing, didn't say believed killed or anything like that. They had a wretched four weeks worrying about it, then they heard I was all right. Father went up to London and ordered parcels to be sent. Most of our food came from England. I got back on Christmas Eve, 1918. I said I'd like to stay in the tanks because I was very devoted to the tanks and my father said "No, no, you've had your ration. I think you'd better go up to Oxford." I said all right and went to University College in 1919. I had played a bit of golf, of course, before I went up to Oxford. I first started to play at Blackheath when I was a very small boy. Although he [my father] wasn't a member, he used to go and play there in the mornings, and I played golf and I also played tennis. In fact when I was 15 I think I was rather better at tennis than I was at golf. My handicap when the war started was plus one. I went up to Oxford not with the idea of getting a golfing blue, but I wanted to get a cricketing blue, because I played a lot of cricket as well and, well, the competition to get a cricket blue was rather harder than I expected. I played for the College XI, but I never got a trial for Varsity cricket. We had in due course our Varsity match at Sunningdale in 1920, and I should think it was about the end of April and I was in the High one morning when I came into Wethered. He said, "The entrance for the Amateur closes today, you're meant to play up there at Muirfield, aren't you?" I said, "Oh no, I'd much rather play cricket – I made 50 yesterday against the Oxford Police and anyhow I like playing cricket in the summer." He said, "Oh, I can't go all that way by myself, to Muirfield. Anyway, we shan't do very well, but it will be a wonderful experience." I said "No, I'm not going." Anyhow, he argued and finally I said, "All right, you don't want to go alone, I'll come with you." So I hurried home and sent a telegram to Arthur Croombe: "Please enter me for the Amateur Championship." My entry was 168 – the last one received for that tournament. In due course we went up to Muirfield, and Wethered was beaten, I think in the second round and came back to Oxford with whooping cough at the same time, and left me up there all by myself. I went on playing. There was a very big American contingent there and then from almost out of the blue I found myself in the final, to play Bob Gardner, who was one of the best American players. It was a 36 holes final. He was two up at lunch.

I played pretty well in the afternoon and got one hole back, then another, back to all square, then I won a hole and had a few halves, then won another and a few more halves until finally I was three up with four to play. The 15th hole was a drive and a firm mashie and he made rather a mess of his drive and was short of the green. I played an absolutely perfect shot straight at the pin and it looked as though it was going to be quite close and I was going to win 4 and 3. But the ball took a bad bounce, went over the green into a bunker. He knocked his up not so far away and I took five and he made four so instead of 4 and 3 I was only two up. The next was a very long hole and took three to get on in those days and I took three putts so that was one up, two to play. Pretty dramatic. The 17th was a very difficult hole in those days – of course, the whole place has been changed – and I had to hole a nasty putt for a half, about seven or eight feet after he holed rather a long one. Dormie. Anyhow, at 18, the 36th hole, he played a beautiful second and got four, I took five, and that was all square. The first extra hole was a short one,

a 2-iron shot, and as I recall, he played a spoon and put the ball on the green. The hole breaks off to the right. My shot went straight at the flag by mistake. I had wanted to play right and have the ball break down. Luckily for me, the ball went straight on and little Ben Sayers came rushing up and said "I think you're dead, sir." When we got to the green (we had a very large crowd) I was furious because the ball was about 14 feet away. I thought, well Ben that's certainly not dead. Anyway, Bob's putt just slipped past. I popped mine in, and won.

People afterwards made a big thing about the five pound note and the caddie. I had a really nice caddie, his name was Solomon and he'd been caddying for a chap called Victor Maude, who was a relation of a famous actor, Cyril Maude was it? He lost in the first round, and since I didn't have a caddie he said "All right, you can have my caddie." So I had this boy. He subsequently worked on the golf course at North Berwick. I promised him that if I won the championship, I'd give him a fiver. I didn't think I would win it, perhaps I was trying to build my self-confidence. As we went to the 37th green I took it out and gave it to him and said, "You'd better have this whilst you can get it!" I really did this just to cheer myself up. I didn't see him for about a quarter hour afterwards.

I met Wethered just before I went up to Oxford. We were entered in the *Golf Illustrated* Gold Vase at Mid Surrey and played a practice round the day before. In those days I could hit a golf ball further than anyone and I was furious because someone was hitting the ball up to me. Bernard Darwin I think won the Vase. I was tied with him after the first round, we did 74s or something like that, then I fell away in the afternoon, .and Bernard did 76 I think, and I finished fifth or sixth. I think it was just timing that let me hit the ball so far. I've always been a swinger, never a hitter, and I had a long swing which wasn't very fast, and with sort of co-ordination over timing and rhythm and balance I used to hit the ball really a long way. Mother would always say she knew who was driving if she wasn't looking because the crack I gave the ball was really different to the crack other people gave, and of course Roger was one of these wiry people with a terrific strong wrist. He gave the ball a terrific crack and it went literally miles, but I've always sort of swept the ball along. He would come under the category more of a hitter than a swinger. Oh, he was a magnificent iron player because he'd got such terrifically strong forearms and wrists. He was a much better iron player than I was, whereas I could drive constantly more consistently than he, and latterly of course he was hitting the ball all over the place. He was inclined to play a type of iron shot with his wooden clubs – I think that was probably the reason why he was all over the place.

Roger is a senior partner of a firm called Grenfell and Company, stockbrokers. His father was of an artistic temperament who was always keen on painting. I think vaguely they are connected with the Wethered Brewery. I think the father had some money, and he became a writer. He wrote all sorts of books, one on Chinese gardening, one on mosaics, anthologies – he was a most intelligent, literary-minded man. Now Roger's mother, I think the name was Lunn or Lund, came from Yorkshire and she had a good deal of money. So they were comfortably off. Roger was the only surviving son, Joyce the only surviving daughter, but I think they had other children who died in infancy. Roger for some reason was delicate, too. He was supposed to go to Eton, but didn't – he had tutors. Roger got a commission and went to France with the gunners for a short time. I think I'm three years older than him. I still see him. I was playing in a county croquet tournament at Hurlingham, and I stayed with him. He has a house just beside the first tee at Royal Wimbledon. He still plays golf. I haven't played since 1963. I had blood pressure and the doctor said I shouldn't play golf. I also played bowls and he said stooping is no good. So I said how about playing croquet. He said, "That's the very game for you!" So now I play croquet. it is a marvellous game. If I had discovered it sooner, I should not have wasted all that time playing golf.

I became a member of the Stock Exchange about 1922 with a firm called Bower and Ray. Well, if you know anything about Association football, there was a Corinthian footballer called Bower, A. G. Bower, and he was up at Oxford playing a match against Oxford, you see, with the Corinthians. And he said, "Oh, what are you going to do when you come down from Oxford?" And I said, "Well, I don't know, I had thought of going into politics, at the moment I am reading law." He said, "Have you ever thought of going on the Stock Exchange?" I said frankly I hadn't. I had an uncle on the Stock Exchange, my mother's brother, who was a jobber in the money market. Bower said "Well, think it over, but if you come to London come and see father, he'd very much like to meet you." In due course, I was up there and gave him a ring and I met his father and his brother, Theodore Bower,who was really a very good golfer – A.G. was a pretty good

golfer too. They'd both been in the H.A.C. in the First World War. And we had a chat and the old man said, "Well, if you'd like to come to us on half commission we'd be very pleased to have you." So I had a chat with my father about it and he said, "Well, you know a certain amount of people, and if it's the life you want, you'd better go there." And so I went to them. I was what is called a blue button, you wear that for two years or something, then you get half fees. In due course, I became a partner in the firm of Bower and Ray, where I stayed until 1929.

I went over to America in 1929 to play in the American Championship at Pebble Beach in California, and I'd been doing a certain amount of American business for a firm called Tucker, Anthony. There were four of us who went over – Lord Charles Hope, Dale Bourne, who was killed in the Second World War, Eustace Storey and myself. When we were in New York, Storey, who was connected with Tucker, said Maxwell Tucker would very much like to see me. I went to see Tucker and he said that I had been doing a lot of business for them in London and did I ever think of coming to live in America and doing business for them there? I said I hadn't thought of it. That was when the market was way up, and people were becoming millionaires overnight. So I went to California and played pretty well, got to the last eight and really ought to have beaten Dr Willing. He got to the final. On the way back I saw Tucker, Anthony again and they offered me a pretty good retaining fee. So I said I would go back to London, sell my seat and give up the partnership. On the way back to America, the crash started and the banks were closed for four days. When I walked into Maxwell's office, he said, "What the hell are you doing here?" I said "Ten days ago you said you wanted to have me – how was I to know a crash was coming?"

I took an apartment as they call it on 52nd street and stayed there on and off for about four years before coming back. I enjoyed it very much – of course I played golf in a good many places. As I said, when I was playing in that championship at Muirfield in 1920 Bob Gardner was one of a big American contingent, and they came over primarily to talk rules with St Andrews, and amongst their delegates was Herbert Walker who at one time was President of their USGA. He conceived the idea that it might be a good thing for the amateurs to play an annual match. It was arranged before he gave this gigantic cup in 1921 that we should have a trial run at Hoylake. They sent over a pretty impressive side, but we felt perhaps a little sorry for them because we thought we couldn't fail to win. We had Raymond de Montmorency, who was a housemaster at Eton as Captain, we had Armour playing for us, we had Jenkins who had been champion in 1914. J. Gordon Simpson was a very good Scotch player, who did well in championships without ever winning. He always said he played well until he ran into someone who produced fireworks and knocked him out, and actually at Muirfield against him I did something like 31 for the first nine holes. Colin Aylmer was another, a dear little man who I think had been a regular soldier in the cavalry, but after the war went to Ranelagh as golf secretary. He held the record there of 55 for 18 holes, staggering.

The Wethereds used to go up to Dornoch in the summer, as did Ernest Holderness and de Montmorency. They had a lot of competitions up there and Roger's father had a house there for a time. De Montmorency was the man really responsible for the graded lot of clubs we have now 1–9. When he was at Eton he played a lot at Stoke Poges, where Sherlock was the professional. He produced quite beautiful clubs, and Monty had the idea of having them numbered. He was probably the first one that had these clubs. In those days, we used to buy our wooden clubs from the one pro and then we'd go round on our travels and suddenly see a big iron you liked, then somewhere else you'd find a light iron and so on, not all made by the same maker. At about that time there was controversy about the ball, to standardise the ball. Monty said, "It's much better if you standardise the clubs. You see the way I play, I sweep the ball away, don't take any divots." I said, "Monty, the only time you take divots is when you're putting."

Holderness was one of the Dornoch people. He used to go up with his father and mother. He had an awfully nice father, he was Sir Thomas Holderness, Indian Civil Service, was he? Anyway, he was the first baronet and Ernest is the second. He played at Walton Heath, went to Radleigh. He was about the finest young athlete Radleigh ever had, but he had a terrible operation, some duodenal trouble. He had to give up his athletics, and took to golf. He was the most beautiful player you've ever seen. He was a lovely player, won the championship twice. Roger won it once, at Deal, Ernest won at Prestwick, and at St Andrews, I think. Very slight, tall and very slight, highly intelligent, hit the ball dead straight, never went in the rough, putted well. If he could have given more time to playing – he was with the Home Office – he could have beaten them all. Made a point of winning the President's Putter, you know

the Oxford–Cambridge Putter at Rye. Won it five time I think.

Roger Wethered, and Joyce, had perfect temperaments. Nothing seemed to irritate them. Some things upset me. You'll see in one match of a Walker Cup when I played Bobby Jones and he beat me 12 and 11. That was entirely due to something happening in the middle of the round when we were all square on the 13th green and I had a long putt to put dead, to remain square. The tail-end match was on the 5th green, 6th tee. And just as I was going to strike the putt, a friend of mine, who was in charge of the other match, bellowed "Fore!" I jumped and hit the ball halfway and I was absolutely furious with him for not waiting. I took three putts and for the rest of the round didn't hit a shot. I was furious. I never did mind what the general public did because they didn't know better, but when you have somebody who knows the game, who knows all about keeping quiet, to suddenly shout like that . . . I went into lunch five down and I never settled down. I couldn't I was so cross. It was very important that I should win that match. We only lost the whole thing by six to five, or something of the kind. If I'd beaten Bobby, we would have probably beaten the Americans. But that's one of the few instances when I've been thoroughly furious with anyone. In 1921 at Hoylake, I remember my single against Chick Evans because he was champion of America and I was champion here. Armour was in our team. Tommy Armour was a beautiful player, even as an amateur. Just after this he went to America, became a professional and had an outstanding career. I played him in the final of the French Amateur, in 1920 I think.

Perhaps I didn't behave particularly well the night before, in Paris, but we did get to the first tee in good order. There were lots of trees down the right side, it was his honour, and he hit one straight into the trees, out of bounds. I thought, well, that's a good start and so I had a crack, and mine went out of bounds, too. He had another go, and that went out of bounds, and I had another go and that went out of bounds. You would hardly believe it. His third effort he hit right on the top, so it didn't go out of bounds, but my next, my third, did. The penalty then was distance, not stroke and distance, and he eventually won the hole in seven to eight, something of the kind. Then we had a pretty good game, perhaps all square or one hole in it at lunch. Anyhow, we played the 19th and the 20th. The third hole is downhill, a little short hole. He made rather a mess of it and I had a chance to win it and go one up for the first time. Then he laid me a dead stymie. I wasn't worried. Just before I played, a butterfly rested on top of my ball. I hit the shot perfectly, it jumped over his ball and went straight into the hole. Well they had little raised metal things in the middle of the hole, where the flag goes and my ball bounced on it, popped out of the hole, and came right back to me, over his ball. You'd hardly believe it possible. I tried again, but needless to say, missed this time. He finally beat me something like 2 and 1.

Norman Boase was Chairman of the Championship Committee and was the king at St Andrews for a while. There was one Walker Cup match at Wheaton, Chicago, which I didn't play in but I spoke to Eustace Storey when they came back. I was the only one who had seen the Wheaton course before they went, and it was a farcical team to send, because it was a very long-hitting course. Anyhow at the particular time they didn't want me to play and I said to Eustace, "How did you get on with Tony Torrance?" He said, "You know, Tony's hopeless to play with. We won the first two holes and he said, 'Now Eustace, all we've got to do is play for halfs'" which was perfectly silly, but the point of the story about Norman Boase is that, I think, I haven't looked at it for a long time, you'll find that Tony Torrance was the only one who didn't lose his single. In fact he won. He beat Chick Evans. According to Eustace, Tony was dormie one and sliced his drive away to the right, while Chick hit a good one. Tony didn't like the look of the lie and said to Norman, "By the way, do you think this is ground under repair?" Norman had a look and said "Yes . . . drop it clear." He did, hit a good shot and got a half. Eustace said, "At least one thing Norman Boase did – he travelled 3000 miles to give a local ruling."

As you know very well, Americans are extremely hospitable, and in one of these early matches over there we were taken to the Follies in New York, and I can tell you a little story about John Cavan. They took us as I say to the Follies and Fritz Byers, one of their delegates – he was an immensely rich man in steel – had arranged for a lot of girls to come so that we could have drinks with them, and dance. John Cavan, a Scot, I don't think he had ever seen an American actress before, and he was getting on jolly well with this girl – I wish I could remember her name – I do sometimes – Peggy Kirton, that's the name – she was a beautiful girl and it was about two o'clock in the morning. Little John went up to Bob Harris and said, "Bob, I like this little girl, Peggy. I haven't got much money on me, could

you lend me five dollars so that I can take her home?" "Five dollars?" said Harris, "You'd need to have five hundred dollars!"

I played a good deal with the Hartley brothers, Rex and Lister. They used to play in the Sussex Championship and I'd meet one in the final one year, the other the next. They played at Addington and used to carve up all the people there. They were quite rich – Hartley's jam. Rex once told me that if you ever saw women making the strawberry jam, you'd never eat it. Poor boy took to drink in the end, and committed suicide, just walked out of a nursing home. He got rather spoiled because he used to play golf with the Prince of Wales and it rather went to his head, I'm afraid. I'm told he was ticked off by the Prince once, and told he'd never play with him again. I think they'd been playing at Sunningdale and went back to their flat, in Hans Crescent I believe, and he gave the Prince a drink or a cup of tea or whatever and something appeared in the Press. The Prince was furious.

In one championship, I was beaten by Alex Hill and they put him in the Walker Cup team. They did that with almost everyone who beat me. We had an absolutely staggering game. I didn't know Alex's game at all. Someone said, "Oh, he plays quite well, but he can't putt." Going to the 7th hole at St Andrews, I was two up. He did the 7th in three, the 8th in three, and did the next nine holes in something like 27. I did the next nine holes in 33, and lost five of them. I won the 16th and 17th, and had a putt to beat him on the 18th and missed. At the 19th my second looked as though it would be stone dead, but trickled past the hole. He just got over the burn, then putted up quite close. I had been putting well and thought I would go for it, and left myself a stymie which I missed. So he beat me. When we came in, Norman Boase was there and he said, "What a bloody fool – fancy taking three putts on the 19th green." I did nothing, just walked in. But Leonard Crawley was there, and he went for Norman Boase, he tore strips off him. He said, "You drunken old sot, why the hell don't you come out and watch and see what happens". Boase practically collapsed in fury – he was still Chairman of the Championship Committee.

Crawley was always rather against those people at St Andrews. He's got red hair and bristles sometimes. He could fly off the handle and get very cross. He occasionally made himself very unpopular. They didn't like him. Of course, a lot of these people have now gone. Normally, Leonard is pretty popular wherever he goes. He was a beautiful player, worked hard at the game, had lessons from Henry Cotton and so on. He was rather like J. H. Taylor, in rifling the ball at the flags. He hit the ball straight – like a shot from a gun. One incident with Leonard I shall never forget. It was shortly before he went to America. His mother died, she was driving a car, and fainted or died in the car. About the time he was invited to go to America to play in the Walker Cup, he was also invited to go to Australia to play for the M.C.C. The other thing – on the boat going over, he struck a match and the box of matches exploded and fell on his hand, so one hand was rather doubtful. On a practice round the day before the Walker Cup, Leonard hit a very good drive at the 18th hole, then a 4-iron which put the ball nicely on the green. When he played his match, he hit the same sort of drive and the same kind of second shot, although he didn't realise the wind was helping him. This beautiful shot went too far, beyond the pin, pitched on a huge piece of concrete and the first bounce knocked the Walker Cup, on display on a table behind the green, off its stance. Crawley felt that the dent he put in the Cup should have been allowed to remain there as an honourable battle scar, but the Americans had it mended.

The 1926 championship was at Muirfield. None of us played very well, and it was won by Jesse Sweetser, the American. Norman Boase and the selectors were at Muirfield and we said to them "How about the team?" They said, "We are not going to pick the team until we know how you've played." It was the first time, and probably the last time, that Ernest Holderness became a Bolshy, and he said "If you want me to play, I'll be at Gleneagles with Roger . . . we're not coming over to St Andrews for you people to look out of the window to watch us drive off. You know how we play." That very upset the committee. We went off to Gleneagles and we'd hardly arrived and a message came to say that we were in the side. Roger had said, "I'm not going to drive off that first tee and have you looking out of the window at my first drive going over the fountain to the right of the course." That was probably the first time that there was an ultimatum given to the committee.

Now I'm trying to think of something – oh, yes, Andrew Jamieson. He beat Bobby Jones in that particular championship and they said he should be in the Walker Cup team, probably rightly. Well, two days before, he came to me and said, "Mr Tolley, I don't think I should play in this match. I can do nothing but hit the ball off the socket." So I said, "Well, we'll go over on the New course and see what's wrong." I spotted it at once. His feet were wrong, and he was coming round with a loop and I got him back and he began to hit the ball beautifully. Bob Harris said something to me about "I thought of putting you with Jamieson in the foursomes." I said "That suits me – I like the boy." And in due course we went off and played. Well, I got absolute stink from the Press. They said I was snooty, didn't like playing with an artisan golfer because I never walked with him, never consulted him. The reason I did it was because if I had come near him when he was playing one of those big shots, he might think, well, am I doing as he told me, so I kept well away. He played pretty well and I played pretty well but I was very upset by the Scottish papers. I liked the boy very much. I'd have walked round holding his hand if it had done him any good, but I kept away from him for that reason.

Ronnie Hardman, now he was a Lancashire player, poor fellow he died in his garage . . . I don't know . . . some wife trouble . . . I think he hanged himself . . . G. N. C. Martin, now he was an Irish golfer, became a Major General, regular soldier, gunner. I used to see him in the last war. He was full of bounce . . . one of the most beautiful putters I've ever seen . . . would hole things from 20 yards . . . he would tell everyone who he was going to beat. I played him down at Deal, played remarkably well and only just managed to beat him . . . but he told everyone who he was going to beat.

I hope I've been able to help you. Only too delighted and I'm sorry but a friend of mine rang me up last night – she's over from Denmark and I haven't seen her since 1950. She's staying at Eastbourne with a conference. I stayed with them in Denmark.

| CAREER HIGHLIGHTS | |
|---|---|
| | British Amateur |
| Cyril Tolley | 1920, 1929 |

# SIR HENRY

**T**homas **Henry Cotton** was born at Holmes Chapel in Cheshire on the 26th of January, 1907, the son of an iron foundry owner who later owned several garages. The family moved to Dulwich in London, and Henry was educated at Alleyn's School. And in that plain fact may lie the first key to the most complex personality in all the line of great golf champions. In simple terms, Cotton is remembered as the first modern British player to have won the Open Championship three times; the first to do that since the days of the Triumvirate before the 1914–18 war, and, when he won at Royal St George's in 1934, as the British player who ended 11 years of dominance of the Open Championship by the Americans from Walter Hagen in 1922 until Densmore Shute in 1933. Further minor clues to the Cotton personality may lie in the fact that there was a brother, Leslie, older by one year, who first became a professional golfer, and older brothers usually have some influence on a younger, plus the fact that father George – he was 47 when Henry was born – was an indifferent but enthusiastic club golfer who encouraged the boys to play. But there was no family history of golf in the usual sense.

If not exactly a major public school – no Winchester, no Eton – Alleyn's was rather more than a minor school and surely put its mark on the boy from a reasonably prosperous, middle-class family. It was the mark of class, that unique element of English life, which, depending on your point of view, is either an out-moded, inhibiting evil, or one of the most artful and effective systems of personal relationships ever devised by society. Henry Cotton wanted to be the best, to have the best, to mingle with the best, in short, to be a "Toff". By and large, certainly in the context of international golf, he was

the first middle-class champion. He wanted to dine in the Savoy Grill, and did, to play golf with the Duke of Windsor, and did. In his best years, his was a world of first class travel, of the immaculate wardrobe, of dashing around Europe in a shining, street-long Mercedes to such exotic destinations as Marienbad, Biarritz, Monte Carlo and Le Touquet. He lived for some years in a suite at the Dorchester Hotel, then in a handsome town house in Belgravia's Eaton Square, and always, always he had the keenest of noses for business and for money.

He had no compunction at taking money from the rich. He would charge £100 for a golf lesson when the going rate might be £5, on the grounds that the rich could well afford it, and – another insight on his view of the world – in any case they were usually boring. His attitude to money must have come from somewhere deep in his roots – in his career, he earned a great deal of it, but, even in his final years at the Penina course in the Algarve of Portugal, he would be serving visitors with golf balls and tees in his shop. It is difficult to imagine Arnold Palmer or Jack Nicklaus doing that.

Henry Cotton was immensely successful, but he worked, indeed slaved, for his success from his earliest days. Henry and his brother Leslie were made members of the Aquarius Golf club, which had a modest nine-holes course, then became schoolboy members of the Dulwich and Sydenham Hill Golf Club, his father's club. When his father took both boys to the great J.H. Taylor at Royal Mid-Surrey for an appraisal of their potential, the verdict was that Henry might be the better prospect as he seemed to have more determination, more powers of concentration. It was one of Taylor's most profound observations. A school fracas over cricket thrust the young Cotton further along the road to professional golf. As a promising cricketer, he had progressed quickly to the school first XI. After a match at Marlow, six prefects in

Henry Cotton making a speech after winning the Open Championship at Sandwich in 1934.

the team left Cotton and four other youngsters to man-handle five heavy bags of cricket gear back to Dulwich, by train and bus. Henry took a poor view of this, expressed his feelings to the prefects and the whole thing developed into something of a school scandal. The headmaster suggested that Cotton should be caned. Henry demurred at this, and was forbidden to play cricket until he accepted the caning. When the headmaster asked him what he would do without his cricket, the young Cotton declared that he would play golf. He was quite bright at school and contemplated a university course and a future in civil engineering, but, by the time he had matriculated, Leslie had become a professional golfer. Henry opted to follow him.

He found a job at Fulwell, where he was a junior in the professional's workshop, shaving hickory shafts, sandpapering iron heads. It was good for strengthening the hand, but did little for his golf game, and he moved on after a few months to Rye, where he had more time for practice and tournament play, such as it was in the 1920s. Helped by Cyril Tolley, he got his first full professional appointment at the Langley Park club in Beckenham – he was all of 19 years of age. At Langley Park, as he had at Rye and indeed as he had done as a schoolboy, Cotton slaved at practice, often lunching on a chocolate bar or a sandwich to save time, then, after dinner at home, where he still lived, spent more time hitting shots into a net in his father's garage. All of this was to have a long-term effect on his health, when in later years he had stomach problems and was afflicted by the golfer's posture – left shoulder up, right shoulder down – and perhaps something of a twist in the spine.

Increasingly in the 1920s, he thrust himself into the tournament scene. Increasingly he became irked at the American domination of the Open Championship. He saw that to become a champion, to be considered a champion, he must become THE Open Champion. That governed all his subsequent thinking: the title and the influence and wealth that might flow from it. Some early tournament successes meant that the time came for Henry to leave home, to set up his very own castle. Typically, he did something different – he bought of all things a church hall, St Mary's Hall, near Bromley. The name was chiselled in stone above the front door lintel. Henry, again typically, engaged an architect to convert the place. They chiselled out the word "Hall" from the door way and it became simply St Mary's. Much attention was given to the creation of a luxurious bathroom, and Henry got his

old nanny to join him as his housekeeper. It was the first of many Cotton residences, almost all of them with a touch of exotica and an expression of his need to be different. George Gibson, then of the Spalding Company, later to be managing director of the PGCA, recalls going to lunch there: "Henry had a unique living room, furnished with low coffee tables and at least one hundred cushions, which you were supposed to pile up against the wall. We went in there for coffee after lunch, and it was so surprisingly comfortable that I all but fell asleep before the coffee came."

The Langley Park committee allowed Cotton ample time for practice, which he put to good use, chipping and putting, hitting thousands of balls, his sessions ending often in the darkness and in tears of frustration if he didn't quite get it right. It would be true to say that Henry was not a naturally gifted golfer, but he made himself a very great player by sheer determination, even bloody-mindedness, as Gary Player was to do subsequently. Increasingly he tested himself in competitive play, increasingly his competitive hunger grew. He played in the Open Championships of 1926 and 1927 as a very young man. He finished in eighth place in 1927, commendable for anyone at the age of 20, at St Andrews, in a Bobby Jones year. This was in the decade of Jones and Hagen, of American dominance in the championship when, it seemed, the home players were overwhelmed simply by the appearance of Americans on the first tee. Henry resolved to find out why, to find out what made the Americans so much better. In 1928, he had a good tournament year, among other things beaten in the final of the *News of the World* Match Play Championship, then considered second in importance only to the Open. With £300 to sustain him, he set off for America to discover what magic formula, if any, the Americans had. Typically, he went first class, on the *Aquitania*, arriving in New York in November, 1928.

Henry spent the entire winter in the US, making the tournament swing through California and round to Florida, and came home in the spring with his £300 intact. From that point of view, the trip could have been deemed a success. More important was what he learned. He saw that the Americans were inveterate practicers, which did not alarm him – he had been just that since boyhood. But they were also ferocious competitors – a persistent historic American trait – taking chances to shoot for the lowest possible score, and be winners. They were outgoing, brash, confident and above all respected by the public. They had a proper place in the social scheme of things, and enjoyed the good life. Young Cotton missed none of this.

He was befriended to some extent by Tommy Armour and Walter Hagen, who thought he had promise but "lacked polish". Henry was busy acquiring it. More important, this American safari brought Cotton a significant swing change. He had gone there with a rather stiff, upright swing which he had manufactured for himself and which some of the British writers had dubbed "artificial". It gave him a slight, left-to-right fading shot which he had nicely under control, but which cost him some distance. At Armour's insistence, he worked on a rather flatter swing which gave him a right-to-left flight, a draw, and the extra yardage he needed. Later in the year, he played in his first Ryder Cup match, winning his single at the bottom of the team by 4 and 3 against Al Watrous, and helping the British team to a win. The following winter, he and Aubrey Boomer made a long trip to Argentina, where he won the Mar del Plata Open. Cotton was impressed by the aristocratic nature of the game there, by the quality of the facilities for playing, practising and teaching and by the fact that the local professionals were considered professors of the game, had a proper social status and were well-rewarded for the instruction, as were the Americans.

In 1930, Henry won the Belgian Open, the first of a rash of Continental championships he was to win, but more and more he had this fixation about the Open Championship. In 1930, he was a joint leader after the first round; in 1931 leader after two rounds. In 1932, Sarazen's year, he was down the field, as it were, but it was an important year for Cotton – he left Langley Park in suburban London to become professional at the Waterloo Club in Brussels. This was the true Cotton element, the sophisticated Continental club with a huge membership, the lavish professional's shop with a bar installed in it, a membership happy to pay him handsomely for his services, Paris within a reasonable drive, and above all an escape from the second-class citizen status which the UK professionals still had to suffer. Thus, on his sorties back home, he was able to arrive at tournaments in Walter Hagen-style, in the limousine, spurning the clubhouse, being his own man. Cotton had a solitary rather than a gregarious personality, with little time to spare on chit-chat with the other competitors.

In the championship of 1933 at St Andrews, Walter Hagen's last serious shot at the Open, Cotton was joint leader after three rounds, but eventually finished three strokes behind. Yet his time was nigh. The championship of 1934 was scheduled for Royal

St George's, and the week before the event Cotton went down to prepare with four different sets of golf clubs, and his game in disarray. He was fiddling with swing changes with little real control of his game. So much so, he left the place and over the weekend did not hit one golf shot. On the first qualifying round, he went out early on Monday morning and scored 66: ". . . 18 of the most perfect holes I have ever played . . . without a long putt going in, a 66." His second qualifying round at Deal next day was 75 and meant that he was to lead this Open from beginning to end. In the championship proper, over St George's, Cotton started 67, 65 and had broken the back of the championship, with a seven stroke lead. The 36-holes record stands to this day. A third round 72 on Friday morning made his lead nine strokes and it seemed that all he had to do to win in the afternoon was to walk round the course. But a funny thing happened on the way to the title – his last round start was delayed because of crowd control problems and Cotton sought refuge in a little empty tent beside the first tee to escape from the well-wishers and back-slappers. There, he was suddenly seized by a powerful stomach cramp so severe that he could scarcely stand up, and which had him believing that he would not be able to play. He had had the lightest of lunches – no doubt it was psychosomatic. He had waited, plotted and planned for this Open for many years. Not to be able to finish it was unthinkable. When he did start he was as weak as a kitten, hit the ball all over the golf course, was out in 40 strokes and in clear danger of squandering the huge lead. However, he holed a stiff putt at the 13th, pulled himself together at last and finished with a 79, surely the highest final round from an Open champion in modern times. His aggregate of 283 equalled Sarazen's record of two years earlier and was to stand until Locke did 279 at Troon in 1950. Henry Cotton was Open Champion. He was 27 years old. And happily the great champions of another day were all there to see him do it – Harry Vardon, J.H. Taylor, James Braid and Sandy Herd.

Henry Cotton dominated the game in Britain up to the 1939–45 war and beyond. He was "King Cotton" or "The Maestro" and many of his friends asserted that, at least for a few seasons, he was the finest player in the world. His 1934 championship had two rather droll postscripts. His second round 65 led to the production of the Dunlop 65 golf ball, the most famous ball of them all and still in production. Henry was never consulted about it, was given no bonus, and for years afterwards he was paid a paltry £150 for playing the ball. "It was the worst

deal I ever made," said Cotton, looking back on it. And George Gibson, then managing director of the PGCA, told how Henry, like most of the prominent players of the time, had been anxious to have a profitable line of autographed clubs, and sought his advice. Gibson had counselled him to wait until the manufacturers were "really desperate to have him", and persuaded him to hold off. Now was the time. Gibson thought that, since Spalding made both clubs and balls, that was where the best deal might be found. He spoke to his old boss there, a Mr Elliss, who thought it a fine idea until Gibson indicated that Henry was thinking of at least £2000 as royalties, a staggering sum in the trade at the time. Elliss told Gibson that he was, in effect, out of his mind. Then Gibson explained that the PGCA had 1000 customers, club professionals who had accounts with him, and that his initial order would be for 1000 sets of clubs – at that time there was no limit to the number of clubs in a set. Thus there should be enough money in the deal for Spaldings, the club professionals, and Henry. The deal was done, and Henry enjoyed it for several years.

The 1935 championship was won by Alf Perry, a man of whom it was said he came from nowhere and went back there. Oddly, the same could have been said of the 1935 US Open Champion, Sam Parkes. It was an Open which Cotton, once again, had the chance to dominate from the start. He played a quite brilliant 17 holes of golf on the opening round at Muirfield, coming to that stiff, finishing par-4 with thoughts of a birdie three and a 65 which would have terrorised the entire field. His drive tailed off into a fairway bunker, and in trying to force the ball all the way to the green he left it in the hazard, taking six for a 68 – not a bad start to any championship, but somehow it took the steam out of him, and he never quite got to grips with the rest of the championship. Alf Perry, the winner, got rather less than his due. He took the trophy, the medal and the cheque back to his club at Leatherhead and was little heard of again. He had played the two final rounds with one golf ball. "I found a good one," he said, "and stuck with it." Modern players will change the ball probably every three or four holes. Perry had a sloppy, right hand grip and a heaving swing that had him spinning on his left foot, but nevertheless he equalled the Sarazen/Cotton low aggregate with 283.

In the championship of 1936 at Hoylake, Cotton played as well from tee to green as he had ever

**Cotton, in 1937, during a £500-a-side Golf Challenge Match against Desmore Shute.**

done, but failed with his putter although he was but two strokes out at the finish, including two penalty strokes in a final round of 74. The winner, Alf Padgham of the massive hands and elegant swing, had won almost all the professional tournaments that year and was an impeccable putter. It was said that, when he went to South Africa the following winter, he completely lost his putting touch on the grainy greens there, and never regained it. An American counterpart in a sense was Ralph Gulhal, winner of the US Open in 1937 and 1938, and a man of whom it was said that he woke up one morning, and could no longer play. Towards the end of 1936, Cotton was approached by Lord Rosebery, president of the Ashridge Golf Club in the Chiltern Hills, to come back to England as club professional, to "help the club get ahead". Henry had his conditions. He was to be made an honorary member of the club, unheard of then; they were to build a practice ground with covered sheds for winter training; there was to be a new professional's shop, with fittings, show cases, hide-covered seating brought over from Waterloo. Henry came back fluent in French, built a handsome house for himself in Ashridge Park (he called it "Shangri-la") and he was done with chasing back and forth across the Channel, the double-taxation legislation of the time restricting him to a total of three months spent in the UK each year.

He joined Ashridge in January, 1937. It was to be possibly his greatest year. He gobbled up the German and Czech Open titles, and in the championship at Carnoustie he played one of the historic foul-weather rounds, with a final 71 through a gale of wind and rain that left flooding all over the course and threatened the continuance of play. Through it all, Cotton chipped and putted, for many the weakest part of his game, in an inspired manner, using only 26 putts. This Carnoustie field included the entire American Ryder Cup team of that year which had won for the first time in the UK by a 7–3 margin at Southport and Ainsdale, captained as ever by Walter Hagen. To Carnoustie came the old hands, Guldhal, Sarazen and Shute, and the brilliant newcomers Byron Nelson and Sam Snead. Immediately after the championship, Cotton met Densmore Shute, the reigning US PGA Champion in a 72-holes match at Walton Heath. Shute had been nominated by the US Ryder Cup team, the *News of the World* had put up the £500 prize. Cotton won by 6 and 5, with rounds of 71, 70 and 69. The US Press voted him "Golfer of the Year".

This seemed to be the very climax of his championship life. Certainly there were many tournament victories to come, and one final championship. In 1948 at Muirfield, along its narrow fairways and on baked, glassy greens – he putted superbly well – his second round of 66, all of it witnessed by King George VI, broke the back of the championship, and with a 284 he won by five strokes from Fred Daly, the defending champion. During the war, Cotton had served in the Royal Air Force but was invalided out because of gastric trouble. In the championships of 1946 and 1947, he was in leading positions after 36 holes, but two rounds on the final day were more than he could cope with in his physical condition, and at a time when war-time food rationing was persisting in the UK he took himself off to America again to re-build his strength. He was reasonably successful there, winning one tournament, but there were suggestions from some American players that Henry was sometimes rather liberal in applying the Rules of Golf. Yet from 1934 for a couple of decades, and in another sense for the rest of his long life, Henry Cotton was a dominant figure in British golf. On the course there was an aura about him, an aura of superiority, of invincibility. His powers of concentration, as J.H. Taylor had suggested, were immense. As a striker of the ball with all the clubs through the bag, from tee to green, he was quite magnificent. Perhaps only Sandy Lyle for example has used a 1-iron with the command of Cotton. And, rather like Lyle, he stood square to the ball, square-shouldered, with his head cocked to the right, left eye on the ball. The first movement took the club rather low round his legs, then it lifted into a three-quarter swing. It was by no means a classic swing, a natural swing with which such as Snead was blessed. There was the impression that the years of practice and thinking about the swing had in some way programmed Henry, that everything had been computed, done by numbers, fed into the machine, and that all of it was the result of punishment, of self-flagellation. On the course, he lived in a cocoon of concentration, seldom speaking to playing partners. Off the course, he was never much for socialising with the boys – a million light-years from a Hagen, a Palmer, a Trevino, was Henry. And unlike "Arnie" or "Seve", no one ever called Henry Cotton "Hank".

His ultimate motivations were probably social status, fame, money. Henry wanted to mingle with the upper crust, the aristocracy, and he did. Off the course, his manner and his presence, as much as his achievement, left the world slightly in awe of him. He had a keen appreciation of money, of what it could do and the doors it could open. He would say that he always did things either for a great deal of money, or nothing at all. Paradoxically, until almost the end, he always saw to it that he had a club to use as a base – Langley Park, Waterloo, Ashridge, then, after the war, Royal Mid-Surrey. At a time when, like Walter Hagen, he could have been simply a tournament professional as Hagen had been, as the modern professionals are, it seemed he needed to cling on to the "profits from the shop". Henry always had a keen nose for the "deal". But he worked hard at everything and was successful at almost everything he did. Booked to do a week's show before the war at the Coliseum, then a leading London music hall (on the same bill were Nellie Wallace and George Doonan), he was retained for a second week, then went on to do 14 weeks up and down the country for a handsome salary. He played in the Open infrequently after 1948, but in 1956, at the age of almost 50, he finished sixth. He ran a winter golf school in Monte Carlo; he wrote a succession of successful books on golf; for many years he wrote a golf column in the *News of the World*, this originating from his friendship with the Carr family, the owners. George Nicholl of Leven had a Henry Cotton autographed club on the market long after Henry had stopped playing. In the 1960s, he designed Penina in the Algarve, the first of many golf architecture ventures, and, if the course was not absolutely the best in the world, Henry's achievement was – he had been given a rice paddy with which to work. He had a spell as a BBC TV commentator on golf. Henry, in a word, prospered. He also kept busy. He was a worker.

If Cotton raised the status of the British professional, as Hagen had done for the Americans, that seemed almost incidental to the thrust of his own career, his own life. Henry was first and last concerned with his own status. He was his own

man. He walked, if not quite alone, then with no one but "Toots" by his side. She was Maria Isabel Estanguet who became Mrs Moss who became Mrs Cotton, an Argentine lady who had married Henry just before the war, and was a powerful personality who pushed and cajoled and occasionally slapped Henry onwards and upwards to further success, at the same time tolerating no criticism of him whatsoever from any outsider. As strong characters both, their tiffs were not always private, but they were indifferent to public opinion while at the same time being quite masterful in publicising any of Henry's business ventures. There were strange paradoxes in the man. He squabbled with the PGA, yet was twice captain of the organisation and sat in committee for many years. He was made an Honorary Member of the R & A. He exploited his friendship with the wealthy, saw no reason why they should not buy the wine. In his final years, he suffered much serious illness, and surgery, bravely. He never became a father, and was addicted, in any company, of telling raunchy, risque, even pornographic, stories, rather badly, but with much glee. He was selfish, but always took the trouble to write a note of thanks, believing that it didn't hurt and might be a little investment for the future. He was meticulous about dress and hygiene and thought there was no excuse for having, for example, dirty finger nails. At all times, he encouraged the young, and his ultimate credo for playing the game was hands, hands, hands. Hand action, he insisted, was the key to the whole thing.

He lived to be 80, and died in a London hospital on the 22nd of December, 1987. Shortly before, he learned that he was to knighted. Thus, at the end, he was Sir Thomas Henry Cotton MBE. On the whole, it was well-merited.

| CAREER HIGHLIGHTS | |
|---|---|
| | British Open |
| Henry Cotton | 1934, 1937, 1948 |

# THE HAWK, MR GOLF AND THE SLAMMER

**B**en Hogan was interviewed by an American golf writer on his 75th birthday. The last question asked was along the lines of how he would like to be remembered. Hogan said, "I would like to be known as a gentleman first, and next as a golfer. That's all."

If any man could put the contemplation of his life into one single sentence, that sentence is not bad, not half bad. William Benjamin Hogan, by any standard, is one of the three or four finest golfers in the long history of the game. And his declaration reflects precisely what we know and have seen of the character and personality of the man. If you wanted just one word for Ben Hogan, it might well be "correct". In the purity of his striking of the golf ball, he was correct. In his treatment of opponents and fellow competitors, he was correct. In his appearance, his dress, his public behaviour, he was correct. In his preparation for the great championships, he was meticulous and correct, and in the winning of them, he was resolute, remorseless – and correct. When Hogan and Sam Snead represented the USA in the Canada Cup matches (later titled the World Cup) at Wentworth in 1956, they won the team competition, and Hogan, in winning the individual title, by the quality of his play somehow made the West Course look like a different, lesser golf course. At the prize-giving ceremonies, Hogan made an introduction to his speech of startling precision and correctness, addressing the assembled lords, generals, admirals, the club captain, the entire official party in sequence and without a single mistake. It was a tour de force. When Snead's turn to speak came, he said "Ladies and Gentlemen – and that goes for all you admirals and generals and everyone . . ."

Hogan, Snead and Byron Nelson are usually branded together like some latter day triumvirate.

**Sam Snead pictured during the 1953 Ryder Cup.**

They have one thing in common. They were each born in 1912. They have little else in common. Hogan was born in Dublin, Texas, near Fort Worth. The family was poor, his father a motor mechanic. When Hogan was nine years old his father, plagued with health and money worries, shot himself. This surely is the first clue to an intense personality, and the young Hogan's early traumatic experience was mirrored in an odd way by that of two other great champions, J.H. Taylor and Gary Player. Taylor's father died when he was 11 years old, Player's mother when he was six. Strangely, all of them reached adulthood with physical similarities in height and stature and with one overwhelming quality in abundance – a singlemindedness that verged on bloodymindedness, a determination to improve, to get there, to get to the top, to leave a mark on the world. Each of them did, more successfully than they might have imagined in these young, seminal years.

The boy Hogan sold newspapers, hustled, took to caddying at the nearby Glen Garden club, where, left-handed by the way, he started to knock balls around. As he gathered an odd collection of right-handed clubs, he switched to the other side of the ball. Also in the caddie ranks at Glen Garden was Byron Nelson, by six months Hogan's senior, and from there they set out on what were to be long eventful roads in golf. Both boys entered amateur state events as and when they could afford to. Hogan turned professional at 19 and set off for the California winter tournaments with some $75 in cash, the plan being to keep that intact and live off his winnings. He was home after one month. He tried again the next winter with little more success. For the next few years he soldiered on with little more success, taking odd jobs to pay the bills, but still slaving at his game. He qualified for US Opens with no success, but he was slowly improving. In 1937, he married Valerie Fox. There were no children. Ben

Hogan was to come to see that this was the best single thing he had done with his life.

Two things were emerging – Ben Hogan, unlike another youngster on the other side of the country, Sam Snead in the mountains of West Virginia, had not been blessed at birth with an abundance of natural talent, but the same Ben Hogan had a burning intensity about him to prove that he could play, that he would succeed. There were all kinds of dramatic stories of Ben and Valerie on the road, down to their last five dollars, living on oranges when no cheques were coming in, having the wheels stolen from their car outside the motel, and many another. But Ben practised as no one had ever done before, or perhaps since, both before and after each round, and by the late 1930s some cheques were coming in and Hogan became just about the longest hitter in the game. In 1940, the dam burst. He won at last, the North and South Open at Pinehurst, in April. He was 28, the age at which Bobby Jones had retired. He was leading money winner that year and repeated the achievement in 1941 and 1942. In the US Open of 1940, he finished only three strokes behind Lawson Little and Gene Sarazen. In 1941 he was third. He tied for the 1942 Masters with Nelson, but lost a play-off to some quite brilliant play from his boyhood chum. In the summer of 1942, he entered the US Army Air Corps, served for three years, was back home in the summer of 1945, and within a month or two was back to tournament golf. In 1946, he three-putted the very last green of both the US Open and Masters Championships where two putts in each case would have allowed him to tie. Finally, later that year, he won his first major championship, the PGA.

Through his earlier years, Hogan had wrestled with one particular demon in his game, the unexpected hook shot. In order to keep up with "the big fellows", he had to give the ball a fearsome smash from a huge backswing which had his club drooping halfway down his back. And such was the power and speed of his swing that, on completing his follow-through, his whole upper body would be swivelled round to face not the target, but well left of the target. Hogan sought to eliminate this hook in favour of a shot that faded slightly, that is moved from left to right through the air. He sacrificed some length for accuracy and did it in simple terms by having his left thumb pointing straight down the shaft, his right hand riding higher over his left. He also used a rather shorter backswing under firm control at the top. Such are the fine margins great players play to; there were other tiny adjustments,

but Hogan had his game under close control.

Yet it took him most of 1947 to make the changes to his satisfaction. In tournament play, the year was fine; in championship terms, it was lean. The next year was to be perhaps the most eventful year of his life – it almost brought it to an end. He won his first US Open, his second PGA title. In the 13 months to February, 1949, Ben Hogan had won 13 tournaments. In four events in January, 1949, he won two and lost a play-off to Jimmy Demaret in a third. Early on the 2nd of February, 1949, Ben and his wife Valerie were driving home from Phoenix to Fort Worth, on a two-lane road. A Greyhound bus, coming in the opposite direction and overtaking another car blindly in morning fog, smashed into the Hogan car, head-on. An instant before the impact, Hogan threw himself across the seat to protect Valerie. The steering column went through the driver's seat. Hogan suffered a double fracture of the pelvis, a broken ankle, a broken rib, and a broken collarbone – injuries almost clinically designed to put an end to any golfing career. He was in hospital for two months, during which time he had further surgery on his legs to eradicate blood clotting. When he arrived home in Fort Worth, he weighed 95 pounds. His legs were encased in bandages from hip to ankle.

Characteristically, Hogan set about not only getting well, but getting back to golf, with a schedule of rehabilitation. By summer, his doctors allowed him to accept a US PGA invitation to be non-playing captain on their Ryder Cup team for the match at Ganton in Yorkshire, in early September. At Ganton, Hogan, a stickler for correctness in every aspect of the game, complained that many of the British clubs had illegal punch marks and grooves on their faces. A good-sized international incident was brewing until Bernard Darwin was called in as an adjudicator, and said, "Nothing that a little judicious filing cannot put right." What had been in the main overlooked was that, at the preceding match at Portland, Henry Cotton had made a similar fuss about the American clubs. Hogan had been the American captain then, and Hogan did not forget. Needless to say, the US won both matches, in Portland and at Ganton.

By the late autumn, Hogan was able to go out to the Colonial Country Club, and chip and putt a little. Then he played a few holes, and finally 18 holes. Not only that, but he entered for the Los Angeles Open, due in January, 1950. The accident to Hogan the national champion, and his convalescence, and now his intended return to golf so quickly, made national news. And his performance in Los Angeles stunned the whole world of golf, indeed the nation. He scored 73, 69, 69, 69 for a total of 280, and, all things considered, these may just have been the most astonishing four rounds of competitive golf ever played in the entire history of the universe. In hindsight, this Los Angeles Open (he lost a delayed play-off to Snead) can be seen as a critical turning point in the life of Ben Hogan. He had started without the slightest privilege, worked long and hard at his craft, and suffered for it. He had reached a point in the weekly tournament golf schedule where he was a dominant figure and almost always the man to beat. He had given, as had many others, three valuable years to war service, and he had emerged to win the US Open Championship at last. Then he had been shattered by an appalling car accident which few men would have survived. Los Angeles proved to Hogan that he could still play, and still play well enough to win. And it set his mind on the pattern of his future golfing life, which would be to pace himself, to focus his thinking and his energies on the major championships. He played in the Masters in the spring of the year, and played well enough with 73, 68, 71 but was forced into fourth place by a rather tired final round of 76.

Hogan still walked with a perceptible limp, and rather slowly, but between the Masters and the Open he won a four-day tournament. At that time, the final 36 holes of the Open were played on one day. Could Hogan survive that? He tied for the championship with Lloyd Mangrum and George Fazio, then won the play-off decisively with 69 against Mangrum's 73, Fazio's 75. Hogan really was back. The Hogan story was on every front page in the country. In the spring of 1951, he won the Masters with careful rational play. If the Hogan swing was now more composed, more rational than had been the slashing, smashing action of the 1930s, so Hogan, approaching 40, had now attained a massive maturity, not only in the purity of his striking of the ball, but in the management of his golfing life, in analysing a golf course, in knowing where were the places, which the circumstances, to gamble, or to play conservatively, who would be the dangerous men in the field from one championship to another. Ben Hogan never missed a trick. So steeped was he in the totality of the game, he knew all the tricks.

Ben Hogan knew how he was, where he was. It would not be unreasonable to assume that, following his road accident, he was absolutely in control of the management of his life from then on. He may well have felt that he owed nothing to anyone, that no one owed him anything. This rather steely attitude to his world was perfectly exemplified in his prize-giving speech after he won the 1951 US Open at Oakland Hills. This was the championship for which the USGA had asked the architect Robert Trent Jones to make the course a more severe test. Jones did that with a vengeance, so much so that Hogan was quite angry about the demands of the course, reflected no doubt in a first round 76. After that round, he decided to meet the Trent Jones challenge head on and succeeded with a vengeance with progressively better rounds of 73, 71 and finally a stunning 67 over a course of 6927 yards with a par of 70. The final round of Clayton Heafner (who finished second) was the only other round under par in the entire championship. The winner's speech on these occasions is usually stiff with platitudes about the excellence of the course, the excellence of its condition, the excellence of the organisation, the excellence of this and that. Hogan remained true to himself when he said pointedly and perhaps slightly bitterly, "I am glad to have brought this monster to its knees." Oakland Hills apart, this is a prime insight to Hogan's attitude to any golf course – that it was a direct challenge to his skills, a tiger with which he had to wrestle, which he had to dominate.

In 1953, Ben Hogan won the Masters, the US Open and the Open Championship, the ultimate accolade for the professional golfer. It has not been done by anyone since and may well never be. It was compared favourably with the 1930 Grand Slam of Bobby Jones, when he won the Open and Amateur Championships of both Britain and America. Indeed, many considered it a greater achievement since two of the Jones victories had been in amateur golf. And Hogan had been unable to complete a professional grand slam since the fourth competition generally included, the PGA Championship of America, had conflicted directly in scheduling with the Open Championship at Carnoustie. This was Hogan's only appearance in the Open, and the manner of his entering said a good deal about the man and the workings of his mind, as did the manner of his playing of the championship.

For several years Hogan's friends, and others, had let it be known to him, sometimes deviously, that no golfer could be considered a great champion until he had won the Open, or at least competed in it with distinction. Gene Sarazen was perhaps the chief proselytiser about this and about British links golf. There were suggestions that Hogan had not played in the Open because he was perhaps not such a good wind player, and that in Britain the wind doth blow – as though it doth not in Texas, where Hogan grew up. He might not care to face the problems of switching to the small ball in unpredictable weather. There were more personal reasons why Hogan had not given too much thought to a tilt at the old trophy. His only experience of the UK had been at Ganton in 1949, when Ben, little more than six months after his accident, had captained the US Ryder Cup team, and with Britain still plagued by post war rationing, had found the whole experience trying and uncomfortable. Valerie was not a particularly good traveller, and Hogan's mother had weighed in with the thought that they should not travel "overseas".

But Hogan had clearly been giving some thought to such an adventure. After he won the Masters in 1953, he said to Valerie that if he won the US Open, he would certainly play at Carnoustie. Hogan's rationale was that it was a major championship to be won; that he wanted to accept the challenges of the small ball and the variable weather and links golf; that the USGA and R & A had lately made the rules uniform so that the centre-shafted putter which he had long favoured would now be legal in Britain, and probably most of all, there was the man's pride in the face of all the people who implied that he could not win, could not do it, in Britain.

He was at Carnoustie more than a week in advance and laid a surveyor's eye on the hulking, brutal, 7200 yards course. He walked it front to back, noting every hazard, every danger zone. He played two or three balls, small balls, on every practice round, assessing where the pins would be set come the championship, thinking about the wind, pondering on the distance that little ball flew, the talents of the other players in the field. Then he went out and scored 73, 71, 70, 68 for 282 and victory by four shots over Cerda of Argentina, Thomson of Australia, Stranahan of the US, Rees of Wales. The first day had been played in rain, the other days in wind, rain, sun – heavy sweater weather. Hogan came through it all.

Hogan's playing of Carnoustie's sixth hole amounted to a demonstration of his mastery of one of the fiercest challenges in the game. This hole is perhaps the most severe par-5 hole in golf. Its championship length was some 540 yards. From the tee, it is flat, nondescript, straightaway, running to the west and therefore usually into the wind. There are two central fairway bunkers, staggered, set out from the championship tee at around 250 and 270 yards. Down the left side of the fairway, all the length of the hole, is an out-of-bounds fence. Down the right side is rough. Between these bunkers and

the fence there is a gap of some 15 yards. The gap to the right of the bunkers is not much more. The back of the more distant bunker is 300 yards from the green, so that to bring the green within reach of a second shot the drive must be past these central bunkers, either right or left. The entire right side of the second half of the hole has massive defences. The rough encroaches. A ditch enters diagonally from the right, crossing the fairway towards the out-of-bounds fence and diving underground leaving a gap of 20 yards to the fence, some 90 yards short of the green. Two powerful bunkers are sited on the right about 80 yards out, and the right side of the angled green is completely screened by a greenside bunker. If ever a hole had to be calculated backwards, from green to tee, it was Carnoustie's sixth. The green had to be entered from the left front. The second shot had to originate from the left side of the fairway. Thus the drive must carry past these central fairway bunkers and finish on the left side, in spite of the terror of the out-of-bounds fence. Passing those bunkers on the right meant an immensely difficult second shot. Hogan resolved it. On each of the four rounds, he drove the ball hard down the out-of-bounds line with a little fade which took the ball past the bunkers and brought it down primly into the fairway – on the left side.

It was his first, last, only Open Championship. He was 40 years old. In the space of six years, 1948 to 1953, he had won four US Opens, and lost another on a play-off; two US Masters championships and lost another on a play-off; two US PGA Championships; and one Open Championship. It is a record surpassed by no other golfer. Ben Hogan was first among equals. There were people, very many people, who said he was the greatest golfer who ever lived.

Hogan at Carnoustie held the attention of the world, as Bobby Jones had done in his time. America was convulsed and clearly deemed it the sporting achievement of the year. There was the ticker-tape welcome in New York for the Hogans, frenzy when they got back to Fort Worth. Carnoustie in 1953 was the last major championship to fall to Ben Hogan, and somehow, following in the same year as the Masters and the US Open, and played on great courses – the Augusta National, Oakmont, Carnoustie – it seemed not unfitting. On the course, there was an aura of inevitability around Hogan, as there had been around Henry Cotton in the 1930s

**Ben Hogan, the perfectionist.**

in Britain and Europe. When he strode onto the tee, there would be a tremor in the crowd of awe, almost of fear. When he hit the perfect shot, or more precisely the satisfactory shot, which he did almost all the time, his features remained impassive. When he hit the shot that was less than satisfactory, there was nothing more than a tightening of the lips, the narrowing of those slanted eyes. When he holed the final winning putt, it never could be imagined that he would jump for joy, punch the air, throw a club or a cap – that would be unthinkable. He would simply touch the white cap – always the white cap – above the conservative grey slacks and sweater and walk quietly off to shake hands with his playing partner, and check the card. He walked with a stiff-hipped, deliberate stride, down the fairway, through an airport, down the street. Everything was, well, correct. One could not imagine Hogan carousing with the boys, being caught in a back-slapping crowd, or even being approached for an autograph. It would be a brave stranger who would call him "Ben" and not "Mr Hogan". The square jawline, the high cheekbones, the slanted eyes that had squinted into a thousand hours of sharp sunshine gave him the look of a Plains Indian, impassive, masked, his emotions tightly controlled. Everything correct.

In the business of golf, he was the business man supreme. He never needed a manager, an agent, and to every offer, he said immediately "No". If they wanted him, they would come back, and the offer would be better. When he captained yet again a US Ryder Cup team at Houston in 1967, Arnold Palmer, his team member, was at the peak of his career (on arrival, Arnold had buzzed the Champions course in his own private jet plane). Every reference Hogan made to Palmer before play started, during the preliminaries, was along the lines of "Arnold Palmer – if selected". At a gala, fund-raising, meet-the-teams dinner on the eve of the matches, before hundreds of guests, Hogan encapsulated his character yet again in one single sentence. Dai Rees, the British captain introducing his team, had each player stand up in turn and prattled on about what they had won, how they had qualified for the team, and so on – rather Welsh, verbose, and to polite applause. Then Hogan instructed the audience to applaud only after he had finished, named his players in turn, and when they were all standing, said, "Ladies and gentlemen, the US Ryder Cup team – the finest golfers in the world." Storm of applause.

The Brits were down before they started. This directness could be misunderstood. People who knew him only slightly dubbed him as distant,

remote, a cold fish. Yet in that same Ryder Cup match, he went out of his way to approach the British journalists and to cooperate with them saying that they should ask him anything at any time concerning his team. And when his career was over, he didn't hang about, didn't become a broadcaster, didn't pontificate about the game. He simply went back to Fort Worth, where he attended to his clubmaking business, spending a few weeks each winter in Florida, and lived his own life. From first to last, Ben Hogan, "The Hawk" as they called him, was his own man. There has never been a finer golfer.

**John Byron Nelson**, son of a Fort Worth grain merchant, was brought up in a house close by the Glen Garden club, and by the age of ten was in the caddie shed there, to be joined by another boy named Hogan. John Byron turned out to be an altogether softer personality than William Benjamin and his career was to move along a step ahead of Hogan's – a step ahead in time, that is. By his early teens he had decided that golf would be the life for him, for hadn't he seen his first idol, Walter Hagen, win the last of his four successive PGA Championship finals at Dallas in 1927? At one point, Nelson and Hogan, in friendly youthful rivalry, shared the caddie championship at Glen Garden, but Nelson was first away in 1930 when he won the important Southwest Amateur Championship. He turned professional in 1932 and earned no more than a fistful of dollars on the winter circuit (not yet, even in America, was there a tournament every week of the year). In a pique of disappointment, Nelson virtually quit the game and went to work in the oil business, but it was not long before his employer sensed that the Nelson heart was elsewhere and arranged a job for Byron as a professional at the Texarkana club.

In 1934, by now married to Louise, second place finishes in Texas tournaments put the Nelson finances in better order, but, more important, the year brought the move to the Ridgewood club in New Jersey as an assistant pro and into the bigger, busier world of the East. His first important win was in the regional Metropolitan Open of 1936. That year, he finished ninth on the money list with a total of $5400. The leader was Horton Smith, with $7800! The next year, young Nelson – he was still only 26 – won the first of a series of major championships that were to be studded with play-offs, brilliant scoring,

**Byron Nelson whose career was always one step ahead of Hogan's.**

118

dramatic incident. He won the Masters, stole it in a sense from Ralph Guldhal. With seven holes of the final round to play, Nelson was four strokes behind the leading Guldhal. The championship turned on the 12th and 13th holes at the Augusta National, as it would do so often in the years to come. On the insidious little 12th, the par-3 with its tee shot across the water to the narrowest of greens, Nelson birdied. At the lovely par-5 13th, he accepted the challenge of the second shot to carry over Rae's Creek, fronting the green and promptly holed for an eagle. Nelson had scored these intimidating holes in 2, 3. Guldhal found the water twice and scored them in 5, 6. On two holes, Nelson had picked up six strokes on his fellow Texan, and played out the remaining holes conservatively to win. Consolation for Guldhal – if consolation it was – came that summer, when he won the US Open at Oakland Hills.

Byron was promptly named for the Ryder Cup team to play against the UK at Southport, won his foursome match with Ed Dudley against Cotton and Padgham by 4 and 2, but lost his single 3 and 1 to his British opposite number, the young Dai Rees. He also finished top American, in fifth place, in Cotton's Open Championship at Carnoustie. In 1938, he moved to the Reading Country Club in Pennsylvania, won a couple of tournaments, but was concerned with what he saw as a lack of consistency in his play, and set about working on his swing. The outcome was a very distinctive action. He worked for a high, straight-up backswing, a straight left wrist at the top of the swing and a slide of the hips, a dip of the knees, through impact. All this hard work – changing the swing habits of a lifetime is a major chore for a player at this level – was rewarded in 1939 when Byron won what was an untidy US Open. This was the year of the ordeal of Snead, the first of more than a few US Opens he "should" have won. Snead came to the last hole of the Spring Mill course in Philadelphia seeking a par-5 on the hole to win, a six to tie. He hooked his drive just off the fairway. In forcing his second from there, he muffed the shot into a fairway bunker. His third went into a greenside bunker; he needed two shots to get out, then three-putted to score eight on the hole and leave himself in deep shock. When he had recovered enough to speak, he said he hadn't realised exactly what he had to score to win. But his championship may well have been lost on the 71st hole, where he left a six foot putt a good 12 inches short.

In the event, the championship was left with a three-way tie – Nelson and two of the older school

in Craig Wood and Densmore Shute. After 18 holes, Shute was out with a 76, Wood and Nelson tied on 68. On the second 18 holes, Nelson had it won on the third and fourth holes. He birdied the third, and on the 453 yards par-4 fourth he holed a full 1-iron shot for an eagle and an eventual 70 against Wood's 73. The year 1939 also saw the start of a remarkable run of match play success for Byron Nelson in the PGA Championship. He was beaten in the final that year by Henry Picard at the 37th. He won in 1940 and 1945, was a finalist in 1941, losing at the 38th, and again in 1944, losing by one hole. Five finals in six events (it was not played in 1943) evoked comparison with Hagen's record in the 1920s.

Hogan and Snead pushed Nelson hard. For the next few years, before he went into the Army, Hogan topped the money lists and scoring averages. In 1942, Snead won the PGA, then went into the Navy. In the same year, Nelson and Hogan tied in the Masters and produced shimmering golf in the play-off. After five holes, Hogan led by three strokes. He played the next 11 holes in one under par but lost. Nelson's 69 to Hogan's 70 was described by Byron as "the best golf of my life". Hogan then won the Hale America tournament, a US Open-substitute, sponsored by the USGA for war charities, before going into the Army. Nelson, who had haemophilic tendencies, did no military service. Championship golf went into wartime suspension, but some kind of tournament golf, played for charity and with war bonds as prize money, soldiered on. By 1944, when Nelson was 32, sport began the start back to peace-time normality, and Byron Nelson set out on two years of golf scoring which were quite unparalleled. In 1944, over 85 rounds, he averaged 69.67 strokes. He won seven tournaments. He won war bonds to the value of $35,005, almost twice the previous money record. He was voted Athlete of the Year. Many of the events were played on short courses. Sometimes preferred lies were allowed. The 14 clubs maximum rule was relaxed, strangely, to 16. Many of the best players were still in service. But even if Nelson had gone out alone, with only a marker, this would have been staggering scoring.

It was no more than an overture. Snead came back late in 1944, invalided out of the Navy with vertebrae problems, but was soon back in action, but Nelson took off on a rampage of golf. He won 19 PGA-sponsored tournaments in 1945, 11 of them in succession. In 30 events, he returned a stroke average of 68.33 per round for 120 rounds. He was never over par in a stroke play event. In 17 stroke play tournaments, he averaged three under par per round. He finished in the money in 100 successive tournaments, and during the year he totalled $66,000 in prizes. He was voted Athlete of the Year by the journalists again, surely unanimously. The physical, mental and emotional pressures on any man doing this are difficult to quantify, but it helps if one considers just one aspect of it all. Nelson covered by train and car the entire continent, winning in Pheonix, New Orleans, Durham, Atlanta, Philadelphia, Chicago, Toronto, Fort Worth, Montreal, Spokane and Seattle. Lord Byron had become Mr Golf.

Ben Hogan came out of the Army in August, 1945, and could scarcely have been pleased with what he found, since, in the early 1940s, he had been top dog. Throughout that winter and most of 1946 he was in hot pursuit of Nelson and, more important, of that first major championship win. In fact, he missed short, last hole putts in the Masters to tie Herman Keiser and in the US Open to tie Nelson, Vic Ghezzi and Lloyd Mangrum. Mangrum only just prevailed after 36 extra holes. But Nelson had had enough. The grind of endless travel, endless competition, could not go on for ever. He was ready to call a halt to it, and declared that after the PGA Championship he would retire. He was beaten in the quarter final round. Ironically, with Nelson gone, the winner was – Ben Hogan. They had been seeded to meet in the final. So Nelson, at the age of 34, was gone, winner of one US Open, two Masters, two PGAs. He went back, with some relief, to his 1500 acres of cattle land in Texas. He became for a spell a successful television commentator, and came out of retirement to play the occasional tournament, winning the Bing Crosby event one year, and in 1955, aged 44, the French Open at La Boulie in quite brilliant style, unleashing a torrent of iron shots which flew like darts at the flagsticks, like the old days. By and large he was happy to remain in Texas, coming out each year to start off the Masters event with Sarazen in an annual pilgrimage, working with younger players like Ken Venturi, Tony Lema and Tom Watson in turn. Nelson's two magical years represented a sustained miracle of consistency and excellence. It is difficult to place this miracle in the context of championship achievement – Nelson won "only" five of the big championships. But these bald statistics will surely stand starkly in the record book as an achievement which is quite simply unique and incomparable. Nelson the golfer will not be recalled as a player with the grace of a Vardon, a Jones, a Snead. He was quite simply efficient, an eliminator of errors once he had established his action, perhaps

almost verging on the bland. He was a pleasant man of much charm, but, if there were any burning fires within, they were well damped down. Passion was not a word to apply to John Byron Nelson, Mr Golf.

Nelson had never much sought publicity; Hogan was quite indifferent to it; Snead generated an abundance of it by being Snead. When he emerged from the Allegheny Mountains in 1937, an innocent but country-cocky 24 years old, he was manna to the writers, a mountain man, a backwoodsman, a barefoot boyo who was a breathtaking hitter and a golfer in a hundred. **Samuel Jackson Snead** had a mountain drawl – he never did lose it – that would have sat well beneath a coonskin, Davy Crockett hat, and he had the most gorgeous golfswing that enabled him to pole out drives of 300 yards and earned him the immediate title of "Slammin' Sammy". In spite of the fact that Hogan, for one, always insisted that there is no such thing as a natural golfer, whatever gods of golf there may be blessed Snead with the closest thing imaginable. It was a swing of, at once, grace, power, rhythm and balance. He took the club back in a wide, slow backswing that had traces of Jones in it, went through the ball with immense power and finished high and handsome, in perfect balance. And since there was no history of golf in the family, the conclusion was that Snead had brought these natural gifts with him when he entered this world. The swing came with his genes, but there was no explaining it.

He was born in May, 1912, neatly between Nelson and Hogan, near Hot Springs, the resort town on the borders of Virginia and West Virginia. His father had a small-holding, and the boy Snead, one of five sons, took his turn at milling, chicken-tending and, on school vacations, caddying. He made his mark as an all-round games player in high school, being adept in baseball, basketball and football, and was also a pretty good sprinter. A football game brought him a broken left hand, and he took to swinging a golf club and playing the game in the hope that it would mend and strengthen the hand. On leaving school, he found a job at the Hot Springs course as an assistant caddiemaster and general dogsbody, later moving to the Cascades course in Hot Springs, and within a few weeks he had knocked round its 6800 yards in 68. Fred Martin, manager of the Greenbrier in White Sulphur Springs nearby and an altogether more posh resort, invited him there on the strength of what he had seen of Snead in local events. In 1936 he was winning state tournaments and more than holding his own against visiting tournament players in exhibition matches.

By the end of the year, he had finished sixth in the Hershey Open and felt ready to tackle all those other happenings beyond the mountains. The Greenbrier people sponsored him.

Sam Snead reached California in January, an unknown. He finished sixth in the Los Angeles Open, then won at Oakland and at Rancho Santa Fe, an event sponsored by Bing Crosby. He was no longer unknown. The newspapermen fell on this hillbilly, naive yet with a native, mountain cunning, and soon the stories poured out of how Snead was a hunter after coon and possum, even wildcats, a fisherman who could take trout with his hands, of how he could play golf just as well barefoot. Much of this was fed to them by Fred Corcoran, a Boston Irishman who was tournament director for the PGA, an instinctive publicist who was for many years afterwards Snead's manager. Corcoran latched on to Snead from day one. Thus was started a career that was to extend to victories over six decades; 84 official PGA tournament wins and 135 victories in all; three PGA Championships; three Masters Open Championships; one Open Championship; and nine Ryder Cup appearances over 20 years; great wealth, but alas not one US Open win. The US Open was to be a cold hand laid on the shoulder of Sam Snead.

In that first year of 1937 when Snead, lean, strong, supple, athletic, first appeared, he went into the championship at Oakland Hills as favourite. He finished second, five under par, but two strokes behind Ralph Guldahl. In 1939, there was the disaster at Spring Mill. In 1947, he had a putt of less than a yard at the 18th hole of the play-off with Lew Worsham to tie, and missed it. In 1948, he was fifth behind Hogan at Riviera in Los Angeles. In 1949, he dropped a stroke at the par-3 71st hole and finished joint second. In 1953, he was second to Hogan at Oakmont – Hogan's fourth championship, Snead's fourth runner-up position. Happily, he did win the Open Championship, when he finished steadfastly in a gale of wind at St Andrews in 1946.

Sam Snead, the Slammer, was probably the most naturally gifted golfer between Harry Vardon and the coming of Severiano Ballesteros. He was blessed with good health and took his golfing skills and physical talents for granted – well into his middle life he could pick a golf ball out of the hole without bending his knees. Hogan said of him that if he had worked harder at the game, given it more thought, he would have been so much better. But it was all very easy for Snead.

Snead could not be described as a cultured man. He came out of the woods in 1938 a hillbilly, and never changed. He was not much concerned with, or even aware of, the world outside golf and sport, or the world outside America, holding that when he left the US he was "camping". He was never a gracious man, given sometimes to rough language and raucous stories in the manner of the later Henry Cotton, although at that game he could always give Cotton a two-up start. And certainly in his early days, he threw his tantrums, more than once walking off the course in mid-tournament, or "toonament" as he called it. Golf enriched him. For many years, as Tommy Armour had done, he taught at the lavish Boca Raton club in Florida – for cash – and many were the stories of Snead finding $500 bills in odd pockets and in the linings of the straw hats which were his autograph, or money buried in tomato cans in his garden because of the country boy's suspicion of banks, and similar nonsense. The fact was that Snead had a mountain shrewdness that saw him buy up large slices of Florida when the price was a few cents an acre. And, whatever can be said of him, there is no denying that there has never been a golfer with a more beautiful swing than Samuel Jackson Snead.

| CAREER HIGHLIGHTS | | | | |
|---|---|---|---|---|
| | British Open | US Open | US Masters | USPGA |
| Ben Hogan | 1953 | 1948, 1950, 1951, 1953 | 1951, 1953 | 1946, 1948 |
| Byron Nelson | | 1939 | 1937, 1942 | 1940, 1945 |
| Sam Snead | 1946 | | 1949, 1952, 1954 | 1942, 1949, 1951 |

**Sam Snead, known as the Slammer and one of the most talented golfers of all time.**

# THE COLONIALS

Arthur D'arcy Locke, known from childhood as "Bobby" because of his worship of Bobby Jones, and **Peter Thomson**, never known as anything but Peter Thomson, dominated the world of the small ball in the 1940s, throughout the 1950s, and even into the 1960s. From South Africa and Australia, respectively, they were probably the greatest golfers produced by these British Empire countries before the empire came to its inevitable end. Here again, although they always seemed to be bracketed together, they were quite different in personality.

Locke was the son of immigrants from Northern Ireland, and was introduced to golf by his father when little more than a child. From the time he won the South African Boys' Championship in 1931, aged 14, his career had an almost inevitable progression. He won the South African Open and Amateur Championships in 1935, aged 17, and repeated that double in 1937. He turned professional in 1938, only just out of his teens, and promptly won the Irish Open, the New Zealand Open and again the South African Open. It was almost a declaration of the pattern that his golfing life would follow. He was to play everywhere in the world and to head for the starry places. As a professional, he set about dethroning King Cotton. With the tournament schedule much lighter than it is today, challenge matches were the order of things, and although Henry saw no profit in defeat by the brilliant young South African, he eventually agreed to a four ball, £500-a-side match at Walton Heath, with Henry partnering the reigning Open Champion, Reg Whitcombe against Locke and his fellow countryman, Sid Brews. Over 72 holes, the Brits won, but only just, by 2 and 1.

Locke served in the South African Air Force as a bomber pilot, mainly in the Western Desert and Mediterranean zones. Before the war he had been a slender, almost skinny youth, with rather spindly legs, weighing perhaps 11 stones. By 1949 he was better than 13 stones, and later in life, his tournament career behind him, he probably reached 16 stones. In 1946, he won two British tournaments and yet another South African Open and was ready to descend on the US tournament scene (Walter Hagen, on a pre-war exhibition tour of South Africa, had told the young Locke that his golfing education would never be complete if he did not play in the US).

Locke in America was a sensation. He won four of the first six events he entered in 1947, a total of six in all, plus the Canadian Open Championship. He was second money winner in the US that year, and in 1948 he won three more tournaments. It was an exceptional achievement for a newcomer, and to its lasting discredit the US PGA sought unsuccessfully to ban him from playing there. He won at least once every year in the US until 1952, and in five US Opens from 1947 to 1954 he finished third, fourth, fourth, third and fifth – for a foreigner, almost unheard of since the days of the Scottish immigrant professionals. By 1949, however, Locke had substantially finished with the great republic and entered the most fruitful decade of his life, embracing the rest of the world of golf. With a 1949 Open behind him, he went on to win again in 1950, 1952 and 1957. He was second to Peter Thomson in 1954. His career brought him the championships of France, Germany, Switzerland, Egypt and Australia, as well as those of New Zealand and Canada. He won professional events galore in Britain, the US and at home. He was made an honorary member of the R & A in 1977 when he was 60.

If ever a golfer made the point that champions come in all shapes and sizes, it was Bobby Locke. He was a plain man, with a big body perched on still-spindly legs, with a small mouth beneath a moustache set in a fleshy, round, jowly face – the

**Peter Thomson, the great Australian Champion.**

Americans called him "Old Muffin Face". Nevertheless, he was immensely charming, particularly with ladies, what with a twinkly smile and particularly white, gleaming teeth. Locke was clean – the fingernails were always well tended, the dark hair slicked down in Fred Astaire fashion, the white shirt, always the white shirt, perfectly laundered. Locke in fact had a personal uniform for the golf course. He wore plus fours, usually navy blue in Britain and Europe (often lightweight, white "knickerbockers" in the US). He always wore white shoes, with white or grey socks, and he always, always wore a necktie – white shirt and necktie. The tie would be SAAF, or the South African Golf Association, and, towards the end of his life, the R & A tie. The tie should have a small, tight knot. The street shoes were always highly polished. On the course, he wore a white cap, which would be tweaked nonchalantly in response to applause. On a cold day, he would wear a Cambridge blue sweater. The uniform was unchanging and therefore perhaps boring at times, but in a subtle, and no doubt calculating way, it identified the man. There was no mistaking Bobby Locke – in his middle years when he was quite portly, he would progress down the fairway with the deliberation of an Edwardian bishop.

Locke was sometimes accused of slow play. The truth was that, although he walked rather slowly, by the time he had reached the ball, he would have done most of his thinking, and the shot would go away quite briskly. But the style was the man. It was part of a routine, a pattern, a rhythm that he applied to his day as to his play. He might take 20 minutes to shave, 15 minutes to put one sock on. He never seemed to spend much time on the practice ground. There is a delightful, revealing vignette of Locke with Peter Alliss at the 1957 Open at St Andrews. The championship, off the course as it were, was a good deal less sophisticated then than it is now – no vast hospitality complexes or tented villages, no organised practice grounds. Out where the Swilcan Burn reaches the sea, there is a little patch of rough ground with room for perhaps two players to hit balls along the beach. Locke was there with seven practice balls, and had sent his caddie Bob Golder across the burn and out on to the beach. Alliss arrived with his caddie, Joe Mamby, and some 30 balls. Locke had a pitching wedge in his hands, with a long grip, an awful leather grip stretching half way down the shaft. They were due to play an exhibition match on behalf of Cancer Research at the City of Newcastle G.C. on the Sunday following the championship and chatted about that. Locke was simply waggling his club when

he suddenly looked at his watch and said, "Must be going." He had not hit one practice shot. With that, he walked over to the first tee, took two practice swings and drove off in the Open Championship. He won it. Today it seems that the young bucks of the game need an hour of practice plus an hour of meditation before going out to finish 30th. That championship had a rather bitter-sweet ending for Locke. In replacing his ball on the 72nd green, he forgot that in marking it he had moved the ball one putter blade-length to the side, and so replaced the ball in an incorrect position. There was a feeling abroad that another competitor had made a formal report to the committee. Bobby Selway, the chairman of the championship committee, later wrote him a reassuring letter saying that, as far as the R & A was concerned, he was the Open Champion, and he should feel free to show the letter to anyone interested. Locke had been shaken by the entire affair, and made the bizarre, irrelevant promise of a penance that "he would never again wear plus fours in competitive golf!"

In the 1950s, golf tournaments ended on Friday. One round would be played on Wednesday, one Thursday, and two on Friday. The tournament over, the British players would chase back to their club jobs to tend to their weekend members. The leading players of the day were in demand for Sunday exhibition matches, usually for charity, and their chasing might often be to the other end of the country to make the exhibition date at a country or provincial golf club which seldom had an opportunity to see the professors in action. The player's reward would be £20 in cash, plus another four pounds for expenses, which seemed reasonable at the time – after all, only in 1955 did the first prize for the Open Championship reach £1000. Locke was in demand for these, and here too he maintained that regularised pattern to his life. He would get to the relevant town on Saturday night, and always had breakfast in bed on Sunday, in those days considered rather grand. The room would be rather untidy, scattered about with sweaters. He would take rather a long time to shave, his shaving kit assembled in neat, leather cases. He would reminisce about earlier times, how he had brought a block of flats in Johannesburg, his experiences in America, and how the hustle and fast pace of life there had taught him to pace himself quite deliberately, to let nothing fluster him or divert him from the business

A D Locke, known as "Bobby" because of his worship of Bobby Jones.

of the day, which was playing golf. He dressed with the deliberation of a bull fighter getting into a suit of lights. Then he would proceed to the golf course, and go to work. Locke had a ukelele. It travelled with him everywhere. After a weekend exhibition match, he would sit in a corner of the bar with a glass of beer to hand and entertain the members, singing two or three choruses in which he would make up lyrics bringing in the captain's name, the professional's name, the secretary's name, and so on. It was a rather weird sight – here was this man who had won two or three or whatever Open Championships 16-handicap on the ukelele, entertaining the troops. But they would never forget him, the singing Open Champion! And he had a remarkable memory. He would remember the name of a committee man he had met at a small, suburban course where he had played ten years earlier. Perhaps he saw this as just as much part of the rich tapestry of the game as one of the great championship occasions.

Technically, Locke was close to being unique. As a young player, a slim young man, before the 1939–45 war, he had hit the ball routinely straight or with a slight draw. After the war, as his girth expanded, increasingly he drew the ball until the flight became a downright hook. In his prime years, he would often start a drive 30 yards to the right of his target line, but draw the ball back unerringly to the centre of the fairway. His greatest assets were judgement of distance, from around 100 yards in to the flag, and putting. Locke was one of the greatest putters in the history of the game, and always the procedure was the same – a look at the line from behind the ball, crouched, the putter held out in front of him by two fingers; a very close scrutiny of the green 12 inches around the hole; back to the ball; two practice swings; and away it would go, targeted on the hole. His two basic thoughts on putting were that "every putt is a straight putt", meaning that you hit the ball straight and directly along the target line you have chosen, and second "You hit the ball and only the ball", meaning that the putter blade should not scrape along the grass. South African golfers, particularly those from the High Veld, the Johannesburg area, and brought up on strong Bermuda grasses with their extreme and progressive breaks, are adept at reading lines on a green. Locke was a master. Time and again his putts would take that final turn into the hole when they seemed to be short. His action from a slightly closed stance, right foot behind left and both feet rather close together, made it look as though he was hooking the ball, which cannot be done on the

greens. He acknowledged the influence of Walter Hagen on his putting style, and wrote later "The term he used for taking the blade back and keeping it square was that you hooded the face. He proved to me that this backswing applies true topspin to the ball, and is the only type of backswing with the putter which will do it. Hagen was the world's greatest putter – I was happy to learn from him."

A fearful accident marred Locke's later years. On the 17th of February, 1960, his wife Mary gave birth to their daughter Carolyn in Cape Town. On the evening of the 19th, Bobby and a friend, Maurice Bodmer, professional at Clovelly Country Club at Kalk Bay, were on their way to the nursing home. Prince George's Drive, Wynberg, a very busy road, crosses a railway level crossing with double tracks, quite near the Royal Cape GC. It is controlled by flashing lights. Locke stopped the car to let pass a train coming from Cape Town. When the lights stopped flashing, Locke started the car across. Unknown to them, a train was coming in the opposite direction. It hit the back end of the car – if it had hit the centre of the car, both would certainly have been killed. Bobby Locke was somehow catapulted through the rear window and was found by the ambulance men head down in the boot with severe head injuries and injuries to his left hip. Maurice Bodmer had been thrown out through the passenger door and had several broken ribs, one of which punctured a lung. Locke was unconscious for several days and his left eye was permanently damaged. Eleven days after the accident he left the hospital. On the 21st day after the accident he went to the Clovelly Club and said to Bodmer, "Come on Maurice, let's have a few holes – would you rather die in bed or on the golf course?" After some persuasion, Bodmer agreed. They played four holes. Within the week, Locke was playing 18. Comparisons with Ben Hogan's experience are obvious. In June of that same year, Locke partnered Gary Player in the Canada Cup matches at Portmarnock, Ireland. He played with a patch over his left eye. They each scored 289. South Africa finished fifth in the competition.

Bobby Locke could be cryptic, sardonic. He would say to young players, "Great round, son – what did you score?" or "Tell me about your round – start at the 18th." His greatest asset was one he shared with Peter Thomson. It was a kind of containment, an impression that they walked around inside a bullet-proof shield, that they were not in the slightest concerned about what other competitors were doing. That was only partly true – they were always aware that, on the last day in particular, there

**Peter Thomson, one of the most relaxed and rational golfers.**

would always be someone making a birdie that would change the whole complexion of the thing. But there was the impression that the others could make the mistakes, and their concern was simply reaching the greens, making pars, the importance of planning the round, knowing the potential birdie holes, the putting together of the score. It was a certain selfishness, of ignoring other people, of pacing themselves. Both men had a keen awareness of the necessary rhythms of the game, of the round, of the four rounds, of the championship week.

Apart from the urges that young people from the "Empire" countries of South Africa, Australia and New Zealand had to visit the "Old Country" at least once, urges that happily still apply, Locke and Thomson had much in common. They each knew from the beginning that the nature of world golf meant that they would have to go overseas, first to the UK, then America. They were both full-time tournament players at a time when the British tour-

nament players were still obliged to hold down club jobs. When they complained about this, saying it cut down on their tournament skills, Thomson used to say, "Why do it, then?" Both travelled thousands of miles to advance their tournament careers. In the 1950s they made exhibition tours together to South Africa and the Pacific countries, and no doubt Thomson, 12 years the junior, learned much from Locke.

**Peter Thomson** from Melbourne, that gracious Victorian city that considers itself a cut above bigger, brasher Sydney, was born on the 23rd of August, 1929. Not too much is known of his early career as a boy or youth golfer (he never seemed to talk much about that) although there is a suggestion that his first aim in life was to be a chemist, but, after finishing leading amateur in the Australian Open of 1948, he became a professional in 1949. He was second in the Australian Open of

1950, won by Norman Von Nida, and won his first New Zealand Open that year. In 1951, he won the first of his three Australian Opens, and was clearly precocious. The future was to bring him the championships of Italy, Spain, Germany, Hong Kong, India, the Phillipines and above all the staggering total of five Open Championships, three of them in successive years, the first time it had been done in the 20th century, the first time since Bob Ferguson of Musselburgh back in the 1880s, a distant age ago.

There has never been a more rational champion than Peter Thomson, a more self-contained person. His creed seemed to be that we all live in an imperfect world, and that we simply need not be surprised at anything, should take everything as it came along. He gave the impression always that he knew exactly where he had come from, where he had been, where he was and where he was going. He was one of the most relaxed, at least apparently so, of golfers, and seasoned observers never stopped marvelling at his jauntiness on the course, the air that it was all just a brisk and rather pleasant stroll. Even as a young man he had a rather fleshy countenance, twinkling eyes, a sardonic sense of humour and a striking ability to switch off from what should have been the pressures of the moment. He never did suffer fools gladly. If he was invited to do something, go somewhere and didn't care to, he would say simply "No, thank you." Nothing more – no waffle about frightfully sorry old boy or previous engagement or the like, just "No, thank you."

After a round, he would sometimes have a drink in the clubhouse, talking to the other fellows briefly, but when he had finished his drink he would say quite pleasantly, "I've had enough of you fellows," and be off. Even in his earliest days, Peter Thomson carried an air of grandeur, even of superiority. He would travel over from Australia first class at a cost of around £200, a lot of money in the early 1950s. He would have a flat in London. He would pay his caddie £5 when £1.50 was the going rate. He was about as relaxed as a champion could be and no one could ever tell whether he was playing well or badly. He played every year for a spell in America, won a tournament, always made a profit. Indeed in 1956, the year of Cary Middlecoff's win at Rochester, he made a very strong run at the US Open, finishing fourth.

Although Bobby Locke was established when Thomson arrived on the scene, their careers were drawn together and they were the world's finest small ball players for most of two decades. From 1949 to 1958, they won eight Open Championships

and had two second places. Just as Locke's hero in his youth had been Bobby Jones, so Thomson's hero was Ben Hogan – two impressive mentors, perhaps offering clues to the personalities of their disciples. By the standards of professional golfers, Thomson was a sophisticate, with an enquiring mind. He was much taken with the Orient. He wanted to know everything about India and Russia. He wanted to know why Hindus could starve and yet give food to holy cattle. He read the life of Gandhi, listened to Mahler, could rip off the entire Professor Higgins/Rex Harrison part in *My Fair Lady*. He became a journalist, a television commentator, a golf course architect, almost a politician. He stood for a Melbourne constituency, Pirran, as a conservative, tramped the streets, knocked on doors, reduced hugely the margin, but didn't win. Being Governor of the State of Victoria would not have been beyond his wildest dreams, nor perhaps his capabilities. He said later that when he had reached 50 he wanted to do something "more important", as though his career in golf had been no more than pleasure. There was an idealistic streak – he wanted to work with drug addicts. He was a giver, but perhaps found it difficult to let people see that he was, or that he enjoyed it. And he had a relaxed attitude to money, always saying that there would always be another "money-tree". At a time when the money was perhaps running a little low, Thomson the pragmatist went back to the US, and on the burgeoning Seniors Tour he won half a dozen events and a huge sum of money, something more than $300,000.

In terms of his technique, the style was the man. When he first experienced links courses, he quickly saw that the key to steadfast scoring was to keep the ball in play. His forte was a relentless rhythm and simplicity of action. You could imagine him saying to someone who asked him how golf was played, "Why, you just hold it like this, stand like this, swing it back like this, swing it forward like this, swish it away down the fairway, get on the green and don't three putt." He was no more slavish a practicer than Locke. If he was playing "badly", he would just go back to the hotel, sit down and think about it, go back and hit half a dozen balls – that's it, by George he's got it! In his playing days, he never seemed concerned about money – there was always an exhibition match, or something, around the corner. He dressed conservatively in greys and blues, and always wore white shoes. He had a rather strong left-hand grip, with his right hand slightly under, left shoulder high, hands slightly forward. There was just a suggestion of lateral movement as

130

he started the backswing, but it was a simple swing through the ball, rather than a hit at it. In putting he had a rather more upright blade than Locke, took a longish backswing, then a pop straight through, with very little follow through. Locke's putting action was perhaps more inside, more closed, then came through like the closing of a door. Thomson was not an outstanding short game player, possibly not outstanding at any particular thing, but, put the whole package together with a sharp mind, and it was, rather like Nicklaus, almost unbeatable. Someone once said that the greatest club in his bag was the clearness of his brain and Thomson was once reported as having said that, the tighter the situation, the more clearly he saw the challenge.

Nowhere was this more true than at Birkdale, in the 1965 Open, his fifth and finest victory, the last year in which 36 holes were played on the final day. Thomson spent the lunch hour with Tony Lema, defending champion and his playing partner, over a sandwich and trying to explain to Lema the intricacies of an England-Australia Test match showing on television. Thomson was a cricket lover. The two closing holes at Birkdale are very severe, a par-5 and a long par-4. On the 71st hole, Thomson threaded a long iron shot into the green, pitching 30 yards short and running on to eagle range. He did exactly the same at the 72nd and won the championship by two strokes. These strokes were on a par with Tom Watson's iron to the same last green when he won in 1983 – boldly, coldly, clinically done.

These long iron shots, under such circumstances, seemed to be the absolute essence of Peter Thomson, just as a 30 foot putt, perhaps downhill with two breaks, would have been the absolute essence of Bobby Locke. Thomson was a perceptive thinker

on the game, in the manner of Jones and Hogan. He spoke knowingly for example of that singular moment at the climax of a championship when the potential winner stood on the 72nd tee, facing the final drive and concentrating his entire being on getting the ball out to one single patch of fairway, perhaps only 100 square feet in area, and how with that shot a championship could be won or lost, a man's life changed for ever more. There is one other anecdote which is vintage Thomson. Long after his championship career, he was asked about memorable moments. There was not one to be found from his five championships. Instead, perhaps impishly, he recalled a Match Play Championship tussle against John Panton at St Andrews. He had played the three final holes in 3, 3, 3, to tie the match, going on to win at the fourth extra hole. "That was rather pleasing," he said. But the best of Peter Thomson emerged when he said that he felt no one should win six Open Championships, that Harry Vardon should be left "with his immortality".

Bobby Locke and Peter Thomson had other contributions to make. Before Locke, Sid Brews was the only South African professional of note and he never played internationally to any extent. Thus it was Locke who opened the way for Gary Player, the Hennings, and generations of South African international golfers. Before Thomson, Norman Von Nida, a firebrand from Sydney had played a few feverish seasons in the UK, winning several professional events and making two or three good runs at the Open Championship. But it was Thomson who blazed a trail for such as Bruce Devlin, David Graham and more recently Greg Norman. If in golf's pantheon, the highest places must to to Vardon, Hagen, Jones, Hogan and Nicklaus, Bobby Locke and Peter Thomson are close behind.

| CAREER HIGHLIGHTS | |
|---|---|
| | British Open |
| Bobby Locke | 1949, 1950, 1952, 1957 |
| Peter Thomson | 1954, 1955, 1956, 1958, 1965 |

# THE BIG THREE

**T**he advent of the gutty ball in the middle of the 19th century, the coming of the rubber-core ball at the start of the 20th century, and to a lesser extent the appearance of the steel shaft in the 1930s, were milestones in the evolution of the game. All of them changed in some way the manner of playing the game, of swinging the club, of striking the ball. Then in the 1960s another milestone in the game, in no way less important than the others and in many ways more significant, came with the "Big Three". The coming of the Big Three coincided with the development of colour television, the most potent advertising medium yet devised by man, and the emergence of the jet aircraft which brought fast, cheap travel within the reach of millions, and the coming of the Big Three made championship golf a spectator sport to rival in its dramas a heavyweight championship fight or a World Cup final. And it convulsed the earning potential of all championship golfers.

The Big Three was, or were, three champion golfers – **Arnold Deacon Palmer, Gary James Player** and **Jack William Nicklaus**. There had been triumvirates before in golf – Vardon, Braid, Taylor, and Hogan, Nelson, Snead – but no three men ever convulsed a sport as the Big Three did. Their contrasting personalities, their achievements and the manner of their achievements over a decade or more, made golf such a major sport that the greatest public corporations in the world embraced the game and these players as prime media for advertising and marketing products, and for publicity, public relations and promotional activities such as had never before been imagined. For golf, it was the best of times, and the impetus and influence of the Big Three and their decade persists. For those of us who lived through it, and nostalgia being what it is, the 1960s was a

**Palmer, Player and Nicklaus played a major part in the golf explosion of the 1960's.**

decade to remember. It was a time of rock music, the beginnings of drugs, of sexual indulgence and revolution; of the Beatles and the Rolling Stones and Bob Dylan and mysticism; of the assassination of President Kennedy, student riots in Paris, the Russian invasion of Czechoslovakia; the coming of commercial television and betting shops in Britain; flower power and San Francisco and Cassius Clay; and, alas, the permissive society. And so affluent was the US in this decade that it could conduct a major war in Vietnam and at the same time indulge in a hugely expensive space programme. Through all of this, golf and the Big Three were untouched, in that the sport was clean and proper and as well-administered as it had been for 100 years. The Big Three did not "wear flowers in their hair".

Palmer, Player and Nicklaus were contrasts and complements. Palmer was five years older than Player, Player five years older than Nicklaus. Arnold Palmer had won the American Amateur Championship in 1954, narrowly, by one hole from Robert Sweeney and turned professional the next year. Gary Player had been a professional since he was 17, in 1953. In 1958, Palmer won the Masters, Player finished second in the US Open. In 1959, Player won the Open, Jack Nicklaus won the first of his US Amateur Championships. For the three men, all of this was but an overture for the shining 60s to come. In 1960, Palmer won the Masters, the US Open and in going for the Ben Hogan Grand Slam of three championships in the same year, lost the Centenary Open at St Andrews to Kelvin Nagle of Australia by one slender stroke. In 1961, Player won the Masters, Palmer won the Open, and Nicklaus won his second US Amateur. In 1962, Palmer won the Masters (after a play-off with Player and Dow Finsterwald), Nicklaus (in his first year as a professional) won the US Open, Palmer won the Open, and Player won the US PGA Championship. In 1963, it was Nicklaus winning the Masters and PGA, Palmer losing the US Open in a play-off to Julius Boros. In 1964, Palmer won the Masters, the last of his major championship wins. In 1965, Nicklaus won the Masters, Player the US Open. In 1966, Nicklaus won the Open and the Masters, and Palmer lost yet another US Open play-off, this time to Billy Casper. In 1967, Nicklaus won the US Open. In 1968, Player won the Open. It was an astonishing sequence. From 1960 to 1965, they won six Masters in a row, three Opens, three US Opens and two PGA Championships, and dozens of other events such as the World Match Play Championship and the Canada Cup. At every major championship, it seemed, the television cameras were hypnotised by Palmer, Player and Nicklaus. At every prize-giving, it seemed, the trophy went to Palmer, Player or Nicklaus.

Palmer was first on the scene, all fire, all boldness, going for everything, always attempting the impossible and sometimes succeeding. And when he failed, his failures would be Wagnerian. Player was the little man from distant South Africa, all intensity, dressed in black, fidgeting over diet and exercise, but perhaps the greatest international player the game has known. And finally there was Nicklaus, Johnny-come-lately, the big, blonde, powerful boy who had been indulged if not spoiled by a doting father in his childhood, who was to go on and amass more championship victories than the others combined.

And behind the Big Three was a big fourth, one of the greatest significance, Mark Hume McCormack, a grey eminence who became a blue-chip eminence. Just as much as did the players, McCormack changed the face of the sport irrevocably. McCormack was a Cleveland lawyer who, in a word, "managed" all three players and made for each of them, and for himself, a fortune, as we shall see.

Palmer, Player, Nicklaus – and the greatest of these was Arnold Palmer, not so much for his achievement as simply for being Arnold Palmer. A generation or more on, it is difficult for contemporary golfers to appreciate, even comprehend, what Arnold meant to golf, to America, in his time. Quite simply, he became a folk hero, a John Wayne figure who seemed to exemplify all the qualities with which Americans identify – the poor boy who "made it big", with a Gung-ho, go-for-broke attitude to the game of golf. Palmer tackling a golf course was like the US Marines storming some foreign beach, the 7th Cavalry coming to the rescue of the wagon train. He laced out long, thrilling drives down the fairway. He poured immense iron shots not at the green, but at the flags, regardless of inhibiting hazards. If he caught the rough, and he did it often, he plunged in and smashed out prodigious recoveries. And he putted with a silent futy, as though he could glare the ball into the hole, as though a putt missed, even from 40 feet, was an affront to his manhood. Golf to Arnold was essentially a charge, as though "Forward, Forward" was the only watchword. And if occasionally it became a Charge of the Light Brigade, the open-mouthed galleries identified with his disasters from their own experiences, identified with his towering drives, his remorseless putting, his successes, from the depths of their own fantasies. The Palmer galleries were vast, whooping, screaming, whistling at his every shot – "Go get 'em, Arnie" was the cry that thundered across the fairways of America.

He would tee the ball rather forward, opposite his left foot, and stood away from the ball, as though reaching out to it. His grip was vice-like, his hands enormous. The swing, on the quick side, was inside all the way back, then from inside slightly to outside at impact, and with a slightly closed face, the clubhead sent the ball flashing off, thrillingly, with a slightly right to left pattern. He had a tremendous extension of his right arm through the ball which sent his follow through not round behind his head as in the classic Snead manner, but straight up in the air, spinning sometimes above his head, sometimes even in front of it. He would cock his head to the right, following the ball, then, satisfied with what he saw, he would stride out quickly down the fairway to the uproar of the crowd, chasing after the ball as though he couldn't wait to hit the next shot, to get to grips with all of it again.

He was physically well-ordered for the work, with wide, strongly-muscled shoulders, slim hips, strong legs and immensely powerful forearms and hands. He looked like none other than the middleweight champion of the world. His face was a glorious mirror of the man, above all else an honest face. No golfer was ever more anguished than Palmer when the golf ball did not behave as he had decreed. His habits, his characteristics, were essentially human. He hitched at his pants; his shirt tails hung out from time to time; he sniffed; he dragged deeply on cigarettes on the course until what amounted to a national outcry forced him to stop for a time – in public, that was. On the putting green, when the other man was putting, he would sometimes turn and glare at the gallery and it seemed he was always looking at YOU, so that you would say inwardly, "My God, what did I do – did I make a noise – did I jingle coins in my pocket, or what?" But he was really looking over and beyond the gallery, thinking distant thoughts. He quickly realised that when the little red

134

light on top of the television cameras shone, that meant the camera was transmitting. Arnold always knew which camera was the live one. Over the ball on the green, he locked into a stance that would have taken a hurricane to topple – knock-kneed, slightly pigeon-toed, body still. Three little practice putts, and off the ball would go.

Arnold was not the most handsome of men, but exuded above all else virility and, we are assured, sex appeal to a remarkable degree. He had star quality, and he was strangely gracious, a word you might not think of using for him. Off the course, he would suffer gladly fools, bores, drunks, the media and would sign autographs in a way that Hogan, for example, never could do. Arnold was a simple, honest, conservative man. Above all else, he was a physical animal. He would surely never sit down to read a book, and paid little attention to newspapers. Arnold had to be *doing* something – filing and fiddling with golf clubs in his workshop, flying the length and breadth of the country, latterly in his own jet plane, to exhibition matches, tournaments, sales conferences, advertising photography sessions, television matches, dining at the White House, walking with kings and presidents and keeping the common touch. He appeared a dozen times on the cover of *Sports Illustrated*, the leading US sports magazines and – the ultimate American ennoblement – on the cover of *Time Magazine*. He was Arnold Palmer, the folk hero.

He was born on the 10th of September, 1929, in Latrobe, Pennsylvania, son of Deacon Palmer, who was greenkeeper/professional at the local 9-holes course (it subsequently grew to 18-holes, and Deacon became the head professional). Latrobe is a small town east of Pittsburgh, a steel town with a population of 12,000, small enough for almost everyone to know almost everyone else. In such a place, and with such a background (father a golf professional), Arnold grew up on the golf course. There was never anything else for him. With his father, he had a rather abrasive surface relationship which masked the deep affection they had for each other. Arnold wasn't so much taught golf by Deacon as directed by him. Deacon was above all a club professional who would enter the clubhouse, modest as it was, by invitation only, and, like an old Scottish professional, "knew his place". No doubt Arnold's conservatism came from such early influences. A friend, Bob Worsham, received a golf scholarship to Wake Forest and persuaded the college to do the same for Arnold, and he became one of the best college amateurs in the country. Worsham was killed in

a car crash in 1950, which so shattered Palmer that he promptly left Wake Forest and enrolled in the US Coastguard for three years. That done, he went back to Wake Forest briefly, then moved to Cleveland to work as a salesman in what was obviously a restless period in his life. There was never to be another such period.

After his US Amateur Championship win, he turned professional. He was 25. He won the Canadian Open of 1955, in his first full year. The Palmer career was on the move. General Eisenhower, during his presidency, gave golf a tremendous impetus in the US, notwithstanding the quality of his play (he was to become a close friend of the Palmers). The outstanding champion of the hour was still Ben Hogan, the austere forbidding perfectionist, although his last tournament success was the Colonial Invitational of 1957. The personality of Palmer, the derring-do of his play by contrast, made him a natural entertainer, made championship golf nothing less than theatre for the television companies, so much so that not many years passed before grumbles came that there was too much golf on television. For Palmer there were only two places at the end of a championship – first, or everywhere else. His greatest joy, the whole thrust of his life it seemed, was in winning, in beating the others, in beating *all* the others so much so that it could almost be said he wasn't interested in golf, but only in *competitive* golf. All of this was picked up by the small screen.

Almost all of his victories were last-minute affairs in which he came from behind to overtake the leaders with a burst of birdies, winning over the last few holes. More than once his failures came from the impossible shot which he could not resist, or from the lapse of concentration when he had already decided that he had won. In 1960, a golden year, he birdied the 71st and 72nd holes at the Masters to win – it saw the beginnings of "Arnie's Army", the thousands of fans who cheered and held up banners exhorting him to even greater deeds. In the same year at the US Open at Cherry Hills in Denver – one of the greatest, most evocative Opens, since it saw a Palmer victory, the first appearance of young Jack Nicklaus the amateur (he finished two strokes behind) and the last challenging appearance of Ben Hogan the veteran (he finished four strokes behind) – Arnold was seven strokes behind with one round to play, and 12 players ahead of him. The first hole, a rather short par-4 down a valley, had irritated him all week. He was convinced he could reach it. On that last round, he smashed out an enormous drive onto the putting surface. Two putts gave him a birdie.

He chipped into the hole from off the green at the 2nd for another, then birdied the third and fourth – four under par after four holes. He went to the turn in 30, and with all the others falling away scored 65 and won with a record low last round. Yet over the next six years, he was to be in three US Open play-offs, and lost all three.

In the 1961 Masters, he came to the last hole seeking only a par-4 to beat Gary Player. Earlier, Player had been in the bunker to the right of the green, and splashed out successfully for a single putt and his par. Palmer hit the same bunker, knocked his recovery clear over the green, chipped back over-strong, scored six and presented the Masters to Player. Later that year, in the Open Championship, he hit two shots which are firmly planted in the history books. The championship at Royal Birkdale had experienced the worst gales since Sandwich in 1938. Palmer gave a quite stunning exhibition of long iron play, hitting shots that seemed no more than a head high, but which drilled through the wind without deviation. On the third round, his pitch to the 16th hole, than a par-5 of 510 yards, missed the green on the right and finished on a high bank above a narrow green, pin high but deep in willow scrub, scarcely playable. Arnold made a ferocious smash at the ball, got it on the green and made his par. At the 15th hole of the final round, leading the championship, his drive tailed off to the right, a yard or so into calf-high rough. With a 6-iron, again he tore through everything and got the ball to the middle of the green – the narrowest of gaps, the toughest of lies, the tightest of pin positions, Arnold would "go for it". His philosophy was "If you can hit it, you can hole it." The Birkdale club later put a commemorative plaque on the spot. The only other on a championship course is on the 17th at Lytham, commemorating a similar Bobby Jones shot in the championship of 1926.

In the US Masters of 1962, he tied with Gary Player and Dow Finsterwald, scoring two birdies over the last three holes to do it. In the play-off, he was three strokes behind Player with nine holes to play. He scored them in 31 strokes to win. In the US Open that year, he tied with Jack Nicklaus and lost the play-off. Over the five rounds, he three-putted ten times, Nicklaus three-putted once. In the Open at Troon that year, Palmer played his finest championship, matched only by his fourth Masters win in 1964. On a course parched dry by drought, where the ball kicked and bounced unpredictably, Palmer scored 71, 69, 67, 69 for 276, a championship record. In second place was Kel Nagle, six shots behind.

The third man, Bob Charles, was 14 shots behind. In the Masters of 1964, his last major success, he again scored 276 and both championships brought from Palmer masterly exhibitions of long, telling driving, of iron shots which peppered the flagsticks, and putting of an inevitable aggression.

Of course, there were other times. In the US Open of 1963, he tied with Julius Boros and Jackie Cupit, names not likely to cost Palmer much lost sleep. But a stomach ailment did. He was up and down most of the night before the play-off, went to the tee next day weak as a kitten and lost to Boros. But the greatest of Palmer disasters, a king-sized disaster, came in the 1966 US Open, in San Francisco, and it came from two typical Palmer shots – ridiculous, melodramatic, impossible shots. He was five shots ahead of Billy Casper at the 15th tee on the final round at the Olympic Club. The championship was surely won. This is a short hole, the pin on the day cut perilously close to the right side and a defending bunker. There was lots of target space to the left of the flag. Arnold shot straight at the flag, caught the bunker, scored four on the hole. Casper cannily dumped his tee shot into the middle of the green, and holed the putt. Two shots gained. At the 16th, a very long par-5, Palmer hooked his tee shot into very dense rough, and actually tried to force the ball out with a 3-iron. He failed, advancing the ball not many yards. He eventually scored six on the hole thanks to an excellent bunker shot and one putt. Casper meantime had played conservatively down the fairway, was on in three, and of course holed the putt. Two more shots gained, and, when Arnold hooked yet another drive on the 17th, they were tied. Palmer had lost a six stroke lead on the round, and lost the play-off, 69 to 73. At least the man stayed in character. There were other nonsenses – he once scored 13 at a hole in Los Angeles (there is a plaque confirming it) – by hitting four consecutive drives out of bounds. When asked what had happened, he said, "I missed a short putt for a 12." And at the Open Championship of 1987 at Muirfield, he scored 10 at the 14th hole of the second round. Playing steadily, almost certain to qualify for the two final rounds, he played five shots in a bunker. It was vintage Palmer – the ball had to be advanced at all costs. The first of them could have been played out comfortably, backwards to the fairway, but even at the age of 58 that was not the Palmer way. "Forward, Forward" was still the cry. Arnold Palmer was then,

**Arnold Palmer with his characteristic follow through, during the Piccadilly Match Play in 1965.**

as he had been 30 years earlier, just the most exciting golfer the game had known since Walter Hagen.

Marching along with Arnold Palmer, seldom more than a stride behind him in these early years and from time to time ahead of him, was one **Gary Player**, just possibly, and certainly arguably, the greatest international player the game has known. Gary was born in Johannesburg on the 1st of November, 1935, and that is the first critical fact in his career. Any South African golfer intent on success at the highest level must leave home, must play away from home, must live away from home through most of his active years, for the great events of the game are in Britain and America, thousands of miles away. The second critical fact must be that Gary's mother died of cancer when he was six years old, scarcely old enough to comprehend his loss. His sister Wilma is four years older, his brother Ian eight years older. Wilma married when she was 17. Ian had enlisted in the Army before he was 17 and fought in Italy with a South African armoured regiment. And, by the time Gary was 17, he was an assistant professional on the other side of the city, all of which says something of the nature of the Player home life after Mrs Player died. Gary's father, Harry Player, was a gold mine "captain" in Johannesburg, a powerful man who introduced Gary to golf when he was 15. The third critical factor in the early life and times of Gary Player, one that stayed with him, was that he was small, five feet eight at best. At school work he was no star, but he excelled in all the school sports – football, cricket, swimming, athletics – winning a trophy as best all-round athlete in the school, this against all the big fellows, the sixth formers.

Within a month of his first golf game with his father, Gary had the bug. He discovered the golf course at Virginia Park where Jock Verwey was the professional, and started to haunt the place. Jock had a daughter Vivienne, a year younger than Gary – he thought her rather special – and a son Bob, and all three of them grew up as it were on Jock Verwey's course. Gary became his assistant at £29 a month, charging five shillings (25p) for lessons, when he could find customers. In between times, he slaved at the game from morning to night. Practice was a way of life for Player, even into his 50s. There has never been a more obsessive practiser in golf, Ben Hogan not excluded; the Ben Hogan, whom, at long range, Player worshipped.

Although there were 18 years between them, the life and experiences of Bobby Locke were much in Player's mind, and he realised quite quickly that professional tournament golf in South Africa was very limited. If he wanted to make his mark on the game, it meant going "north", going to England, the "Mother Country". As with Locke and Thomson, and all the "colonials", the call of England before her empire was totally wound down, was strong. Gary moved from Virginia Park to the Killarney Golf Club in Johannesburg, an altogether more prosperous club, where he met George Blumberg, who was to prove a benefactor. The call of the north was strong. In 1955, he had failed to qualify for the South African Open and, with only the East Rand Open to boast of, and aged 19, he set off for England. The Killarney members raised money for him. His father arranged an overdraft at his bank. George Blumberg gave him £50, a healthy sum then, and the young Player, with those big, brown eyes wide open, an air ticket, and £200 in his pocket, set off for England and a career beyond the imagination of any of his sponsors. If he was careful, these funds might keep him alive for a couple of months. On the way, he played in the Egyptian Match Play Championship and won, beating his friend Harold Henning 4 and 3 in the final! It was his first tournament outside South Africa. To a young man, the first prize of £300 was quite simply a fortune.

In England, he had a difficult time. His little band of South Africans – Henning, Brian Wilkes, Doug Evans, Harry Middleton and himself – lived in digs, travelled in trains and buses and other people's cars, and had to watch their pennies. Player was criticised by a few leading British players. They didn't care for his grip and swing – probably rightly, for there were imperfections – his wardrobe, his hairstyle. Their attitude was that he would never get anywhere in golf. It hurt, but it did nothing but make the young fellow more determined to succeed, and determination verging on bloody-mindedness was to characterise the entire golfing life of Gary Player. The next summer he was back, this time as South African Open Champion (he was to win the title 13 times over three decades) and he won a five rounds Dunlop Tournament at Sunningdale, beating Arthur Lees, the club's professional, who could nominate a score on either of Sunningdale's Old or New courses in matches with members, and go out and do that score.

Next year, America, at a time when the flight from Johannesburg took the best part of two days. And he

**Gary Player, the evergreen South African, a model of professionalism.**

has made that journey at least once every year since. There are many facets to the life of Gary Player. Like all the rest of us, he is a complex personality. His place of business throughout his working life has been essentially the US golf tour, more recently the Seniors Tour, all of which takes place some 12,000 miles from his residence, which must make him the world's champion commuter. In addition, he has played extensively all over the world. He has won the Australian Open seven times. He won in Chile, Brazil (where he scored a 59), Japan, the Ivory Coast, Britain and Europe, and has won more than 130 events in his career. In doing all of this, he quickly came to terms with travel and its pressures, developing the ability to sleep in aeroplanes and ignore their claustrophobic environment. He is said to have been asleep in his seat more than once before take-off. He would often spurn all meals and drinks on long flights, and cat-nap on the aisles of first class compartments.

What is quite remarkable is the vision and courage that he showed as a young man in knowing where his future lay, in making the progression from South Africa, to Britain, to the US, and in coming to terms with being on his own for long periods in cultures that were at least in part foreign to his own. Ultimately, the essence of Gary is that he is a small man from a "small" country, at least in the golfing sense, who beat all the big men in the big countries. He did it from unbounded ambition, from a massive determination, and with practice, practice, practice. In only his second year in the US, he won the Kentucky Open, scarcely a major event, but finished second to Tommy Bolt in the US Open at Tulsa, Oklahoma. His reward was $5000. He played one round with Ben Hogan, who told him that he had played well, there was nothing much wrong with his swing, and that he must keep practising – "I never stop practising," Hogan said. For Gary, this was accolade indeed. The next year, he won the Open Championship at Muirfield, at the age of 22. Over the next 20 years, he won the Open twice more, the US Masters three times, the US PGA twice, and the US Open once. He became the third man, after Jones and Sarazen, to do the Grand Slam. He won the World Match Play Championship no fewer than five times in eight years, played for South Africa in the World Cup 16 times and won both individual and team titles. In doing this, he spent hundreds of hours in the air, and travelled thousands upon thousands of miles to become surely the greatest international player there ever has been. If ever a little man ran fast enough to keep up with the big men, it was Gary Player.

There is a delightful photograph of Gary after the presentation of the Open Championship trophy, the old claret jug, at Muirfield. He is walking back to the clubhouse, holding the trophy, his face aglow with joy, flanked by two strapping Scottish policemen, and he is wearing a white suit. Soon afterwards, his golfing uniform became black, all black, which he said retained the heat and gave him strength. Gary became a faddist, obsessed with fitness. He convinced himself that diet was critical to his form and indulged in honey, nuts, raisins, wheat germ, fruit juice, fresh fruit, fish, bananas – he had a contract to endorse bananas for a time. Out went tea, coffee, white bread, potatoes, fried food, sugar. He took weightlifting courses to build muscle. He never used tobacco and was against stimulants. And he came to believe in premonitions, that all was ordained, that the Lord, at least from time to time, was on his side. He has written that in practice rounds for the US Open at Bellerive, St Louis, in 1965, when he won, each time he passed the scoreboard by the first tee, listing all the previous winners, he saw clearly "Gary Player, 1965".

As his career developed, he gave more and more attention to public relations, press relations. When he won that US Open, he handed his winning cheque of $26,000 to Joe Dey, executive director of the USGA and asked him to use it for cancer research and to help junior golf. At exhibition matches, he would compliment the locals on their lovely course, before he had seen it, saying how it reminded him of his farm in South Africa, and he would trot out a series of jokes and stories, rather like Bobby Locke, adapted to the place and personalities. He learned a sharpness, a kind of street wisdom, in dealing with the writers. Over the early years of the World Match Play Championship at Wentworth, it seemed that each year, on the morning of the first day, the newspaper preview stories would lead with Gary Player doing or saying something, regardless of what else was happening, or who was in the field. One year, he declared that in practice he had had a lesson from a police officer(!) and that he would "never hook the ball again in my life". He then went to the first tee of his first match and hit a high, handsome, looping hook. More than once he declared that the World Match Play Championship was the fifth major championship in the world. Having won his last Masters championship at the age of 42, then becoming the oldest winner, he claimed that there was no reason to doubt that a man of 50 could win a major championship.

All this was part of a public persona he built up over the years. Sometimes he seemed preposterous – his public statements were inclined to be rather extreme. But he would say all these things from behind large, wide, brown eyes with the intensity that he brought to his golf, so that not only did he intend you to believe it, but you almost felt that he too believed it all. There was a certain ruthless streak in Gary. He missed few tricks on the course. In the 1973 World Match Play final, Graham Marsh suggested to him that he had teed his ball ahead of the markers on the 35th tee. As they left that green, Gary told Marsh exactly what he thought of him. Marsh incidentally had been two down with four to play, but produced three birdies in a row to go one up at the last hole, where Gary holed from six feet to save himself. At the 37th and 38th holes, Player, from greenside bunkers, saved himself each time by getting "up and down" in two each time, confirming yet again that he was the world's best bunker player. At the 40th, Gary holed from eight feet, Marsh missed from four, and Player, in the longest final of all, won his fifth World Match Play title. The handshake was perfunctory.

Earlier, in a 1968 semi-final, Gary faced Tony Jacklin, the darling boy of British golf, Open Champion the following year, US Champion in 1970. This one had almost as much drama as the Lema match (see p. 209). They finished all square when Gary missed from four feet at the 36th, in a downpour that completely washed out the next day's play. The explosion of cheering which had greeted that miss left no doubt in Player's mind that the huge gallery was partisan – in favour of Jacklin, that is. When they got to the 37th tee, 36 hours later at 9 am, to finish the match, a crowd of hundreds was already spilling down each side of the fairway. Jacklin's second shot found the front of the green, Gary missed on the left. He pitched up about nine feet past the hole. Jacklin left his first putt four feet short. Now Player. He seemed fidgety. He was troubled by some crowd noise. He asked photographers to move. Eventually he putted, smack into the centre of the hole and immediately turned to upbraid the crowd. Someone had said, "Miss it, miss it," as he was over the ball. Gary addressed the world at large, along the lines of "I know you are pulling against me, but at least allow me to putt." All this was going on as Jacklin was moving to his ball. He missed the putt. Some people booed Player, suggesting that they thought his remarks to the crowd smacked of gamesmanship. Jacklin was stunned. Player had won. The handshake was very perfunctory.

Perhaps for all his impishness, for all the Spartan regimes he would have you believe he follows, for the divine help he suggests he is often blessed with, and not to ignore the endless hours of practice the edifice is built on, Gary Player's ultimate quality has been courage. He had the courage to leave home as a boy, the courage to go overseas as a youth, the courage never to quit, never to accept that any cause was lost until the sun went down. In 1978, when he won his third US Masters, he had not won a tournament in America for three years, and, since he was 42, his championship career had the sound of the past tense. But how many times has he said out loud and believed it, "I have never played better in my life", or "That was the finest round of golf I have ever played". When he started that last round at Augusta, he was seven shots behind the leader Hubert Green, and between him and Green were such players as Gene Littler, Tom Watson, Lee Trevino, Hale Irwin and David Graham. Level with him were Severiano Ballesteros and Tom Weiskopf. Jack Nicklaus was one stroke behind. It was clearly going to be a scrimmage finish. The previous evening, Player had said to Mark McCormack, his manager, that he could shoot 65 next day and "still win this thing". Sometimes one feels that Gary invented positive thinking. Paired with Ballesteros, he picked up only two shots on the outward half, but even then was saying to the Spaniard "I can still win this thing." He then proceeded to score 30 on the inward nine, tying a record, and finished with 64, and won. It was a victory for cold courage in the hot Georgia sun and Player, no doubt still blessed, went on to win the next two tournaments – three tournaments in three weeks.

In one sense, Player's courage was exemplified in his putting. When a man birdies three successive holes with single putts at any level of the game the adrenalin flows and each successive putt becomes progressively more nerve-stretching. Player was never afraid of piling birdie upon birdie. For years he was a rap putter, giving the ball a crisp click without much follow-through. In that 1978 Masters, he used a longer, more fluent stroke, still with the simple blade putter he always favoured. From his early days, when he had a fearsome hooker's grip, he changed to an orthodox grip. His swing action featured a very low, straight takeaway to give him the widest possible arc so that he could get to the ball with maximum speed and power, to keep up with the strongest players. It was slightly flat, and when he went for the really big shot, the long shot,

he often toppled over in reaction to the speed of his follow-through. He was a masterly chipper and putter, a brave and very talented recovery player.

Gary Player's career has spanned four decades, from the era of Hogan to the era of Ballesteros. After he turned 50, he won the Senior Grand Slam of US and British Seniors Opens and the US PGA Seniors. In the entire context of world sport, there is a case for saying that Gary Player is not just an outstanding golf champion, but has been one of the world's outstanding athletes.

The tale is told that, when the US team arrived at Muirfield for the Walker Cup match of 1959, Raymond Oppenheimer and another British selector walked over to the practice ground to check on the new players in the American team. They found young **Jack Nicklaus**, blonde, crew-cut, massive, hitting 1-iron shots. After a few seconds of gaping, open-mouthed, Oppenheimer said to his friend, "The jig is up – let us return to the clubhouse immediately." They did, in search of whatever solace was at hand. They found little – the jig was truly up. The Americans won the match 9–3 and Nicklaus, of course, won all of his matches. Over the next quarter of a century, for more than just one Walker Cup match, the jig remained truly up in so many of the world's great championships. Nicklaus collared 20 of them. So what is there to say about this man who has won more championships than any other golfer, more prize-money (some $5 million) than any other player in the long history of the game? One could simply call him the greatest golfer who ever lived, and leave it at that, objectively. But subjectively, as ever, things are different, and the different things must rest in the eye of the beholder. If there are 30,000 people watching a golf tournament, there is not one but 30,000 tournaments being played. Some people may not care for the Nicklaus swing, or his taste in golf clothing. Some people may prefer their champion to take a more dashing approach to the thing, like a Palmer or Ballesteros, or a more tranquil approach as in a Locke or a Thomson. So we are forced back again to the fact that diamonds are diamonds, rubies are rubies, pearls are pearls. And different times, different mores.

Jack William Nicklaus was born in Columbus, Ohio, on the 21st of January, 1940. His father, Charlie, was a big friendly man, successful as a pharmacist – he eventually had four shops – and

**Jack Nicklaus, winner of 20 major championships and some $5 million in prize money.**

had Jack on the golf course at the age of ten. It seems clear that Charlie indulged his only son (there was a younger daughter, Marilyn) along the lines of "just sign a chit for what you want at the club". The club was the nearby Scioto Country Club, where Bobby Jones had won the US Open of 1926, so there was some history around the place.

It was quickly clear that Jack was as much a prodigy as Jones had been. He was taught by Jack Grout, the club's professional, and by the age of 12 had scored a 74 on the full course, and at 13 he was scoring under 70. That same year he played in the US Junior Championship, and at 15 he was good enough for the US Amateur. All this time he had been winning, local and state amateur events, but at the age of 16 the world beyond Ohio heard of Jack Nicklaus – he won the Ohio State Open against a field of the best professionals in the state, and scored a 64 in the third round in doing it. In high school and college (Ohio State) Nicklaus was a good athlete, particularly in basketball and football. He was a big boy, five feet ten inches tall at 13 and just under 12 stone. In vacation time, it was golf all the way under the eye of Grout, who preached that young men should hit the ball hard and that direction and control could come later. When he came to Muirfield for that Walker Cup match, he was a young bull of 19, now five feet eleven inches tall and better than 200 pounds who could lace out a drive of 300 yards as Sam Snead had done if with rather more elegance than Nicklaus showed. Later that summer, he won a classic US Amateur final against Charlie Coe, one of the half dozen best amateurs in America, holing a birdie putt on the last green for a one up victory. The year of 1960 was to suggest that Nicklaus was to be something more than just a very good golfer. In the Eisenhower Trophy matches for the World Amateur Team Championship, he scored 66, 67, 68, 68, over Merion, a US Open course. His 269 was 13 strokes better than the next man. And, in the US Open, he finished in second place, only two strokes behind Arnold Palmer, the Young Lochinvar of the hour. In 1961 he finished fourth in the US Open. His championship aggregate for the two years was better than any other player in the two events. He won his second US Amateur, and sought out Mark McCormack to discuss with him his prospects in professional golf. When he asked Mark what his overall income might be in his first year, McCormack said without hesitation "$100,000". This was almost twice what the leading money winner of 1961 (Gary Player, with $64,540) had won. Nicklaus turned professional at the end of the year. The third man had arrived. The Big Three was complete.

Jack Nicklaus brought to the professional ranks an immense power, a swing that smashed rather than swept the ball away vast distances down the fairway, and simply poured iron shots with a high trajectory into the greens. And he putted like a young man who didn't know how difficult it was, crouched over the ball, taking forever to make the stroke. And he brought with him a substantial arrogance. He was not above keeping the likes of Hogan and Snead waiting on the tee. Jack always had a very clear idea of how good he was, and considering his career up to that time it may not have been too surprising. Above all, the accident of history threw him into direct conflict with Arnold Palmer, the people's champion. There was an almost immediate confrontation, at the US Open of 1962, when he beat Arnold after a play-off. From then until 1986, Nicklaus won 17 more major championships and finished second no fewer than 18 times, an astonishing achievement.

In those early years of the 1960s, as far as the crowds were concerned, Jack was not easy to love. He lacked the warmth, the outgoing friendliness of Palmer, and his game had an inevitability about it, unlike the Palmer autograph of anything-can-happen-next. As someone has written, when Arnold stepped on the tee, lightning flashed and the gallery crowded closer; when Nicklaus stepped on the tee, thunder rumbled and the gallery drew back. So ominous to their hero did Jack become that "Arnie's Army" would hold up banners behind greenside bunkers, saying "Hit it in here, Jack," when Jack was playing an approach shot. Nicklaus went on to outstrip their hero – Arnold's last championship challenge came in that ridiculous US Open with Casper in 1966 – and he also went on to undergo a metamorphosis seldom experienced by any sportsman. Although Nicklaus still wore his arrogance on his sleeve – unlike Arnold he never did suffer fools gladly – he must have known that stepping into Palmer's battleground was stepping into a minefield. Sustained by his massive talent, he simply did it, and avoided the mines. If this partisanship didn't exactly pain Jack – the two men were good friends with a mutual respect – he could seldom have been left unreminded of it. But he made no comment, and by the end of the decade "Ohio Fats" had gone and the "Golden Bear" was very much alive. Indeed in 1969 he began to make a positive effort with his public image. He grew his hair longer, and had it "styled" in contemporary fashion. His golfing clothes were co-ordinated. He dieted and lost 20 pounds in a month, and ate more carefully. He smiled a little more. The death of his father Charlie in 1970, when Jack was scarcely into his 30s, affected him deeply (Ballesteros, at roughly the same age, had the same experience). All of a sudden it seemed that Jack was a different person, a mature man, someone who was re-assembling his values, so that the 1970s would become even more prolific of success on the golf courses of the world.

His triumphs have been well recorded, and it might be tedious to relate all of them again, but two aspects of Nicklaus the man were emerging. He was the most gracious of losers, of sportsmen. In the Ryder Cup match of 1969 at Royal Birkdale, the entire series came down to the last match of the last afternoon singles, Tony Jacklin against Jack Nicklaus. On the final green they were all square, each some three feet from the hole. Nicklaus putted first, and holed. If Jacklin were to fail with his short putt, the Ryder Cup was lost. As Jacklin moved to his ball, Nicklaus picked it up, conceded the putt and the match was halved. The Ryder Cup was tied at 16–16. His action may not have pleased his non-playing captain, Sam Snead, but Nicklaus felt that it was less than fair to ask a first-class player to hole a little putt in those circumstances. And in the 1977 Open at Turnberry, when Nicklaus had scored 68, 70, 66, 66 for a 269 total which was a record in itself, only to be beaten by one stroke and a final 65 from his playing partner Tom Watson, Nicklaus walked off the green with his arm round Watson's shoulder, congratulating him on winning what had been a quite epic battle between them. And five years later, in the US Open as Pebble Beach, Nicklaus had finished his final round a few minutes before the same Watson. He stayed in the recorder's tent, watching a television monitor and saw Watson hole that electrifying chip shot from off the 17th green which gave him a one stroke lead over Nicklaus. And when Watson holed out at the 18th with yet another birdie, Nicklaus was first on the green to congratulate him and to lead him to the recorder's tent.

There is one aspect of the Nicklaus career that is worth detailing – its longevity. His six Masters victories extend over 23 years from the first in 1963 to the sixth in 1986. His US Open record covers 18 years, 1962 and 1980. His Open Championships were 1966, 1970 and 1978 (he was second in 1964, and again in 1979). In the US PGA, he first won in 1962, then took his fifth in 1980. All of this contains the evolution of a champion and of the changes he made in his play and his thinking about the game with the passing of the years. In his early days, he was a prodigious driver of the ball, a fearsome long iron player. He felt he could hit any green in the world in two shots and make his share of putts. His swing then was upright, straight back and up, his "floating" right elbow (swaying away from his right side on the backswing) was quite notorious, and his huge power came from the drive of his legs – "strong below the waist" was a Henry Cotton dictum. It seemed at least in part a Byron Nelson swing philosophy. He later modified his action to make it less upright, more rounded.

As Nicklaus went through his long seasons in the sun, it became increasingly clear that here was the most intelligent, most rational in golfing terms, of all the great champions, Hogan and Thomson included. There was perhaps no single aspect of his game that was so much better than that of Smith or Jones or Brown, but in the management of his game for a particular championship on a particular course (for example in making the change from US courses to a fast British links and the small ball in the 1960s); in assessing holes which would give him birdie chances and could be attacked aggressively, others which should be played conservatively; in the effect of a change in wind direction which would alter shot requirements; in a certain feel for the ebb and flow of the four days of a championship and in identifying the most dangerous of his opponents and what they might do; in all of these things, Nicklaus was without peer. In coming through the final nine holes, the final six, the final three, there never was a more rock-like finisher than Nicklaus. The greatest challenge of the game for him was "Three holes to play, and a birdie to win". And there never was a more resolute putter with the one that mattered – the ten foot putt that just had to be holed. If you wanted someone to hole the putt that would save your life, you would call for Jack Nicklaus, even before Locke, or Palmer at his peak. In the US Open of 1980 at Baltusrol, in holding off the talented Japanese golfer Isao Aoki, he played an impeccable final nine holes, holing everything that absolutely had to be holed. He was so elated at that victory that he spent two hours at his Press interview, with some of the journalists drifting away, saying, "I don't want this day to end." And in the Masters championship of 1986, considering the eight players ahead of him before the final round, he decided that he would need 66 to tie, 65 to win. He went out and scored 65, and won. He made seven birdies in ten holes, again holing every putt that had to be holed

and, like Gary Player eight years earlier, scored the inward nine in 30 strokes, equalling the record. He embraced his son Jackie, his caddie, and walked off to torrential, even hysterical applause from the huge crowd, looking no more perturbed than a benign bishop.

If a very close analysis of the Nicklaus game in its most mature years had been made, the conclusion might have been that, in its separate parts, it was not particularly outstanding. Nicklaus had never been an especially good wedge or bunker player. But, just as the unbridled power of his early years had been cast aside, so his whole game seemed to be in a perfect, peaceful balance, and it was clear that the Nicklaus greatness lay not in any one or two elements of his technique but in the clarity of his thinking about the game, his powers of concentration, his resolution at the climax of a great championship. His experiences did not bring a complete personality change. If he became more mellow, he could still be tetchy. His business associates, sometimes his clients, had to march to the beat of the Nicklaus drum. If the private jet was scheduled to leave at 8.30am, and Jack was ready to go at 8.20am, it would go, regardless of who might be left behind. He became more and more involved with golf course design, construction and management, with large and expensive projects around the world. He has not built a simple, or an easy, golf course.

Jack has always had other interests. He has long been a tennis player, a fisherman, more recently a skier. The walls of his Florida home are adorned – an odd aberration – with elk heads and game fish which he has killed. He has earned some $5 million in prize-money alone and must be considered quite wealthy. He stands in the highest echelon of the game with Vardon, Jones and Hogan. Many hold him to be the greatest player in the history of the game. Bobby Jones said that a man could only be the best of his time, could only beat his contemporaries, could not have beaten those that came before, or after, and Nicklaus has done that. He received the royal nod from Jones after a Masters victory, when Jones said that he played a game "with which I am not familiar". Nicklaus, the third of the Big Three, won more championships than any golfer, more than the other two combined. When it comes down to the debate so beloved of all golfers, we get down to the simple, terminal response – "Look at the records".

All three champions, differing personalities as they were, had some things in common. All three were blessed with wives of quality. Winnie Palmer, Vivienne Player and Barbara Nicklaus were women pre-

Mark McCormack the manager and marketing genius behind the Big Three and many of today's champions.

pared to subordinate their lives to a husband's career and were sensible enough, when it was necessary, to put a brake on the excesses which fame and wealth might bring. And all three of our champions had something else in common. In an odd way, seldom expressed against a background of hero-worship, of mingling with the great and the good, of flying off all around the world, of earning large lumps of compensation for their labours, they all knew that, ultimately, the game is not about money. It is about glory, and a personal immortality.

If all the words that have been written and spoken about the Big Three were laid end to end, they would extend no further than all the words that have been written and spoken about Mark Hume McCormack, their manager and mentor. Born in Chicago, McCormack was educated at William and Mary College and graduated from Yale Law School, joining Arter, Hadden Wykoff and Van Duzer in Cleveland, one of the largest and most proper law firms in the state of Ohio. Mark was a golfer good enough to qualify for four US Amateur Championships and one US Open, not to mention the Amateur Championship of 1966, when he went all the way to the first round before losing a happy match with one Ronnie Shade at Carnoustie. With a friend, he started an agency to book exhibition matches for professional golfers. In the late 1950s, they had the feeling that golf was ready to grow. He first met Arnold Palmer briefly in 1956, then again in 1958,

after Palmer had won his first Masters, and Mark's agency was soon representing him, Dow Finsterwald and a clutch of other tournament professionals. The next year, 1959, Palmer went to McCormack and asked if he would represent him, Palmer, on an exclusive basis. He was getting more offers than he could handle. After some discussion, it was agreed. They shook hands, and from such a simple beginning came the greatest promotional empire that sport has every known, eventually culminating in McCormack's International Management Group, a multi-million dollar company that trades throughout the world in sports promotion, personal management, investment counselling, television production, publishing, merchant banking and a dozen ventures at any one time.

Arnold Palmer had already won the Masters, but his signing with McCormack, and the coming of Gary Player and Jack Nicklaus over the next two years, produced a sequence of events that saw McCormack being dubbed by the golf gossips as just plain lucky. Palmer in 1960 won the Masters and US Open; Gary Player, who joined Mark in 1960, won the Masters of 1961; Jack Nicklaus joined him in late 1961, and promptly won the US Open in 1962. That was probably the first year of the Big Three, since Gary's winning of the US PGA Championship gave them a clean sweep of major titles. The Big Three was a creation of the journalists – McCormack saw no reason to complain about it.

One of his first chores was to check all Palmer's existing contracts. As a young professional, Arnold had signed with the Wilson Sporting Goods Company in 1954. McCormack – he has written amusingly and at the same time bitterly about this – found that the Wilson contract was paying Arnold a meagre royalty and had so many restrictions that Palmer in effect could not endorse any product without Wilson's approval and participation. No matter how McCormack struggled, option clauses allowed Wilson to hold on to Palmer until 1963, by which time the man had won the Masters three times, the US Open once, the Open twice. However, when the divorce was completed, the floodgates opened. Arnold Palmer was a brand name. In a society in which image is all and the advertising of goods and products a huge industry, McCormack soon had Arnold Palmer and Arnold Palmer Enterprises in a torrent of endorsements – golf clubs, clothing, garden tools, automobiles, soft drinks, airlines. There were books to be published, exhibition matches to be planned, television appearances to be arranged. There were only a handful of days in the year when

Arnold was not scheduled to do something, somewhere across the length and breadth of America and overseas. A private jet plane, which Arnold learned to fly competently, helped with mobility, because Arnold Palmer had become a small industry in himself. It was, of course, an affluent decade in the US – almost all of them are – and the same endorsement and marketing opportunities arose for Player and Nicklaus and were handled with like expertise.

By the end of the decade, Jack Nicklaus separated from the McCormack organisation for reasons which have never been made quite clear. It has been said that, while Mark was expert at generating income, Jack was even more expert at disposing of it. By 1970 he had formed Golden Bear companies which handle all his business affairs more than successfully.

In all of this, of course, McCormack, no more than anyone else in the same position, could not remain the world's sweetheart. He made enemies. By and large he ignored them unless they crossed the boundaries of the law or of the contract. His clients' interests he defended furiously – after all, the man was a lawyer. He proved to be a brilliant salesman, a tough negotiator, an expert organiser. He has a prodigious memory for people and places, dates and times, aided by a pocketful of 4 × 2 cards on which he jots reminders. And his time throughout each day is comprehensively organised, aided by a staff that runs into hundreds, in a dozen, hard-driven offices around the world. His huge IMG organisation has grown from a handshake with Arnold Palmer 30 years ago.

McCormack has the great basic American quality of energy. But he has one other quality that sets him above and apart from his competitors and contemporaries. He has vision. He has had the vision to look always beyond the immediate contract, to look for long term relationships with the major corporations with whom he deals. He has had the vision to arrange deferred payment arrangements for his clients, to provide income beyond their active competitive careers. In his early days, he had the vision to see the vast potential of television, and to package, produce and sell television programmes under his own control, such as *Big Three Golf* and *Challenge Golf*. He had the vision to learn about television negotiations and the vicious infighting that goes on between stations and networks, and he has acted for such governing bodies of sport as the Royal and Ancient Golf Club of St Andrews, and the US Tennis Association in arranging improved international television contracts. He had the vision to "create" sporting events, for example the World Match Play Golf Championship, to provide the talent, find the sponsors, arrange the venue and television coverage and keep all parties satisfied – more or less. He has run his companies with the tightest of fists – every employee must list daily their activities and achievements – and allowed them to grow organically into the world's leading sports management and marketing organisations, marketing Papal tours, marketing on behalf of Olympic Games host cities. So don't call him an "agent".

In considering what McCormack has done, one has to resist the temptation, the instinctive thought, of the word genius. What he did achieve for the Big Three and subsequently is simply phenomenal.

| CAREER HIGHLIGHTS | | | | |
|---|---|---|---|---|
| | British Open | US Open | US Masters | USPGA |
| Arnold Palmer | 1961, 1962 | 1960 | 1958, 1960, 1962, 1964 | |
| Gary Player | 1959, 1968, 1974 | 1965 | 1961, 1974, 1978 | 1962, 1972 |
| Jack Nicklaus | 1966, 1970, 1978 | 1962, 1967, 1972, 1980 | 1963, 1965, 1966, 1972, 1975, 1986 | 1963, 1971, 1973, 1975, 1980 |

# Tijuana Brass and the Kansas City Kid

**G**olf champions are just people, in the sense that no two champions are alike. On the whole, and with very few exceptions, two of which might be Bobby Jones and Jack Nicklaus, they have not been blessed with the world's comforts and pleasures in their formative years, and one of them, more than any other, was quite simply underprivileged. He was **Lee Buck Trevino**, born in Dallas, Texas, on the 1st of December, 1939. Trevino's father, of the same name vanished from the scene fairly quickly – the young Lee never knew him – and the boy was brought up by his mother Juanita and his grandfather, neither of whom could read or write. Home at one time was a wooden shack without power or plumbing. Before he was ten, the boy was haunting a nearby driving range. He left school at 14 and found a job at the range where he developed a distinctive, totally self-taught and effective golf swing. At the age of 17, he enlisted in the US Marine Corps, a sobering thought in itself, for a four year stint, and was a good enough golfer to spend some of that time playing "with the officers". That done, he found a job as an assistant professional at El Paso, on the Mexican border, and it was there that his golfing education, a self-education, was rounded out.

Trevino hustled. He had to. He would tackle anyone on the golf course for a dollar because a dollar was important. He would take on any bet, well, almost any bet, with any taker, such as getting down in two from a bunker, chipping and one-putting from 40 yards out, giving a man strokes and a start of 100 yards down the fairway – any of golf's endless stream of permutations on its handicapping system. All this was happening in that distant corner of America that was less fashionable, less sophisticated and certainly less prosperous than New York or Los Angeles, and where much of the news was made by Mexicans

**Lee Trevino, the champion who made it against all the odds.**

sneaking across the border illegally. Trevino learned to be his own man. He had to, since no one was doing him many favours. And he learned to be tough, since nobody was there to protect him, defend him, save himself. Yet, just as a child without shoes sees nothing wrong when all the other children are without shoes, so there was little self-pity in Trevino. He smiled, made jokes, was outgoing, with a smile of dazzling whiteness in a swarthy countenance beneath a mop of jet-black, curly hair.

He had an endless line of chatter and stories, emerging from the fact that if you are gambling it might just help to protect your own money, and relieve the other man of his, if it distracted him a little. Later, when his tournament career was at its height in the early 1970s, and he chattered compulsively with the galleries and his opponents, and if the galleries enjoyed it – and they did – many of the players came to see it as verging on gamesmanship. One prime example of this came in his astonishing semi-final match with Tony Jacklin in the Piccadilly World Match Play Championship at Wentworth in 1972. Trevino opened the 36-holes match with a 67 for the morning round against Jacklin's 72. At the lunch break, Jacklin realised that Trevino had talked him out of his game with his chatter. At the start of the afternoon round, Jacklin said to him "Do you mind if I don't talk this round, Lee?" Quick as light, Trevino said, "You don't have to talk Tony – just listen." As they moved along, Jacklin tagged behind Trevino, out of earshot as much as possible and played what might have been the best burst of golf of his life. He had been four down when they started the second 18, but he scored the opening nine holes in 29 shots, seven under par, and was one up, for the first time in the match. Yet Trevino was never a man to lie down to anyone. Over Wentworth's inward half, which then had a par of 38, he used only 32 strokes for a second 67. Jacklin scored the second 18 holes in 63, but match play being match play he lost by one hole in a match which was manifestly an epic – but Trevino, talking or silent, as he was over the final intense nine holes, won.

In 1965, Trevino won the Texas State Open, placed second in the Mexican Open. In 1966, he qualified for the US Open, finished nowhere as Arnold Palmer and Billy Casper fought out their high drama in San Francisco. The year 1967 was one of revelation for the unknown Lee Trevino. He finished fifth in the US Open and won a cheque for $6000. The affluence of the professional tour, the ambiance of the whole thing, the fact that finishing fifth in the championship meant that he was as good as almost any of the others, was all a revelation and a magnet to him. At 28, he buckled down to more and more competitive play, and the next year he won his national Open in revealing fashion. He went into the final round one stroke behind Bert Yancey – a tall, handsome, blond man, a classic swinger, a man obsessed with the need to win a major championship (he never did) and a complete contrast to the stocky, swarthy, brash Trevino with his "agricultural" swing, as it was dubbed.

That stroke was won back after only three holes, and after five Trevino, playing no more than routine golf while Yancey was playing nervously, suffering from his own imagination as much as anything, was a stroke in front. In the second half of the round, Trevino had swept Yancey aside and was relaxed enough to be joking with the galleries again as he finished with a 69 and a total of 275, equalling the existing record. It was the first time any US Open winner had returned four rounds all under 70. Trevino was always a great final round player, a great last hole player. In this, his first major championship, he drove into the left rough at Oak Hills 72nd hole, left his second shot in the rough, pitched his third a few feet from the hole and clipped the putt in for an unorthodox but perfectly comfortable par. Trevino became a national personality overnight, and he loved it. He loved the limelight and the media, the backslapping and the autographs, he loved "being recognised". But this early, the more experienced observers of golf were noting that, in spite of, or maybe because of, that uniquely ugly swing, Lee Trevino was rather more than just a happy, laughing wisecracking Mex. He could drive the ball unerringly into the narrowest of fairways with a fading, but consistent, flight. He was a magnificent putter, prowling around the green to check the putt from both sides, both ends, before striking it crisply. And he was the boldest of scramblers, getting the ball on to the green and holing the putt time after time

from bunkers, greenside rough or fringe grass from anywhere – pitching and running, pitching and stopping, scuffling the ball, chipping often directly into the hole.

And the joking and talking would vanish on final round, close finishes, when there was work to be done. The swing never failed him. He had an open stance, with the ball opposite his left toes, the perfect stance for a big slice. He had a strong grip. On takeaway, the club would go straight back, even outside the target line, and his hips would slide to the right. At the top of the backswing, the left wrist would be straight, so that he seemed set to hook the ball. As he went into the downswing, there was a pronounced and powerful leg action, with the hips driving through, as though the club was to be left trailing. With his left wrist arched back, he hit the ball very late but with a long extension of his right arm through the ball and a huge spinning follow-through. Somehow the clubhead went into the ball very 'low' and stayed there for a long time, longer than the more upright swingers. It was a remarkable swing, imposing strains on the legs and lower back, but it was above all in control. And the man thought this swing was the most natural thing in the world.

In 1971, he established himself as a true champion in addition to being a highly successful money winner on the US Tour – he won, again, the US Open, and went on to win the Canadian Open and the Open Championship in the space of four weeks. It was a striking demonstration of the man's strength and resilience. Merion, not much more than 6500 yards with a par of 70, featuring above all the narrowest of fairways, was ripe for the Trevino speciality, accurate driving. He tied with Jack Nicklaus on 280. On the first tee of the play-off, Trevino flipped an imitation snake out of his golf bag to the general consternation, and won handily by 68 to 71. In the Open at Birkdale, he won by the tightest of margins – one stroke – from Liang Huan Lu of Formosa, of all people, known affectionately as Mr Lu. Trevino in fact won the US Open twice, the Open Championship twice, the US PGA twice and incidentally the Canadian Open twice which is certainly enough to qualify any man for his share of immortality, and nothing was more compellingly dramatic than his defence of the Open Championship in 1972, at Muirfield.

Apart from anything else, anyone else, he was faced with a Jack Nicklaus who had won the Masters and the US open and was vying to equal Ben Hogan's Grand Slam of all three titles in 1953. Only Arnold Palmer had come close when in 1960 he had gone into the Centenary open at St Andrews with the two big titles won, only to finish second in the third. Nicklaus was to have the same experience. Also very much on hand was Tony Jacklin, Open Champion of 1969, US Champion of 1971 and right at the peak of his career. The championship was to lie between Trevino and Jacklin, with a late intervention by Nicklaus, but Jacklin was doomed to be Trevino's bunny. They were tied after 36 holes on 141. In the third round, Trevino, trailing, summoned up a small miracle by holing the inward half in 30 strokes, with successive birdies on the five final holes. The most outrageous of these came at the short 16th, where Trevino mis-hit a bunker shot, the ball came fizzing across the green, hit the flagstick and flopped into the hole. At the last hole, with his second well through the green, he chipped the ball down the slope and into the hole. Someone was watching over him. His 66 equalled the record of Johnny Miller on the previous day. Jacklin, his playing partner and a witness to all this, held on manfully with a 67.

In the final round, Jacklin hit a 3-wood shot to the long par-5 fifth eight feet away. The putt went in for an eagle, and Jacklin was tied for the lead at that point with Doug Sanders, at three under par. At the same time, Nicklaus was storming into action, with 32 strokes to the turn, birdies at 11 and 12, and birdie chances at the next four holes, none of them taken. Trevino birdied the 11th, Jacklin the 14th, and at that point there was a three-way tie for the lead. The whole thing boiled up into a desperately thrilling final hour to the championship. Nicklaus went over par on the short 16th when his tee shot spun off the green, and he finished with two pars and a magnificent round of 66 which was to prove just one too many. Everything hinged on the 17th hole, 542 yards at its championship length. Jacklin hit two beautiful wood shots and was some 20 yards short of the green. Trevino drove into a bunker, splashed the ball out, hooked his third shot into rough short of the green, then played a rather careless approach which ran through the green and up a slope, again in rough. At this point he had probably decided that it was over, and that Tony Jacklin would be the champion. He pitched on, 15 feet from the hole. His birdie putt, which would have given him control, ran four feet past the hole. Trevino chipped on, and the ball went straight into the hole. Jacklin missed his return putt. Trevino, who had scarcely been on the fairway, had his par-5. Jacklin, who had never been off the fairway, scored six. Someone again was watching over Trevino. With a stroke in hand now, he almost sprinted to the 18th tee and laced out a perfect drive almost before Jacklin got to the tee. Trevino gave him no time to settle. He hit his second shot ten feet from the hole, and two careful putts gave him his championship. Jacklin, shattered, scored five on the hole, and finished third, behind Nicklaus. Trevino had defended his title triumphantly, the first man to do it since Arnold Palmer, a decade earlier.

When Trevino first "appeared", first broke through in 1968, many people dismissed him as little more than a caddie who would vanish as quickly as he came, taking with him that strange, less than credible, swing, and that he was in essence a brassy, unabashed gambler. Yet a very objective look at Trevino the golfer revealed him as a conservative player who hit the fairways relentlessly, found the fat parts of the greens rather than blasting at the flagsticks, and put his trust in an impeccable putting method. And if he holed a chip shot or two from time to time, and was condemned as lucky, that was simply a matter of the law of averages, the odds. If Trevino was a gambler, he was a calculated, professional gambler who never went for the impossible bet.

The man lost a fortune in ill-starred business ventures and simply went out to earn another fortune. He was struck by lightning on a golf course, survived that, then survived surgery on his lower back. Nothing abashed Lee Trevino. He'd engage Severiano Ballesteros in Spanish, in spite of the fact that the Trevino Spanish was pidgin. When it came down to the heart of the matter, the last round, the last few holes, the man was steel. Trevino was a compulsive talker, but much of it was calculated. It relieved the pressures the game put on him, as on everyone else. It bolstered the public image of the happy, carefree Mex, to whom golf was no more than fun. But, if he did any carousing, he did it away from the golf course. When he was featured in the BBC's long-running *Pro–Celebrity Golf* series on television, he would appear on time each morning ready to go. When the day's work was done, he would vanish to his room in Gleneagles Hotel or Turnberry Hotel, have dinner there and watch television, and keep away from the backslapping lobbies and bars and dining rooms. He'd say, "When the cameras roll in the morning, I'm on, and I'll give them my best stuff. When the cameras stop rolling in the evening, I'm off – gone, finished!"

When you start life with nothing, almost everything is a bonus. If ever a man made it against all the odds, it was Lee Buck Trevino. He was a very different animal from **Thomas Sturges Watson**,

151

born ten years later, but they have one quality in common. Both Trevino from the Lone Star State, and Watson from Kansas City, the capital of the endless Mid West plains, in some strange way had powerful affinities with the Scottish game, the game of the links, of the humps and hollows, of the winds and the storms, of managing in their earlier days the small ball, of manufacturing the shots which golf at the British seaside demand, and of the whole philosophy of the game in these tight little islands.

On the evening of the 20th of July, the last day of the Open Championship of 1980 at Muirfield, Ben Crenshaw, who had finished third, resolved to play two more holes of golf in the long Scottish twilight. Crenshaw from Texas is a dedicated student of the history of the game and an avid collector of its implements, and earlier in the week had acquired a gutty ball and five wooden-shafted clubs, all of them a good 100 years old. Shortly after dinner in the Greywalls Hotel which overlooks Muirfield's tenth tee, Crenshaw and friends assembled there. Tom Watson, Open Champion of a few hours standing, if for the third time, helped Crenshaw to tee the gutty ball old-style on a small pile of sand. Ben whacked the ball out some 150 yards, but into the rough. He knocked his next shot the same distance, into the fairway, with the same hickory-shafted club. By this time, Linda, Tom Watson's wife, had been back into the hotel to uncover a piper, and the small gallery proceeded up the fairway to the sound of bagpipes. The ball was found to be damaged, and Crenshaw was allowed to substitute a modern ball, which he hit onto the green with a "mid-iron", holing out in two more. Watson could resist no longer. He wanted to lay hands on one of these old clubs and he challenged Crenshaw to a match over the parallel 18th hole, which returns towards the hotel. With the same "baffing spoon", they both hit good drives along the fairway. Crenshaw's second ran into a bunker, Watson's second, from a careful three-quarter swing was in the fairway, 70 yards short of the green. Crenshaw, without a modern sand club, left his next shot in the bunker but somehow got his fourth to the front of the green. Watson's mashie third went over the green into rough. Crenshaw got his next shot a couple of feet from the hole and Watson, without a modern pitching club, somehow scrambled his ball on, seven feet from the hole, and with an ancient putter, holed it.

Perhaps this frolic was the perfect release for Watson after the tensions of a championship in

Tom Watson, the Stanford educated champion.

which he had played superbly and won by a comprehensive four strokes from the evergreen Trevino. When Nicklaus won his first Open, at the same Muirfield in 1966, he was so exalted that he too went out that evening, but to the hotel tennis court, where he played fiercely for an hour to unwind himself.

The next year, following the championship at Royal St George's, Tom Watson travelled all the way to Royal Dornoch, by plane and by car, simply to play the great course there, the St Andrews of the North, because he had heard and read so much about it. Dornoch is some 50 miles north of Inverness, so that Watson's pilgrimage from Sandwich to Dornoch meant the best part of 700 miles. In the same way, he made visits to Ballybunion, that monumental links in the West of Ireland, surely one of the best dozen golf courses in the world. All of this preamble does no more than affirm that not since the days of Hagen and Jones has any American golfer been so enchanted by links golf, so attuned to the requirements of the Open Championship, as has Tom Watson. He won the Open Championship five times, which might be enough for any man. Yet in a concentrated period of seven years, beginning in 1975, Watson won his five Opens, two Masters and one US Open. In addition, he was second in the Masters in 1978 and 1979, second in the US Open of 1983 (and subsequently in 1987) and second in the US PGA of 1978. The remarkable thing about Watson was that, in one sense like Trevino, he came from nowhere – there was no history of golf in the family, no background, no golf scholarship, no distinguished amateur career. He was born in Kansas City in September, 1949, and if Trevino was one of the under-privileged, Watson was one of the other kind, to be compared only with Jones or Nicklaus in this respect. To this day, he has a little scar on his chin from jumping into a swimming pool at the age of three – the swimming pool was, of course, at the "country club". Tom's father was an insurance broker; his grandfather had been a judge. The family was affluent, liberal and active in politics, living at the better end of Kansas City. Their country club was Prairie Dunes, where the Great Britain and Ireland Curtis Cup team was to win for the first time in America in 1986.

When Tom later married Linda Reuben, like married like – Linda's father was very successful in real estate, specialising in commercial property. The boy Tom went to private day schools, then to Stanford University, the Harvard of the West, the up-market college at Palo Alto, near San Francisco, where he graduated in psychology, not perhaps the worst preparation for the stresses and strains of championship golf. He played on the Stanford golf team, won his state amateur championship more than once, and quite simply turned professional when he was 21.

Like all good young players, he laboured, intermittently good for a 66 or a 65, but seldom in the early days good for four solid rounds when it mattered. Physically he has the build of a good middleweight, rather like Arnold Palmer – strong legs, very powerful arms and hands, wide shoulders. With reddish-blonde hair and fresh complexioned, Tom was quickly described as the Huckleberry Finn of golf, an all-American "country" boy. He was far from being that. If there is one word for Tom Watson, it would be "brisk". He moved briskly down the fairway. He was brisk and business-like in everything he did. He wasted no time. He hit the ball with fearful speed and power – if his game went off, it was almost always because his swing had become over-fast. And, on the putting green, he was just as brisk and business-like. He walked the fairways, as Nicklaus said of him in a wider context, "like a man who knows where he is going", as you might expect from a graduate in psychology. In conversation as on the putting green or the tee, Tom Watson was quick, brisk, decisive.

In 1974, he went into the final round of the US Open one stroke ahead of Hale Irwin, and led the championship. He scored 79. But he did win his first tournament that year, the Western Open, and in the very next year he won the Open Championship at his first attempt. It was a championship with a frenzied finish – Jack Newton, Bobby Cole, Johnny Miller and Jack Nicklaus were all potential winners until they were gobbled up by Carnoustie's fearsome three final holes. The play-off between Watson and Newton was as close as could be, Watson winning by a single stroke when Newton missed from ten feet on the 18th green.

By the time the 1977 Open came round, to be played for the first time on the Ailsa course of the Turnberry Hotel, Tom Watson was a much more assured, much more mature, golfer. He came into the championship as winner of the 1977 Masters, a birdie putt on the 71st hole putting paid to one Jack Nicklaus. They were to clash again in one of the most dramatic personal encounters of the old championship. Their opening rounds were identical – 68 and 70. Paired together for the two closing rounds, they each scored inspired third rounds of 65. Unlike the usual blustery weather on the Ayrshire coast, the final day was like most of championship week, one of brilliant sunshine and no wind in what was a heatwave Scottish summer. Nicklaus began the final round with a birdie. Watson dropped a shot at the second. Nicklaus birdied the short fourth – three ahead. But Watson, unabashed, ripped off birdies at 5, 7 and 8. On the long par-5 seventh, he hit an immense shot with his driver from the fairway to the heart of the green for that birdie. Nicklaus was a stroke ahead going into the par-3 15th. There, Watson missed the green on the left, but from out of the fringe, using his putter, he sent the ball skipping 60 feet across the green to rap the flagstick and scuttle into the hole. They were all square, the others were far behind, and it had resolved into match play. The championship, as they do so often in close finishes, turned on the 17th, the 71st, a par-5 played through a long valley. Watson's second shot went nicely into the green, 15 feet from the hole. The Nicklaus second shot was hit slightly thickly and finished short. He chipped up to five feet, and missed! Watson needed only two putts, and he was ahead for the first time that day. As they walked to the final tee, he said to his caddie, "I think we've got him!"

Some 25,000 fans spilled around and beside them, lining the hole tee to green on either side, down an avenue to the arena of grandstands around the home hole. Arnold Palmer, his championship finished (he was a commendable seventh), sat in a hospitality tent, sipping a drink. Looking at a television monitor as Watson and Nicklaus marched up the 18th hole, he mused to the world at large, "Nobody can imagine what these two guys are going through – no one can imagine the pressure, unless he's been there." Arnold had been there, often enough. Watson played an iron from the tee, hitting perfect position, position A, in the fairway. Nicklaus, in death or glory mood, smashed with his driver, cut the ball across the fairway into an awful lie, almost under a gorse bush. Watson played an immaculate 7-iron to the green, less than three feet from the flagstick. Yet Nicklaus had more to say. He made the most stupendous smash at his ball, gorse bush or no gorse bush, and it came burning out of there to reach the front of the green a good 160 yards away. It was a terrific shot, but even then Jack William Nicklaus had more to say. From there, from a good 30 feet, with a rise and fall and a break between him and the flag, he holed the putt! Watson, brisk as ever, rolled in his putt for a 65 and the Open Championship, by one shot. They walked off the green together, smiling, Nicklaus with an arm round Watson's shoulder. In third place was Hubert Green, US Open Champion,

11 shots behind the winner. The huge crowd was stupefied by the audacity and the brilliance of the whole day.

The Watson swing that carried him to his success was fairly simple, fairly orthodox, but very powerful. His hands poured the clubhead through the ball at startling speed and he was a very long hitter. Since Byron Nelson was his mentor at times, it verged on the upright, but featured Nelson's trademarks of the sliding of the hips, and a vigorous driving of the thighs through impact. Tom was leading money winner in the US in 1977, 1978, 1979 and 1980. His 1980 Open win, as we have seen, was one which he dominated from beginning to end. His 1982 win at Troon was rather given to him when Nick Price, in control of the championship, faltered over the closing holes, and Tom became champion of Britain and America in the same year. In the US Open of that year, he played one of those shots that claim an immediate place in the folk lore of the game. Level with Nicklaus (who else?) at the 71st hole at Pebble Beach, where Watson had often played in his university days, he pulled his tee shot at the par-3 hole just off the left of the green, into ankle-high rough. The lie was clean, the flagstick close to the edge of the green. Watson took his sand wedge, lobbed the ball onto the green and into the hole. The shot won him the championship.

In 1983, his fifth Open Championship had all the tension that Arnold Palmer might have imagined. With nine holes to play, Nick Faldo, Andy Bean, Hale Irwin and Lee Trevino were in contention with him. Faldo went out at the 12th hole, saying when he had finished, "I'm capable of winning the Open one day – I'll be back." Five years later, he proved that to be true. With three holes to play, Watson had a one stroke advantage over the others. Bean and Irwin – who had missed a two-inch putt on the third round – missed the ball completely trying to tap it in; both birdied the 17th, each finishing eight under par. Watson had three holes to play. He birdied the 16th to be nine under, then made a par at the 17th. He stood on the 18th tee needing a par to be Open Champion for the fifth time, and again he was composed, confident, brisk. He hit a huge and perfect drive, then a 2-iron, 213 yards to the green, which flew like a bullet, running perfectly between the two frontal bunkers which flank and narrow the green. "It was the best 2-iron of my life," he said. Two putts later he was champion for the fifth time, and in his time the dominant player in the game.

Watson has played less golf since then, avoiding the week-in, week-out grind of the American circuit. "My desire to win is not all-consuming," he said archly. But his concerns remain the major championships. He may not be finished with them. If Gary Player, Jack Nicklaus, Lee Trevino can win in their 40s Tom Watson can.

| CAREER HIGHLIGHTS | | | | |
|---|---|---|---|---|
| | British Open | US Open | US Masters | USPGA |
| Lee Trevino | 1971, 1972 | 1968, 1971 | | 1974, 1984 |
| Tom Watson | 1975, 1977, 1980 1982, 1983 | 1982 | 1977, 1981 | |

## 14th Hole
# SEVE AND SANDY

The definition of a champion, the assessment of achievement when we are dealing with contemporary players in mid-career, becomes a subjective guessing game. We are dealing with the public persona. The private person may be quite different. Certainly the criteria demand that, to qualify, the golfer must have won more than once in the great championships of the game, and preferably on both sides of the ocean, in Britain and America. That hard rule eliminates such fine contemporary players as Nick Faldo and Curtis Strange. Two players qualify: one with the greatest natural talent the game has known since Sam Snead, and before him Young Tom Morris; the other an exasperating enigma.

**Severiano Ballesteros Sota** and **Alexander Walter Barr Lyle**, Seve and Sandy, the contemporary game's outstanding champions, have everything in common – save personality. Ballesteros lopes the world's fairways, prowls the world's greens, in a capsule of concentration and with a dark, burning Latin passion that says he wants to prove that he is the world's greatest golfer, and to prove it over and over again until the whole world thinks of Ballesteros before it ever thinks of Jones or Hogan or Nicklaus. Lyle by contrast saunters the world's fairways, potters across the world's greens, with a blond, fair, open Anglo-Saxon outlook of blandness that almost suggests that he knows he is the world's best golfer, sees no particular reason to keep on proving it, and if people don't quite agree with him, there is no reason to make a fuss about that, one way or the other, and so forth and so on.

Seve, pronounced "Sebbie" in the Spanish language, is a diminutive which if not quite polite is convenient for our purposes. Sandy is an acceptable contraction for Alexander. They were both born "on" a golf course, the Spaniard at Pedrena

Seve Ballesteros, one of the most naturally gifted golfers of all time.

on the Bay of Santander on the north coast of Spain, the Scot on the Welsh Marches of England at Shrewsbury. They were born within the same 12 months, Seve on the 9th of April, 1957, Sandy on the 9th of February, 1958. They were both the products of golfing families, Lyle even more so than Ballesteros. The Lyles of Clober were famous in golf in the West of Scotland.

Sandy's paternal grandparents had a farm at Clober, near Milngavie, on the outskirts of Glasgow. When Clober Farm fell on hard times, they decided to make it a golf course, and started it simply by cutting nine circles for greens. They later cut nine more, and there was some kind of an 18-holes golf course. In time, Clober Golf Club was formed, and developed, and the land and course were subsequently bought by the members. There were three golfing sons in the family: the late Walter, in his time a useful tournament player in Scotland; George, still professional to the Clober club; and Alex, father of Sandy, lately retired from being professional at the Hawkstone Park club, near Shrewsbury. The young Lyle was brought up there, in a house some 75 yards from the golf course, and his entire life seemed pre-ordained – there was no possibility of Sandy Lyle being anything but a golfer. By the time he was 12, he was virtually a scratch player. By the time he was 15, he was a boy international. In one year, 1975, he represented England at boy, youth and full amateur international level. He reached the final of the Boys' Championship twice, and lost twice. And when he played in his only Walker Cup match, at Shinneock Hills in 1977, he played three, and lost three. Perhaps this early, Sandy was a stroke play man, a golfer who simply did not relish match play, man to man combat with its personality clashes, its eye-to-eye contact and its tactics, as important in match play as the shot-making. He was to be a finalist four times in the World Match Play Championship, losing each time, narrowly. At the age of

157

11, he sat in the grandstand by the 18th Green at Royal Lytham and St Annes and saw Tony Jacklin win the 1969 Open Championship. He resolved there and then that he would become a professional golfer and "win the Open".

The career of the young Severiano Ballesteros at Pedrena, almost 1000 miles away, marched in parallel. Seve's grandfather had developed a family dairy farm in Pedrena, where his mother's family, the Sotas, had farmed for generations. His mother's father, in fact, had sold land in 1928 which became part of the first, fourth and sixth holes of the Real Club (the "Royal" club) de Golf de Pedrena. The course dates from 1929, under the patronage of the then King Alfonso XIII and was designed by H. S. Colt of Sunningdale fame and his partners Allison and Morrison. The Ballesteros family house overlooks the practice ground. It is essentially an unpretentious house, much extended, but the impression that Seve had to fight his way out of poverty, like a Trevino, is quite untrue. Over the years, the family had added to the patrimony by accumulating a good deal of land locally, and Seve, like Sandy, had a perfectly comfortable, if not grandiose, start in life.

Golf intruded on the child's life simply because it was there, at the door, and because his mother's brother, Ramon Sota, was, like the Miguel brothers Sebastian and Angel, among the first of the international golfers from Spain. Through the 1950s and 60s, he won the championships of Spain, Portugal, France, Holland, Italy and Brazil and played more than once in the US Masters, finishing sixth in 1965, a Nicklaus year. Since Seve's three older brothers, Manuel, Baldomero jun. and Vicente, were to become professionals too, there was talk of golf and little else. At the age of seven, he had his first club, a 3-iron head to which he fixed a stick, shaved to the form of a shaft. At eight, he had his first proper golf club, again a 3-iron given to him by Manuel, the oldest brother and he began to play and caddie when he could. Since Uncle Ramon banned caddies from playing the course except in their annual competitions, Seve would sneak on illicitly – or practice on the beach or whatever open space there was. Thus he learned how the golf ball will react, or spin, or otherwise, when struck in a certain manner by a certain club, for long shots, short shots, recovery shots. By the time he was 12, he had scored the full course in 79 in a caddie competition, and by the end of the same year he was a scratch player, with a quite exceptional feel for the ball in one so young.

He caddied for Manuel in the Santander Open of 1969 at Pedrena, when he was 12. In the 1970 Spanish Under-25s championship in which Manuel played poorly, the teenaged caddie upbraided his older brother, saying that he, Seve, could have played better. The boy was locked into the game, obsessed with golf. School had little interest for him. Golf in Spain was beginning its apparently endless expansion, centred mainly on the Costa del Sol in Andalucia, in many ways almost a world apart from Cantabria in the north. There was no real culture, no history of the game there, such as would engulf a boy in Fife or Ayrshire, save that created by the family, but the example of his uncle, Ramon Sota, had proved that there was a wider world, and a boy from such a village, from Pedrena, could conquer it. No costly, time-consuming amateur career for young Ballesteros – he became a professional, Spain's youngest, at the age of 16 years and eight months in January of 1974. Five years later, he was Open Champion. Sandy Lyle, the prodigy, did have such an amateur career, and turned professional at 19, after the Walker Cup match of 1977. Eight years later, he was Open Champion.

That a champion of the stature of Ballesteros should emerge from such an environment is something of a minor miracle. That a champion of the stature of Lyle should emerge from his environment could be considered inevitable, if with some reservations. As they entered their professional careers, so much more might have been expected of Lyle – when his father heard that he had won the Open Championship of 1985, he said, "It's about time." Both young men had God-given gifts, but often it seemed that Sandy did not know quite how to use them. Seve did, from the very beginning. Of all the elements that make up his complex personality, the most obvious is the burning desire for victory, a neurosis of perfection. And he has never kept it from the world, in the flashing grin, the anguished glare, the brooding frown. Sandy on the other hand gives the impression, rightly or wrongly, that it isn't really that important. Not for Sandy the emotional tantrums of a John McEnroe. An outburst of passion, of anger or frustration from Sandy Lyle would be demonstrated with a gentle slap of his right thigh and a pursing of the lips. What fires may blaze underneath there is never any way of knowing.

Both young men in their formative years would have been exposed to class, in the case of Ballesteros "upper", in the case of Lyle "middle". The club at Pedrena is one of the most exclusive in Spain, serving Santander, a royal city in its time, and to this day a prime resort to which wealthy "Madrilenos" escape the heat of a Castillian summer. The workers of the world are unlikely to unite on the Pedrena golf course – here, there is still an element of Franco country. Sandy Lyle probably caught the end of an era in which the middle classes dominated golf in Britain at club level, when the club secretary would be a retired wing-commander or bank manager, when the club professional would enter the clubhouse by invitation only, and a man, and in particular a boy, would certainly know his "proper place".

In 1974 Seve set out to conquer the world in his first international event, the Portuguese Open, played over the tight, short Estoril course. In his qualifying round, he scored 89. The par was 69. He was on his way home by the time the championship proper had begun. By the end of that year, he had won a couple of regional events in Spain and covered his expenses. One of his victories was the National Under-25s played over Pedrena. Naturally, his game was still unbridled. He smashed at everything as though he should hole out at every shot, perhaps heeding Arnold Palmer's dictum "If you can hit it, you can hole it." Palmer always said that with mischief in his eyes. But allied to Seve's youthful power was a short game that was altogether deft, one single example of which was to bring him international recognition.

In the Open Championship of 1976, played over a Royal Birkdale course baked hard by a heatwave – the course literally caught fire – Seve had been exempted from pre-qualifying as leader of the Continental Order of Merit (later amalgamated with its British equivalent to become the "European Tour"). He was 19, strong and handsome, and brought to Birkdale the flashing smile and a marvellously uninhibited golf swing that provoked from time to time spectacular recoveries. He also brought an opening round of 69, which led the field, and followed it surprisingly with a second round of 69, which again led the field by two strokes. In second place was Johnny Miller, the American champion of 1973, and they were paired together over the two final rounds. They each played slightly ragged third rounds of 73. Miller played the first nine of the last round in 33. Undisciplined driving cost Ballesteros the lead. When Miller chipped into the hole at the par-5 13th for an eagle, Seve was so excited by the whole scene that he rushed over and shook Miller's hand. A six at the sixth, a seven at the reasonably gentle par-4 11th had cost Seve control, but it was a quite impeccable final round of 66 by Miller which won the championship. It was Seve's third

shot at the last hole, televised internationally, that confirmed to the world that a star was born. At the 72nd, he needed a birdie four to stay in second place, tied with Jack Nicklaus, but he hooked his second wide of the green onto a scrubby patch of rather bare ground. He was about 30 yards from the flagstick, cut only 20 feet beyond a pair of bunkers confronting him, with a pathway of only a few feet between them. The routine shot might have been a wedge over the bunkers. Such a shot had little hope of getting any control on the ball, any backspin from that lie – the ball would surely run far beyond the hole. Seve elected to play the audacious shot, the impossible shot, a chip and run which sent the ball up the path to within a few feet from the hole. He holed the putt. If this was typical of the mad abandon of youth, it was to be typical of his entire career.

Much later, when Ballesteros was chided for his wayward golf, and before he had his good command of the English language, he said, "Drive een fairway, heet on green, two potts – ees boring!"

Severiano Ballesteros went into the last round of the 1979 Open at Royal Lytham and St Annes on 213, two strokes behind the leader Hale Irwin, a month or so earlier the winner of the US Open Championship. Demons treading close behind were Jack Nicklaus, Ben Crenshaw, Mark James, Rodger Davis and Isao Aoki. It was the closest the young man, the Kid from Spain, El Cid, had been to the title since Royal Birkdale in 1976 – at Turnberry in 1977, he finished 15th, at St Andrews in 1978, 17th. It was a championship of intermittent rain and cold, north-west winds, difficult weather, yet it produced the youngest champion since Young Tom Morris in 1872 – Seve was just 22 years and three months old when he won a championship which put him into the master class. And he did it with a bewildering amalgam of the exuberance of his youth, smashing immense drives which often finished many yards off the fairway, and with a wisdom far beyond his years in tactical planning when it mattered, in deep concentration, and in putting pressure on the field, and in particular on his playing partner over that last round.

The single exceptional round of that championship, long forgotten amidst his dramatic recoveries in the finale, was Seve's second round of 65. The half dozen finishing holes at Lytham are considered as severe as those of any course on the championship rota. Four of them are very long par-4s, all of them are stoutly defended by bunkers both fairway and greenside, by gorse and mounds and out of bounds areas, and all of them play into or across the pre-vailing wind. Ballesteros played the last five in 3, 3, 4, 3, 3 – four under par over a stretch that, on the day, must have had an even more realistic par of 4, 5, 4, 5, 4. Such was his cavalier attitude to the whole thing that the next day his score was ten shots higher. Both he and Irwin were 75, but maintained an edge on all the others. As they went to the first tee of the last round, Ballesteros wanted an edge on the US Champion, a seasoned player. He needed to hit him hard, and early, putting maximum pressure on him quickly. He did just that at the very first hole, Lytham's par-3 of 206 yards. He hit a 7-iron shot, down the wind, 15 feet from the hole, and holed the putt. Irwin took three – one stroke recovered, quickly. At the second hole, Irwin mis-hit his drive, eventually three-putted for a six against Seve's careful par four, and with only two holes played, the young Spaniard had gained three strokes. Hale Irwin had lost a lead he never recovered. He was shattered.

It was an advantage Seve was never to lose, in spite of a torrent of strokes, appalling and inspired, which were to flow from his clubs and which had him hitting recovery shots from places where no man had gone before. The sixth was a perfect example. At 490 yards, this is a short par-5 which doglegs slightly to the left, in the angle of which the Lytham club had built a huge mound, shortly after Bob Charles's win in 1963. It was soon covered with gorse and rough. In previous rounds, Seve had drawn the ball successfully past this hazard, about 240 yards from the tee, to the fairway beyond. This time, he hit what might well have been the worst drive ever hit in any championship anywhere. In a right to left wind, he hooked the ball monumentally over the mound, over the rough, over the 14th fairway into rough that rightly belonged to the 13th hole, at least 75 yards off line. He found a decent lie, then positively smashed a 9-iron shot that finished 40 yards over the green. From there, somehow, he fashioned a par five.

Another example came at the 13th, a par-4 of 339 yards, turning slightly to the right with a huge sandhill in the angle of the turn. He had played the hole conservatively three times, using an iron club from the tee and pitching to the green. This time, with the adrenalin flooding through him, he went for the big drive, to hit the green. The ball pitched on the top of the sandhill, a carry of almost 300 yards through the air, and fell back into the sand. From there, he pitched the ball 70 yards (the long shot from a bunker is one of the most difficult in golf). It broke off the green to the right, pin-high, in the fringe grass, ten yards from the flagstick.

From there, with his putter, Ballesteros holed it – as soon as he hit the ball, he was chasing after it, shouting in ecstasy. It was preposterous. The last of these examples came at the 16th, where Seve was dubbed by sardonic American writers as the "parking lot champion". The hole is a short drive-and-pitch par-4, doglegged to the right, of 353 yards. An area to the right was used as an overflow car park. Contrary to the general belief at the time, Seve drove there deliberately. He knew that (a) the rough ground there would be trampled down by spectator movement, and (b) if he finished among the cars the Rules of Golf would allow him to drop the ball clear of these obstructions without penalty. And he thought that area would give him a better approach line for his shot to the green. He poled out a long drive right into that area, 25 yards off the fairway. He was allowed to drop then pitched a sandwedge shot 20 feet from the flag – and, naturally, holed the putt for a birdie. The championship was his.

Irwin was to say later, "I saw Seve on the first tee, then on the 18th green – I don't know where he was in between." But Irwin, on the last green, was gracious enough to hole out first then shake the Ballesteros hand and tell the young fellow that he was a great champion, even before Seve had tapped in his short, final, winning putt. He won the 1980 Masters with an irregular last round in which a ten(!) stroke lead came down to two, but he recovered to win by four strokes with 66, 69, 68 and 72 for 275, 13 under par. In 1983, when he won again, this time with 280, eight under par, he complained that he "hadn't hit a good shot all week". At the same time he was saying wistfully, "I wish people would remember my good shots, not just my bad ones." And, in 1984, he won his second Open at the one place where every golfer in the world would want to win – the Old Course at St Andrews. Played in brilliant weather, this is the championship that is remembered above all for a few concentrated moments of the most extreme tension when Tom Watson was on the 17th hole, Severiano Ballesteros on the 18th hole, of the final round. That last day's battle had been between three of the world's finest golfers of the hour – Ballesteros, Watson and Bernhard Langer of West Germany. Now the entire championship hung in the balance.

At the 17th, Seve had driven yet again wide into the left rough. On this, the Road Hole, perhaps the most fearsome in the entire catalogue of championship holes, it was time for an inspired shot. It came. He hit a 6-iron almost 200 yards into the narrow green, took two careful putts and made

*Opposite:* St Andrews: an aerial view of the 1st and 18th holes.
*Top:* Wentworth, built during a golden age of golf architecture
in the early twenties.
*Previous page:* Sunningdale: a view of the 5th hole of the Old Course.

*Bottom:* The Country Club, Brookline, Massachusetts; the start
of the first golf boom in America in the 1890's.
*Overleaf:* Augusta National, Georgia: created by the great
Bobby Jones and home of the US Masters.

*Previous page:* The 16th at Cypress Point, California; arguably the most beautiful hole in the world.

*Top:* Shinnecock Hills, New York: Willie Dunn, winner of the first US Open in 1884, helped lay out the course in the 1890's.

*Bottom:* Pinehurst, North Carolina: developed by Donald Ross who was to have a major influence on American golf course architecture.

a par on the hole for the first time that week. He then quickly laced a long drive up the 18th fairway. Watson, behind, had hit a drive into perfect position on the fairway of the 17th, and came to his second shot. There, perhaps indecisive about club selection, perhaps over-excited, Tom smashed a 2-iron shot clear over the green and over the road to clatter into the infamous wall beyond the road. Ballesteros, seeking the birdie he thought he needed to win the championship, pitched to the 18th, 15 feet from the flag. Watson chopped his third shot at 17 up onto the green, but a good 30 feet from the flag. As he crouched over the putt, an explosion of sound came from the 18th – Ballesteros had holed the putt and danced across the green in a tarantella of joy, punching at the air, screaming at the crowd. Watson failed with his first putt on 17. Now he would need an eagle two at the last hole to tie, and he actually paced off his second shot all the way forward, the distance 93 yards. His pitch carried past the flag. At the shrine of golf, Severiano Ballesteros, the man from the unlikely starting point of Pedrena in the north of Spain, was the champion. And watching the end of it all, from a window overlooking that final green, was Carmen from Cantabria, Severiano's mother.

**Sandy Lyle**, by contrast, pottered quietly into his professional career. He elected to be Scottish for international team purposes, not unreasonably. He was dubbed "Rookie of the Year" in his first year, 1978, and won his first Open Championship that year, albeit in Nigeria. From then on, placid as a shepherd, he won at least one event each year, in Scandinavia, France, Spain, Italy, Hawaii, Japan, the US as well as at home, earning £50,000 in 1979, his second year, and improving on that regularly and progressively. Yet, until his win in 1985, he made little impact on the Open Championship, the one that counts more than any other. Some observers said that he won in 1985 as an afterthought. He had played in the championship of 1975 as an amateur, aged 16, scoring commendably 75, 77 and 84 over Royal Lytham, failing to make the last day's play. But, from 1979 onwards, he finished 18th, 12th, 14th, 8th, then missed the last day in 1983, and in 1984, 13th. His friends were beginning to despair. And even when at last he won in 1985, having, he said, "served my apprenticeship", there were moments of despair a-plenty. For example, he bogeyed the first hole of the first round, double-bogeyed the same hole in the second round, bogeyed it again on the last round.

This championship turned on two holes, if any

championship can. Sandy went to the tee of the 14th hole, two strokes behind the leader, David Graham. The hole is a straightaway par-5 at 508 yards, with heavy rough on the left. Princes Golf Club is beyond an out of bounds fence hard along the right side, and a stream, the "Suez Canal", crosses the fairway 323 yards from the tee. Sandy drove into the left rough, then advanced the ball along the fairway with a sand wedge. He then hit a 2-iron shot some 220 yards to the green, more than 40 feet from the hole, and holed the putt. In these four strokes perhaps lay a microcosm of Sandy Lyle's golf, Sandy Lyle's golfing life. At the 15th, a par-4 of 467 yards, he hit a 6-iron second to less than ten feet. He holed the putt. As others lost strokes here and there, these two birdies put Sandy in command of the championship. Payne Stewart, the American addicted to wearing colourful plus-fours, had sneaked in with a whisper and a 68 and was "leader in the clubhouse" on 283, three over par. Challenging just behind Lyle were David Graham and Bernhard Langer. Both dropped shots at the short 16th hole.

Lyle came to the last hole believing that he needed four to win, and again, perhaps typically, drove into the right rough, then saw his second, a 6-iron, roll off the green, pin high to the left, in rough. He was perhaps 40 feet from the flag, with a mound on the green intervening. His thought was to get his ball to the top of the mound and let it run down to the hole. It didn't. He hit a downright sloppy shot which saw the ball fail to top the rise. It rolled back to him, still on the putting surface, now 25 feet from the hole. Lyle fell on his knees, pressed his forehead to the ground like a Moslem at his devotions, thinking the Open for him had vanished, asking his god to please, please, let him not three-putt from there. He got his first putt two feet from the hole, and somehow got the next one in. He was 282, leading the Open. Graham and Langer came to the last hole, each needing a birdie to tie. Graham dumped his approach shot into the front right bunker. Langer's approach shot ran through, went only just off the putting surface back right. Neither of them could make the fateful birdie, although Langer hit the most valiant chip shot which ran just past the hole.

Sandy Lyle was Open Champion, but there was something in a way untidy about it. In fact, making a comparison between his third shot at that last hole, and the Ballesteros third shot on the last hole of the 1988 Championship at Royal Lytham from an almost identical position – pin high left, off the green – says much about the character of these two champions. In 1988, after a stunning final day in which the Open

resolved itself into a battle of quite magnificent golf between Ballesteros and Nick Price, reminiscent of nothing more than the epic finalé to Turnberry, 1977, between Watson and Nicklaus, and like that one going right down to the 72nd green, Ballesteros got there with a one stroke advantage. Price was on the front of the green in two, a long way, perhaps 40 feet, short. Seve had to score four to be sure of at least a tie, since Price, improbable as it was, could have holed the long putt. From an awkward lie, the Spaniard hit a little pitch and run shot, crisp, positive yet at the same time with finesse, that had the ball rolling delicately across the green to touch the hole and stop three inches away. Price was broken. His first putt went far past the hole, and he missed the return. Seve's final round was 65, Nick's 67.

These two little shots, Lyle at the 72nd at Royal St George's, Ballesteros at the 72nd at Royal Lytham, say much about the two men. Seve can be intense, brooding, introverted, arrogant as a grandee. No one since Arnold Palmer has been so anguished at the shot that got away, no one since Gary Player so elated at the impossible one which succeeds, or at the victory. Darkly handsome, his smile when it does come could light up a darkened room. He expects to win each time he plays. As he stretches out along the fairway, his left shoulder is noticeably higher than his right, his right arm, the one that swings as he walks, an inch or more longer than his left. His swing is orthodox, perhaps a little more rounded, less upright than in his earlier days. His right hand rides rather high over his left, as with the latter-day Ben Hogan. On the backswing, he breaks his wrists quite early, but goes through the ball squarely at immense speed, through to a high, twisting finish. And when he goes for the really big hit, his hands finish above his head, almost in front of his head – it could be Arnold Palmer in action.

Sandy Lyle is an altogether different animal, in an odd sense less of a physical animal than Ballesteros. Seve's interests are listed as cycling, football and swimming, Sandy's as cars and aeroplanes. His walk down the fairway is getting on for a Sunday stroll. He occasionally eases the white visor or the grey tweed cap which he wears from his fairish brown hair, the whole thing suggesting that, between shots, his mind is not too cluttered with golfing calculations. His swing is highly personalised. He takes the club back, low, round and flat, to somewhere around his ankles, it seems before taking it steeply up, down and

**Sandy Lyle, a modest champion with a deceptively calm air about him.**

**Sandy Lyle is one of the game's biggest hitters.**

through the ball, giving no particular impression of leg action, or much in the way of a turn or follow through. The Lyle swing seems to be hands and arms and nothing much else, yet he hits the ball vast distances with all the clubs – his 1-iron will fly further than most professionals can drive the ball. Finding a clue to the real Sandy, finding the key, is difficult. His attitude to golf, to life, might be expressed in an old Scottish saying, "Come day, go day", some kind of almost oriental fatalism, based of course on his huge talents, that nothing is really very important, no matter what happens we each grow a little older each day, and what will be will be.

None of this can be absolute truth, any more than it is true to say that Sandy cannot withstand the pressures that international championship golf can put on a man – in short, that he doesn't have "bottle". He disproved all that in winning the US Masters of 1988, when two birdies over the last three holes brought victory after a rather typical Lyle slump in the middle of the round. Sandy had dumped his tee shot into the water fronting the par-3 12th hole at Augusta, described by Jack Nicklaus as "the most demanding short hole in the world". Sandy may have been unlucky there – if the ball had carried a few feet further, the shot would have been perfect. He dropped two shots there, and failed to make birdies at the par-5 holes, the 13th and 15th, both of which most players can reach in two shots. Thus he lost a lead in the Masters which he had held for two-and-a-half rounds. Thus he went to the 16th tee one stroke behind; he now sought two elusive birdies to win. At the short 16th, he hit a 7-iron shot some 15 feet above the hole. On the most viciously sloped of all Augusta's viciously sloped greens, he faced a fast, downhill putt that would break left to right a good 20 inches. He holed it. It was a stroke of cold courage, a brave and brilliant golf shot, even more critical than his second to the 18th, the shot that was instantly enshrined in Masters legend as one of the most memorable ever seen at Augusta. After a par at the 17th, he hit a 1-iron tee shot some 240 yards at the 18th, but into the first of a pair of fairway bunkers on the left. He was annoyed that the tee shot had not faded as he had planned, but none too concerned at being in the bunker. All would depend on the lie. It was clean. From the sand, he hit a perfect 7-iron, picking the ball off the sand as easily as could be, flying the ball right over the flagstick, 140 yards away. The ball checked on the green, ran back down, and stopped ten feet above the hole. It was a straight putt. Sandy hit it dead straight, smack in the middle of the hole, and became the first British player to win the US Masters. Putting and patience had won it for him. Knowing the Augusta greens, reading them well, putting them well, is the key to the entire Augusta course, and the patience to take the odd hard knock, and wait for the birdies to come, is the other essential there. It may be that patience is what sometimes lies behind that apparent casualness that so many people find exasperating in Sandy Lyle from time to time.

One often feels that the golf course is dominating Sandy Lyle. Seve on the other hand will wrestle a course to its knees and choke it to death if needs must. One dearly wants to believe that inside Sandy Lyle, somewhere, bubbles a volcano of human emotions, while knowing at the same time that you would probably have to say something quite rude about his mother before he would display any anger. With Seve, if you crossed him on a triviality, it would be an insult to him, to his family, to his King, to the entire Spanish nation. Seve is all *orgullo, dignidad,* whatever Spanish word for pride you care to use. Yet he can be pensive. At the players' dinner on the eve of the World Match Play Championship of 1986, still affected by the death of his father earlier that year, he said in general conversation, with a certain melancholy, "I don't drink, I don't smoke, I live carefully – and I am always ill."

Seve acts. Sandy reacts. Seve wants to dominate his environment – he made himself sufficiently fluent in English to crack jokes in the language at promotional and exhibitions days, in making speeches and in more than holding his own with the world's Press. They are both in their fashion gentlemen, and Sandy Lyle is a gentle man. Perhaps that is even more important than being a great golf champion. What is certain is that both of these young men are hugely talented, hugely gifted, and, in the middle of their careers as they are, they both have miles to go before they sleep.

| CAREER HIGHLIGHTS | | |
|---|---|---|
| | British Open | US Masters |
| Severiano Ballesteros | 1979, 1984, 1988 | 1980, 1983 |
| Sandy Lyle | 1985 | 1988 |

# Part III
# THE BEST
# OF THE REST

*15th Hole*

# THE ARCHITECT

### "The Ground determines the Play"

**N**ewmachar is an immaculate, rain-washed village, population 1500, ten miles north of Aberdeen. Charles Keith, a community policeman who serves in Old Aberdeen, moved there in 1975. Keith had been introduced to golf rather late in life by his brother-in-law, a doctor who later left to go into general practice in Timmins, Ontario, but with application got himself down to an impressive 3-handicap. Irked by the traffic on Aberdeen's public courses – more than 200,000 rounds played in any one year with golfers queuing at 2 am on a Friday to book a Saturday starting time, and waiting lists of from five to 25 years for membership of the private clubs – Keith had dreams of simply building his own golf course. This has been the dream, the fantasy, of every golfer since man first swung a stone at a stick, a baffy at a feathery. By November, 1979, Charles Keith resolved to do something about it. His dream was to have overtones of nightmare as he tangled with bankers and bureaucrats, planners and sponsors, quangos and do-gooders galore, through every one of his off-duty waking moments over the best part of a decade.

In November, 1979, he called a meeting in the local village hall to establish support for the creation of a local golf club. Around 100 people attended, and a steering committee was formed. Within a month, a local landowner offered them a farm. They had plans drawn up by the Alliss/Thomas consortium, as it then was, of golf course designers. A club was formed with 170 members contributing between £25 and £40 each, and planning application was made to the local authority, Gordon District Council. The only objections came from the Department of Agriculture on the grounds that they were absorbing 80 acres of good to medium quality farmland. The new club appealed to the Secretary of State for

**Gleneagles, the beautiful Scottish course.**

Scotland, and went through the prescribed rigmarole of a public meeting in the village hall, where the Reporter appointed by the Secretary of State heard evidence and opinions, and with a QC hired in from Edinburgh to act for the new golf club. The finding of the inquiry was that they had established a need for a local golf club, but not an "overwhelming need", and so the release of this land from food production could not be justified. The planning department of the local council then identified three other potential sites in the area, two of which proved useless. The third was the Hawkshill farm, two miles south of the village. The owner was approached, and agreed to sell.

There were approximately 135 acres comprising two arable fields of some eight acres each, and the rest of the land was abandoned rough grazing or heathland, with fairly thick stands of silver birch and Scotch pine. There were several boggy areas due to a neglected drainage system. In May, 1982, David Thomas walked the site and drew plans to give 18 holes which could run to 6800 yards. In June, 1982, Keith and his cronies again applied for planning permission. There were no objections from the local council, but this time, for some reason, they asked for observations from the Scottish Wildlife Trust. Although the site was not of "special scientific interest", the Trust and the local authority insisted that a condition of planning permission was that there must be specified areas of "wetlands" in the design. After much discussion, the club was obliged to agree. In February, 1983, planning permission was granted with a five year expiry date. Funding was the next challenge. The club had set a fee of £300(!) as the contribution required from members to start the project. It would cover an entrance fee of £150 and a first year subscription of £150, and since the club faced a construction period of three years, it could be paid by instalment. With this prospect, and the delay in getting the club moving, many of the original sup-

169

porters drifted away. They were left with about 100 interested members. That year, one Jock Strathie, a British Petroleum employee, joined the committee. Strathie was a one-week offshore, one-week onshore worker in the North Sea oilfields. And Strathie was a hustler. A brochure and packages for corporate sponsorship among local companies was produced. One of these, for £15,000, offered six transferable company memberships and an annual company day to handle 75 people – cheap at the price. Strathie knocked on hundreds of corporate doors in the Aberdeen area, offering membership packages for a golf course and club not yet in existence. They chased the Scottish Sports Council, the Scottish Development Agency, the Scottish Tourist Board, the banks, any agency they could think of. By 1984, the committee men were close to deciding that they would never find the money. The cost of the land and an existing large house on the property which might have some potential as a clubhouse, was £120,000, estimated construction costs would be £400,000. Strathie kept beavering and had some success, when, in March of that year, a local councillor, Paul Miller, suggested that they should approach the council and ask them to purchase the land, and lease it back. After setting up a committee – it did not contain one golfer – the council looked at the situation, and agreed.

The conditions were that Newmachar Golf Club had to have £100,000 in the bank and sureties for another £41,000 (estimated cost of making a start on nine holes), by the 21st of March, 1986. At the time of the agreement, the club had £25,000 in the bank, no major sponsor, and rather less than two years in which to meet the terms. On D Day, at H Hour less 20 minutes, Keith and Strathie, now his vice-captain, charged into the council offices with a cheque for £30,000 which Strathie had extracted from BP, to meet the terms of the agreement. On the 1st of June of that year, Graeme Webster from another local course was hired as greenkeeper and a start was made on clearing trees and defining fairway lines. It proved to be one of the wettest summers in living memory in the area, and much of the initial work was washed out. Bert Macintosh, a local plant hirer was approached. He undertook to supply men and machinery and get the work done, with the club delaying payment until two-and-a-half years after the work had been completed. With good local publicity and at last some active movement on the site, membership applications started to come in and local companies began to approach the club for involvement. David Thomas, supervising the construction, nudged and pushed them in the right direction, kept them informed as to what was going on in the big outside world of design, and worked for a reduced fee. By the spring of 1988, some 14 fairways and greens had been seeded, with nine holes to be in play by the autumn, and the 18 holes scheduled for opening in autumn, 1989, a decade after it all started. "We Shall Overcome" might well be the theme of Charles Keith and his friends.

Thomas incidentally has produced a brilliant design for the site. He has transformed it dramatically, so much so that it may well become the most beautiful inland course in Scotland. The boggy areas have become lakes and streams bounded by lovely "drystone" dykes of golden sandstone. Six holes have water in play, as at a Scottish Augusta National. Half a dozen holes or more stride through pine and heather and might well be at Sunningdale or The Berkshire or Rosemount. His use of mounding, his contouring of greens, has been quite exceptional. Newmachar is likely to find a place in the list of great Scottish golf courses. The achievement of Charles Keith and his friends there in making possible a gem of Scottish golf is a small miracle, all the more remarkable when you consider that Jack Nicklaus, for example, can now command design fees running into millions of dollars and that the same David Thomas has been involved in a Japanese-funded development in southern Spain which runs to 80 million dollars, so much so that Thomas is now resident there.

In a slightly different vein, when Sheikh Mohammed bin Rashid El Maktoum, third son of the ruler of Dubai in the United Arab Emirates, decided he wanted a golf course in the desert he had one started, finished and opened within two years, in spring, 1988. When Sheikh Maktoum, who has made a massive and successful investment in horseracing in the UK and elsewhere, saw some golf on television, squeezed between races from Doncaster, he decided that a golf course might contribute to Dubai's growing ambitions as a tourist destination. After all, it had its own airline, and luxury international hotels to spare, not to speak of fine beaches, like most of the other oil states in the Gulf. The design and construction firm of Karl Litten Overseas was commissioned to build a course which would not disturb the natural beauty of the desert, and would be unobtrusive. The dunes of this scrubby, sand desert were left largely untouched, the holes winding through and between them so that, unlikely as it may

**A miracle in the desert. The recently opened championship course in Dubai.**

170

seem, the final course has something of the flavour of a links. If money was never a problem, planning consents never a problem, water might have been but for the existence of a massive desalination plant which supplies Dubai's water requirements. Thus, through a system of 700 sprinkler heads, as much as 1,000,000 gallons of water per day can be used to refresh the course. That and a hot desert sun could mean instant grass. It was found that a hybrid Bermuda grass strain would be best for the fairways, Tifton for the greens, and cuttings came from Georgia and Florida in refrigerated containers. Man-made lakes were a feature of the design, the course runs to 6700 yards with four par-5s, four par-3s and a regulation par-72. The clubhouse, constructed at the same time, is, needless to say, magnificent. The course is a 20 minute drive from the city and is already considered outstanding. It is certainly one of the wonders of the world – an instant golf course in a desert, whereas Newmachar in Aberdeenshire has needed the best part of a decade, and, by comparison, has cost pennies. One wonders if it is not a little incongruous – an oasis of greenery, totally at odds with its natural environment, like the courses that Jack Nicklaus and others have built in the sun states of the American southwest, in which man simply inflicts himself on the landscape.

The worlds of Charles Keith and Sheikh Maktoum are galaxies apart, but they shared a common ambition – to create a golf course. It is a fantasy, almost never fulfilled, that afflicts every golfer, just as every golfer imagines himself as an expert, not only on the design and lay-out of a golf course, but also is a critic of the placement of this bunker, that pond, these trees and why they should be moved or eliminated. In short, there is a dichotomy between the golf player and the golf architect, perhaps expressed extremely by Sam Snead when he said, "Golf architects are guys who don't know how to play golf – and they're gonna make damn sure no one else is allowed to play." Golf course architecture, more properly stated as golf course design, since the actual construction discipline is another speciality, is a science, and perhaps an art, but certainly in these latter years of the 20th century it is a very sophisticated profession which requires a fairly detailed knowledge of agronomy, geology, chemistry, drainage, forestry, machinery, with some civil engineering and technical drawing thrown in. The earliest golf courses along the eastern coasts of Scotland evolved. Golfers played on the machair, the links, the sand dunes, along paths through banks of heather and gorse which were widened by play into fairways and greens. At the coming of the gutty – the ball made of *gutta percha*, in 1848 – there were perhaps only half a dozen courses which we would call "inland", examples being at Perth, Blackheath in London (1608), Glasgow Golf Club (1787), playing on Glasgow Green originally, and Old Manchester (1818). The gutty ball and the spread of the railway system meant an increased interest in the game and greater ease of movement, and more golfers needed more golf courses.

Thus the earliest golf architects were willy-nilly the golf professionals who as good players were presumed to know what a good golf course should look like. Old Tom Morris was responsible for Royal Dornoch, Westward Ho!, the New Course at St Andrews, Macrihanish and the early Muirfield; Tom Dunn did Wimbledon and George Morris, Old Tom's brother, did the early holes at Hoylake, all of them showing some imagination in their planning. But too many courses, thrown together to meet the demand before the end of the century, featured straightaway fairways, with central cross bunkers and square greens with bunkers front, back and on either side. The time of the dogleg fairway and the green angled to the shot was yet to come.

At the turn of the century, the coming of the rubber-core ball revolutionised the game further, particularly for the poorer player, which meant the majority of players. He could hit this ball further. If he mis-hit, the ball would still bobble along – it would run much further than the gutty. To a degree this made for changes in the principles of course design, although it would be less than fair to dismiss the era of the gutty as a drab time of sameness in golf course lay-out. Many marvellous links courses were created on natural land – Troon, 1878; Formby, 1884; Lytham, 1886; St George's and Nairn, 1887; Portrush, 1888; County Down, 1889; Deal, 1892; and Portmarnock, 1894. What was quite unusual was the fact that landscaping was simply not considered as an adjunct to good design, in spite of the fact that a century or more before 1900, landscape gardeners had laid out the most magnificent parks and gardens at stately homes and large country houses throughout these islands. Not yet was there a Capability Brown on the golfing scene. Around the turn of the century, the great champions Braid, Taylor and Vardon were becoming interested, as were a very few amateurs, golf players not of the first rank but who were taken by the business of course design. Willie Park jun., Open Champion of 1887 and 1889, was perhaps the first man to set down the details of good golf course design in his book of 1896 *The Game of Golf*. On philosophy, he says, "The laying out of a golf course is by no means a simple task. Great skill and judgement and a thorough acquaintance with the game are absolutely necessary to determine the best positions for the respective holes and teeing grounds, and the situation of the hazards." Few contemporary architects would disagree with that. On the subject of hazards, he says, "There should not be any hazard out of which the ball cannot be extricated at the loss of one stroke, and all hazards should be visible to the golfer . . . before playing his stroke." By their deeds in this respect, many subsequent architects stand condemned. And Park, who designed many courses in Britain and America, might have had to make an exception of the Old Course, not to mention the Muirfield of almost a century later. As an aside, many people believe that Muirfield did not become a great course until Colt re-modelled the layout many years later.

The penal nature of some of Muirfield's bunkering persists, to the intense irritation of many of the friends of Muirfield and of golf, not to mention the players. This was cruelly illustrated in the Open Championship of 1987. Muirfield bunkers have been much admired for the craftsmanship displayed in their revetted walls, but in that championship several players had to make a stroke at the ball so that it moved to a more equitable position *still in* the bunker, to a place where they had room for a proper backswing, a proper bunker shot. Willie Park would surely not have cared for that. Indeed, a ball running into the middle bunker on the left of the 13th green might leave the player with no possibility of striking the ball out in *any* direction. Hazards were surely not intended for that.

J. H. Taylor in his book *Taylor on Golf* (1902, ten years after he had been involved in the making of Mid Surrey) wrote extensively on course design, saying that he was not a believer in "sloggers' golf", a cry against the lengthening of the courses to accommodate the rubber-cored ball. In the first decade of the century, Braid and Vardon both wrote books with design content, Braid insisting that every "natural" obstacle be used, and bunkering should be used for "positional" play. He was in favour of the diagonal cross-bunker, rather than the straight across, battlement bunker that had been the vogue. Vardon too wanted diagonal cross-bunkers, with the furthest point on the target line to the hole, demanding of the good player some qualified judgement. Here then were the first inklings of the planned, strategic hazard rather than the penal hazard which gave the player no option, no alternative but to take one route.

So thinking on the nature of the golf course and the golf hole was changing, expressed neatly by one John Laing Low, a St Andrews member who had been a Cambridge golf captain, in his book *Concerning golf* (1903). He wrote, "Every fresh hole we play should teach us new possibilities of using our strokes and suggest to us a further step in the progress of our golfing knowledge." And, "A course which necessitates power combined with great accuracy on the part of the player supplies the first principles of a good test . . . the course which requires, in addition to these things, the playing of the greatest variety of strokes, will be the best test of all."

Giving the nod yet again to the plain fact that golf is essentially a point to point game, Low claimed "A perfect tee shot should make the following shot less difficult, a perfect second shot should only be probable after a perfect first. The heart of golf lies in propelling the ball accurately from one situation to another. Each step in the journey should be hazardous; the links should be almost too difficult for the player, bunkers should more perfectly abound." This last phrase was to be much disputed, but as a philosophy for the player and the designer alike, this was better than just good. If "golf isn't meant to be fair", it isn't meant to be easy.

The turn of the century was an intriguing time in the story of golf course design. It was realised that the virgin stretches of fir and heather around London were ideally suited for golf because of the sandy, quick-draining nature of the soil, which provided grass of the texture of linksland. Fine courses at Sunningdale and Walton Heath were among the earliest consequences. And "amateur" designers began to establish themselves. Willie Park and H. S. Colt worked at Sunningdale, Park laying out the Old Course, Colt the New sometime later. Harry Colt was a solicitor, a one time secretary of the Sunningdale club, and an outstanding designer who did much fine work at Wentworth, for example, and in America, in particular at Pine Valley and the Country Club of Detroit. Indeed it has been said of Colt that Muirfield was never a great course until he re-modelled it. He was later in partnership with Dr Alister Mackenzie, who was to help produce three of the world's finest courses in Cypress Point, California, the Augusta National in Georgia, and Royal Melbourne in Australia. Herbert Fowler, in laying out Walton Heath where he worked through an abundance of heather, was still in favour of cross-bunkers, but noted that, since the vast majority of golfers slice the ball, he would place most of his hazards on the right side of the

173

**Harry Colt one of golf's outstanding course architects.**

fairways. It remains a tenet of the design creed. He suggested that in creating an "entrance" to a green, one bunker might be distinctly short of the putting green, the other hard against the putting surface and continuing along its side. This was perhaps the first notion that aestheticism, visual appeal, might have a part to play. Up to this point, the designer had been at the mercy of the land, and of all previous experience. The coming of the internal combustion engine, the tractor, the motor mower, changed all that. Courses had been built, the ground shaped and landscaped such as it was, by manual labour and by horse-drawn scrapers or drags which could strip off topsoil and dump it elsewhere as required. If it was a laborious, labour-intensive method, it could be carefully controlled and was quite precise, even sophisticated, in its effect.

By the early 1920s, horses, and in the United States mules, had all but vanished from the scene. Progressively, mechanical traction complete-ly changed man's thinking on what could be done in converting almost any piece of land into an acceptable golf course. After the 1939–45 war, with a range of bulldozers, dumpers, diggers, drainers and scrapers at his disposal, the golf architect could move mountains. Too many of them did. Before this was possible, the ground dominated the design and architects were at the mercy, to a large extent, of the ground which they were offered. To this day, in fact, the first thing a sensible golf architect might say to a potential client is "Before we talk very much, show me your land." The coming of the rubber-cored ball, which could be hit a good 20 yards further than the gutty, compromised the game in terms of design and placements of hazards. To a large extent, the earliest designers were greatly influenced by what they had seen on classic links such as the Old Course, Dornoch, North Berwick – the plateaued green, the bunker eating into the putting surface, the flat, ground level teeing ground, the bumps and knolls which can make chipping on to a green a minor art form. Blind shots were not yet out of fashion. This may have reached its epitome in the National Golf links of America, on Long Island, completed in 1911 by Charles Blair Macdonald, a powerful figure at the "birth" of modern American golf. Macdonald, from Chicago, in his youth had been a student at St Andrews and came to play and know the game, the links, the town, and no doubt all its worthies, in particular Old Tom Morris. On his return home, among other things, he created the Chicago Golf Club course at Wheaton, Illinois, now almost a suburb of the great city. It was the first complete 18-holes course in "the West". Macdonald had the lingering dream of designing a course which would feature aspects of, if not exactly copy, holes in the great courses he had seen in Scotland. His dream became a fact in 1911 with the completion of the National, far out at the end of Long Island, under-played, but still an outstanding golf course, even if it is distant, a good 100 miles from Manhattan. In the 1890s golf boomed in America. At the start of the decade, there was one course in the US, the St Andrews Golf Club in New York City, which was rather less than sophisticated and was dubbed by some a cow pasture. By 1900, when Vardon made his tour, there were 1000. Some of them persist in the history of the game – the Country Club at Brookline, near Boston, and Shinnecock Hills, near the National on Long Island. Willie Dunn, the Scottish pro who won the first US Open in 1884 when it was played at match play, laid out 12 holes at Shinnecock in 1891, sponsored by a Vanderbilt, and a year later it was stretched to 18. In 1896, it staged a US Open, and was able to do the same 90 years later. The 1988 US Open was played at The Country Club, 75 years after the famous Ouimet–Vardon–Ray Open. Incidentally, 44 founder members were enrolled by William K. Vanderbilt for Shinnecock Hills, each paying several thousand dollars for the privilege, a thought that would make Charles Keith of Newmachar, some 85 years on, blanch.

The amateur golfers like Colt and Fowler (Abercromby, Croome and the eccentric Tom Simpson were others) became "professional" designers, such was the demand. Many worked with the leading golfers of the time, C. K. Hutchison with Braid at Gleneagles, for example. In time, they formed partnerships and companies not only to design but sometimes to construct courses. One of the most capable, respected and enduring of these has been Hawtree and Son, now into a third generation. A certain body of literature on the subject has emerged. Before the 1914–18 war, Braid, Vardon and Taylor each published books with chapters on design, and Colt wrote a complete section in *The Book of the Links* in 1912. There is now a substantial library on the subject – it continues to grow. Into this epoch, the beginnings of golf architecture as we know it, came a remarkable Scot. Donald James Ross was born in 1873 at no. 3 St Gilbert Street, Dornoch, in a house which still stands, is still ivy-covered. St Gilbert Street is a quiet backwater that runs to the 13th century Dornoch Cathedral, behind the main street of this lovely, ancient, Highland village, stone-built, rain-washed, pin-clean. Dornoch could be Brigadoon – there is a cathedral, a castle in the centre of the village, seven miles of golden sands, a stone on the lower links marking where the last "judicial" execution of a witch by burning took place in 1722, Viking connections, and nearby Skibo Castle, the Highland home of Andrew Carnegie, steel baron of Dunfermline and Pittsburgh. The Ross family were members of the Free Church of Scotland which had broken away from the Church of Scotland in 1843, and become a very strict if often disputatious congregation. For all that, young Donald went through school and engaged in all the village activities normally, as would any other boy. And he played golf.

Golf had been played freely on the local links for a good three centuries. In 1877 the Dornoch Golf Club was formed, and in 1886, at the instigation of John Sutherland, who was to be secretary of the club for more than 50 years, Old Tom Morris formalised the course into 18 holes of championship quality which

have survived seldom touched to this day. Donald Ross was first apprenticed to a local carpenter but the same John Sutherland, noting Ross's talent as a player and his wider interest in all aspects of the game, arranged for him to be apprenticed to Morris at St Andrews. Ross went there when he was 20, to learn the craft of making golf clubs. In 1895, he returned to Dornoch as professional/greenkeeper. They built him a little pro shop/workshop, and his younger brother Alec became his assistant. Later in the decade, a Professor Robert Wilson of Harvard University came to Dornoch, took lessons from and played with Ross. He impressed on the young man the potential of golf in America, its huge expansion, urged him to emigrate and helped him do it. In 1898, Ross set out for Boston via New York. He had to walk the last few miles to Wilson's home in Cambridge, with two dollars in his pocket. He was 25 years old. The next day, he started work at the Oakley G.C. in Watertown, Massachusetts as professional. Next in the Ross story came James Tufts of the American Soda Fountain Company, a local man. He was also impressed with Donald's background, his knowledge of the traditions of the game and his thinking on course design. This, it should be said, was at a time when any immigrant with a Scottish accent and a "Mac" in front of his name could pose as an expert on golf, lay out a course with pegs marking tees and greens and take the money and run. Tufts, not enjoying very good health, had taken to spending much of the hard New England winters in a gentler climate, to wit North Carolina, with its more moderate temperatures. At Pinehurst he had bought some 5000 acres of sandy scrubland at knockdown prices, land considered good enough for growing pine trees and little else. Ross accepted Tufts' invitation to become the winter professional at Pinehurst, and he set about re-designing the existing holes, and building new courses. He had arrived there in 1900, the same year in which Harry Vardon played at Pinehurst in his epochal first tour of the United States.

It is no exaggeration to say that both of these men, in their different ways, had a major, indefinable effect on American golf. Pinehurst was developed and established progressively as a winter resort for influential people. Ross's work was admired, his services in demand as the American game mushroomed. At one time he was reputed to have 3000 men at work on courses throughout the country, and, although it has never been established exactly, he certainly worked on more than 300 courses, perhaps as many as 600 up to his death in 1948 at the age of

75. Ross had been resident in Pinehurst effectively from 1903, became a manager, ultimately a director, of the Pinehurst company owned by the Tufts family which controlled the resort beyond that date unto a fourth generation, Richard S. Tufts, who was a distinguished golf administrator and a President of the USGA. Now Pinehurst has seven golf courses, but Pinehurst no. 2 is considered Ross's masterpiece – a "links in a forest". There were others – Seminole in Florida, Scioto in Ohio, where Jack Nicklaus learned to play, Oakland Hills in 1918, Inverness in 1919, Interlachen of Bobby Jones fame, Aronimink.

Ross wanted golf to be a pleasure, not a penance. Accordingly, he was not much taken with a penal attitude to design, claiming that a water hazard, for example a lake that had to be carried and which was becoming almost compulsory in much American course design, carried too severe a penalty, and that there should be more than one way of playing a hole. Thus he was an early "strategic" thinker, and his philosophy, as does his work, survives. Sadly, he never wrote about his life, nor much about his opinions or methods. Even more sadly, he never worked in his native Scotland, but happily his influence survives. The Ross credo for course design was: "The championship course should call for long and accurate tee shots, accurate iron play, precise handling of the short game and finally, consistent putting. These abilities should be called for in a proportion that will not permit excellence in any one department of the game to affect too large deficiencies in another." To this day, the villages of Dornoch and Pinehurst are linked by golf and the memory of the life and work of Donald James Ross. They have much in common. Pinehurst, with a resident population of some 3000, is a tranquil place, as is Dornoch. It remains a winter resort, as Dornoch is a summer resort. Both are shrines to the game, totally different in landscape but attracting each year thousands of golfers from all countries sharing in the delights of playing truly great golf courses.

The period from the beginning of the Ross courses until the coming of the steel shaft in the late 1920s might be considered a golden age of golf architecture. In the UK, as many as 50 courses each year were being built, among them Wentworth, Gleneagles and West Sussex. In the US, particularly in the roaring 20s when the country seemed awash with money, outstanding courses were built – Merion, Pebble Beach, Cypress Point, Pine

**Pebble Beach, California, a masterpiece of golf course design.**

Scots born Donald Ross shaped many of America's courses including Pinehurst.

Pebble Beach on Carmel Bay, some 120 miles south of San Francisco, vies with its near neighbour Cypress Point as one of the most beautiful courses in the world. Laid along the cliffs of the Monterey Peninsula, its only British comparison might be Turnberry. It was built as part of a resort hotel development, and was designed by Jack Neville and Douglas Grant, amateur champion golfers but certainly not professional golf architects in the accepted sense. Yet they created a masterpiece. A stretch of holes from 4 to 10 ranges along the clifftops, with small greens, narrow fairways slanting towards the sea, and shots that must carry over inlets. The 18th hole, a stunning par-5, turns all the way along the clifftop.

Cypress Point, on the tip of the peninsula and only a mile away, many will claim is even more beautiful. If there is an argument as to whether its par-3 16th is the most beautiful hole in the world, it is certainly the most photographed, calling for a carry of 233 yards all across the ocean from a clifftop tee to a small, tightly bunkered green perched on a promontory. There is surely no golfer anywhere in the world who has not seen a picture of this hole from behind the tee – and has been properly terrified. Dr Alister Mackenzie, the architect, has two par-3s, two par-5s following each other, and what is often overlooked is that the 15th hole, only 139 yards, calls for a challenging pitch all the way over yet another inlet in the coast. On these courses on the Pacific shore, the weather can be as whimsical as it is in Scotland.

Across the continent is Winged Foot, at Mamaroneck, New York, where the West course, designed by A. W. Tillinghast, is among the best half dozen in America. Tillinghast was certainly one of the best and most imaginative of American designers, his work including, among many others, Baltusrol in New Jersey and the Five Farms course in Baltimore. "A.W." built powerful but fair golf courses. He believed that a "controlled shot to a closely guarded green is the surest test of any man's golf." Winged Foot's West course features tight driving lines, severely trapped greens. Half of its holes are par-4s of more than 400 yards, and two holes in particular, 10 and 17, are perfect illustrations of A.W.'s philosophy. The 17th is 444 yards, with a narrow fairway that turns to the right in driving range and with a great mass of bunkers in the angle. The second shot must be long to a narrow green severely protected on both sides by deep bunkers. But it is the 10th which is the ultimately classic hole, with its plateaued green suggesting Ross, all the way back to Dornoch. It is

Valley, Oakmont, Oakland Hills, Winged Foot, and, in the 1930s, Augusta National – many of them, odd as it may seem, by amateurs. Merion, in the swank "Main Line" suburbs of Philadelphia, was designed by Hugh Wilson, an insurance broker, transplanted Scot, and member of the Merion Cricket Club as it was, whose members sent him on a reconnaissance of Scottish and English clubs before he got down to extending their course to championship calibre. Wilson produced a gem of not much more than 6500 yards, featuring beautifully-placed strategic bunkering, lightning fast greens and – a feature he picked up from Sunningdale – little baskets in place of cloth flags atop the flagsticks. Merion's merit is underlined by the fact that it has staged more USGA championships than any other course, including Ben Hogan's Open of 1950 and the first, and less than successful, national appearance of young Bobby Jones.

190 yards. Some way short of the green on the left is a big fairway bunker which is scarcely in play for the talented player but which is visually distracting and perhaps intimidating. The green is raised, tilted to receive the shot, but with the narrowest of entrances which is guarded by two huge, deep bunkers eating into the putting surface, and defending the sides of a green which is slightly angled across the line. It broadens considerably towards the back. Thus what Tillinghast is demanding is a long and perfect tee shot all the way to the back of the green, or, in other words, the controlled shot to a closely guarded green, the "surest test of any man's golf". "Winged Foot" incidentally was the emblem of the New York Athletic Club, originators of the course. They had asked A.W. to "give us a man-sized course". He did just that.

Penal thinking was not yet abandoned. There was Oakmont, near Pittsburgh, designed by Henry C. Fownes, steel magnate, originally with 220 bunkers for which Fownes devised a rake that would produce furrows two inches deep, two inches apart. Not a friendly man, Mr Fownes. If Oakmont is penal as can be, the fact that Johnny Miller won the US Open of 1973 with a closing round of 63 merely proves that the modern player will destroy any course, given reasonable weather conditions, and that Miller on that day was surely touched by some unseen, unknown force. Yet the most penal course of all, it too designed by an "amateur", is surely Pine Valley in New Jersey, near Philadelphia, completed in 1919. It was the brainchild of George Crump, a Philadelphia hotelier, who bought 184 acres of nondescript land running along a railway line, and set his hand to designing the world's most fiendish golf course. Crump laboured for six years on the project, lavishing a fortune of $250,000 on it. He had some professional help from Harry Colt, of Sunningdale and Wentworth fame, and after Crump died in 1918, with only 14 holes completed, the other amateur from Merion, Hugh Wilson, helped finish the four extra holes. The result was a golf course unique, without bunkers in the ordinary sense, because the course was simply one vast bunker, presenting islands in an ocean of sand and scrub – islands for teeing grounds, fairway target zones, greens, with everything in between simply sand or scrub. It is a unique and also a fearsome place with every hole screened from every other by pine trees, of course, and shrubbery, so that the golfer feels not so much isolated as cast away. One golfer after his first experience there said, "This isn't a penal course, it is a penitentiary." Crump saw no need

even for greenside bunkers. A ball that rolled off the sharply sloping greens finished, simply, in sand, the sand of the Crump desert. The fairway islands demanded precisely hit shots of a prescribed length, and if a ball didn't reach, or slid away from, these fairway islands, it too finished in the sand of the Crump desert. Golfers there have run into double figures without hitting a bad shot. The four par-3 holes measure 185, 226, 145 and 185 yards. The one Pine Valley story which never tires in the telling is the experience of Woody Platt, a Walker Cup class golfer. He birdied the first hole, 427 yards. He holed a full 7-iron shot to eagle the second. At the third, he had a hole in one. At the 4th, which comes back to the clubhouse area, he birdied for a 3, 2, 1, 3 start, six under par for four holes. When he left the 4th green, Platt walked into the clubhouse and, wise man, stayed there, never finishing the round.

These are all exceptional golf courses. Many in the latter part of the 19th century and in the early part of the 20th – and even later as the game was stimulated by such champions as Jones and Hagen – were laid out on any suburban tract of land that was to hand, and design suffered. Often this meant nothing more than a series of parallel fairways, squeezed into an over-small site, so that fanciful theories of strategic planning could not be applied. But still, design moved on – dogleg fairways, imaginative bunkering, subtle contouring of greens were matters of concern and discussions to the better architects. One of these was Tom Simpson, who made lovely courses at Spa and Royal Antwerp in Belgium, Hardelot and Morfontaine in France, largely because he taught himself something of surveying, and kept a tight grip on the construction work. Simpson was a qualified barrister who never practised. He saw the golf course designer's function as a defender of the faith against the infidel skills of the professional and the improvements in clubs and balls. The coming of the steel shaft, permitting the matched set of clubs, once again made problems for the designers. The professional players were able to adopt more compact swings, hit the ball harder, sent it flying further. Simpson's instinct of setting up defences against this remained valid, and eventually courses had to be stretched out to more than 7000 yards. After the 1939–45 war, such was the improvement in the players' equipment, in construction equipment, and above all in the advances in agronomy, golf course design changed very substantially, indeed had to change very substantially. In all of this, we are discussing the architect versus the very best golfer, the professional tournament player.

The architect has always had to draw a basic design with the scratch player in mind, since scratch is the only single yardstick that golf has. At the same time, he has to build in factors that will allow the average player, the much less talented player, to enjoy the same course. You might call it the syndrome of strategic options.

Other circumstances applied to the global game. For the economy of America, the one country physically untouched by the war, the 1940s and 50s were boom-time while Europe, devastated, struggled to survive, much less prosper. As they had in the 1920s in Florida, resort developments were an exploding market in the US. The coming of the jet aircraft in the late 1950s made people much more mobile. The marriage of television with golf at the same time brought great championships to millions of people, almost all of them played on the great and beautiful golf courses. The golf course became a core asset in resort property and hotel projects. Landscaping became an essential part of the design game as the developers demanded beautiful recreational courses as essential elements in their business. And since the fairway plot, the house overlooking the greensward of the golf course became prime sites, the developers wanted more of them – ergo "more" fairways, longer fairways. This was the landscaping of the bulldozer, not the natural landscape which had made the classic links courses of a century earlier. In Florida, for example, a state which nowhere rises much more than 50 feet above sea level, vast lakes were excavated, the fill used to build cosmetic mounds and hillocks. Hundreds of thousands of cubic yards were stripped off the land, and simply moved elsewhere, so that a course under construction had the look of a lunar landscape. Huge bunkers were built for no more than their decorative effect. The arch-priest of all this, the arch-demon if you prefer, was Robert Trent Jones. It can be argued that golf courses were needed, and not every work of man is a work of art, but Jones had come to the conclusion that the game had outpaced architecture, that the players were winning the battle. When he was called in to prepare and tighten several US Open courses, he did it so ruthlessly that Ben Hogan, the winner, said of Oakland Hills (which had had the Jones treatment) after the US Open of 1951 and his final round of 67, "I'm glad that I finally brought this course, this monster, to its knees." Most of the players were convinced that Robert Trent Jones was the monster. The word entered the vocabulary of golf. Hogan's winning total was seven strokes over par.

Jones said, "I try to build holes on which it is difficult for professionals to make birdies, easy for the average player to make bogeys." Jones moved mountains, dammed rivers, built some of the most expensive courses of his time and made sure he was well rewarded for doing it. To that extent, he improved greatly the lot of all his fellow architects. His work was characterised by very long, flexible teeing grounds, many water hazards (he thought it too easy for the modern players to play out of bunkers without penalty which they could seldom do from water) and, above all, huge greens with wicked slopes. Jones, born in Lancashire, studied, at Cornell University, engineering, architecture, surveying, hydraulics and landscaping. He was well-equipped for his task. And he has built some fine courses – Sotogrande in southern Spain, built on sand and finished in 1965, was his first in Europe. Twenty years later, he was completing a staggering links course at Ballybunion – no. 2 – while at the same time converting a rubbish dump near London's Heathrow Airport. Robert Trent Jones, now being succeeded by his sons, is certainly the most prolific of designers, helped of course by the sheer affluence of the American economy.

As Europe recovered, something of the same pattern emerged, beginning in the 1960s at tourist destinations, particularly along the southern coasts of Spain and Portugal. Henry Cotton built a hotel course, Penina, on a rice paddy field in the Algarve, and not many of the courses on Spain's Costa del Sol held much distinction. But more and more talented designers had emerged through the century – Dick Wilson and George Fazio, for example, in America; Guy Campbell, Hutchison, Frank Pennink, C. K. Cotton and Hawtree in the UK; Javier Arana in Spain. For the traditionalists, the concept of the "stadium" course, with pre-built mounded grandstands for spectators, with minute island greens on par-3 holes, totally surrounded by water save for a slim walkway, seemed quite ridiculous. Such courses were clearly designed to test tournament players and tournament players only. For the average club player, they are virtually unplayable.

An illustration of another side of the coin came with the Bell's Scottish Open Championship of 1987 at the King's Course of the Gleneagles Hotel. The course was a James Braid design of the early 1920s, laid out on a sheltered moorland plateau. It is an enchanted place of natural golfing country, with firm, crisp turf, waves of golden gorse and heather, well wooded with pine and with streams and lakes. There are four courses now in play at Gleneagles. The dominant feature of the King's course is a long ridge which runs the length of the property, and Braid's design in simple terms had a tee in the valley, drive over the ridge to a green in the next valley, or, alternatively, tees and greens on the ridge with a valley intervening. At some holes the green would be cut into the side of the ridge. There are a few blind shots, and, since it was designed in the days of the hickory shaft, it could be considered old-fashioned. In this lovely place, Braid's brief was, "Make it spectacular, make it look difficult, but make it relatively easy to get round." Not much to ask of a designer, but these are the things clients will say. Considering that Braid did it by hand and horsepower, he did a remarkable job, but, discounting the majestic views, and considered from the point of view of the average golfer, say a handicap 18 player, it is open to severe criticism. The first hole is 362 yards to a wide fairway, large green. But the green is perhaps 30 feet above the fairway, with a huge bunker on the slope in front of it. So it might be two shots up the fairway, then a totally blind pitch from the bottom of the slope. On the second, the green cannot be seen from the tee. On the third, 375 yards, it would mean two shots up a rising and tumbling valley, then a totally blind pitch again, over the ridge. The fourth hole is a fine, testing par-4 of 465 yards, which means a par-5 for the high handicap player, but, again, the putting surface cannot be seen until he is about 60 yards away. On the seventh, the player cannot see the fairway from the tee. He must drive into a dogleg left, over a ridge. The 12th has a blind tee shot, the 18th means driving into a deep valley, then another blind second over a high ridge. This course may be a perfect illustration of how the landscape can overpower all other considerations. To face the challenge of the professionals in 1987, the course was stretched out and stiffened by the building of new tees, in many cases making the angle of the drive quite different to that in Braid's thinking, and not always effectively. The result was that the British player, Ian Woosnam, enjoying a blessed year of success, won the event with a score of 20 under par. In the race with the course designers, the players were still ahead.

It may well be that another factor, seldom considered, has made this and other courses seem larger than life. That factor is fame, fame in the sense of a general public awareness of the place created and heightened by publicity and, particularly, television exposure. The outstanding example of this may well be the Augusta National course in Georgia, the creation and development of which had more elements in its favour than any public relations man could imagine. First and foremost it had Bobby Jones, debatably the greatest golfer who ever lived. The golf course and its Masters tournament are now touted as a memorial to Jones greater than his phenomenal championship achievement, which is manifest nonsense. Jones, like Charles Blair Macdonald, had long had the idea that one day he might build a course to embrace many of the qualities he had admired on the courses he had played and seen during his playing career. Jones knew the small town of Augusta, near his home in Atlanta – his wife Mary Malone was an Augusta girl – and he often played winter golf there. After he retired from competitive play, he met Clifford Roberts, an Augusta visitor, and he discussed his thinking with him and where they might find a suitable piece of land. Roberts, a Wall Street merchant banker and a hard man, even a ruthless man in life as he no doubt was in business, discovered that a famous local nursery, Fruitlands, was for sale. They bought it at knockdown, depression prices, and Jones the amateur set about designing a course on a site that was roughly square in shape, with a mansion house on the top side, the whole of the ground falling away from it through flowering shrubs, pine and fruit trees, as much as perhaps 100 feet down to the bottom end, where there was a stream. Jones had the good sense to enlist the aid of Alister Mackenzie, the Scottish-born doctor who had abandoned medicine in favour of designing golf courses, and whose work, particularly at Cypress Point, Jones much admired. By 1933, the course was built, and Jones and Roberts formed a club "for like-minded men", which generally meant rich men, from all corners of the country, who were invited to join and put up the necessary money. To this day, that persists – one doesn't join the Augusta National club, one may be invited to join.

When the course was completed, it was felt that it might become good enough to stage a US Open Championship at some time in the future, but since Georgia summers are so hot, and since spring is the optimum time for having a golf course in prime condition there, that thought was abandoned. From it grew the notion that the club might have its own tournament, to be called the Augusta National Invitational, to which Jones would invite all the leading players of the day, all of whom he knew. It was quickly dubbed "The Masters", a tag which has stuck. Jones and Mackenzie had agreed on a policy for the course. It was to be one of natural beauty, one which would be pleasant and none too taxing

for the members, average players all, yet testing for the expert players – not exactly a small order. Thus they produced a course without rough, with wide, rolling fairways, huge greens and originally a mere 30 bunkers. Jones was a believer in the old maxim that the game, or rather the golf hole, should be played backwards, from the flagstick back to the teeing ground. The player should know in which quarter of the green the hole is cut; where he wants to land his approach shot to get the ball close to the flagstick; the point on the fairway from which he wants to hit that approach shot; and, finally, the tee shot which will get him to that point. In terms of the expert player who hits the ball vast distances, the greens then were critical. They were to present the major challenge to the expert, and the greens at Augusta have been much altered in contouring over the half-century of their existence. In addition, for the Masters event, they are made fiercely firm and fast, so much so that the contestants, experts all and accustomed to playing soft, holding greens in other places for much of the year, have occasionally experienced four-putt greens and have never been slow to express an opinion of this. pin positions during the tournament dominate the playing of each hole. Each hole has four prescribed pin positions, varied through the four days of play. In theory, each day should provide six difficult, six moderate, six easy pin positions, decided each morning by the greens committee who take weather conditions into consideration. In the eyes of the average golfer, the Augusta course in tournament condition is an immensely severe golf course. You could take a reasonable player, say 6–12 handicap, set him off from the tournament tees, pins in tournament positions, no practice round, and he would not do better than 95. Bet £10,000 on that if you can find a taker, and you would certainly win a great deal of money. Such a player would simply have no conception of the terror these greens would inflict on him.

The course has been changed, modified, improved over the years. In 1947, Trent Jones built a completely new 16th green, opened up a stream to make a lake so that the tee shot was wholly over water, and made the hole 190 yards as against the original 150 yards. In some cases, the fairways, like the greens, have been re-contoured archly to compromise the second shot, but equally suggest a line or an area of the fairway which will profit the bold. For example, the 10th hole is downhill, almost but not quite

**Nicklaus at the 18th tee at Augusta. He has won the Masters a total of six times.**

straightaway – it turns very slightly to the left, and, because it is downhill, is a par-4 of a hulking 485 yards. Incidentally, it may well be the single most beautiful hole in golf. Walking from the tee down the fairway is like walking the nave of a great cathedral, with towering Georgia pines on either side. The driving zone around the 250 yards mark has a ridge across the fairway which, from a drive to the right of the centre line, will insinuate the ball to the right, giving a long second shot. But a drive down a tight, brave line to the left, or drawn to the left from a central line, will see the ball moved on by the ridge and down to a little flat area of fairway which will give the golfer a level stance and a much shorter shot to the green. The same applies at the par-5 13th hole, the "azalea" hole, almost equally lovely. This hole, the same length at 485 yards, is quite different but offers the bold player a similar reward. It doglegs to the left, quite sharply at 90 degrees some 250 yards from the tee, and almost all the fairway slopes down from right to left. Along the entire hole to the left is heavy woodland, and the left side of the second leg of the fairway, round the corner, is bounded by a stream. Just around the corner of the angle, on the lower side of the fairway, is another flat piece of ground. The bold driver, who takes a line down the left and draws the ball round the corner, is richly rewarded by finding a flat and level stance and is closer to the hole than the man who drives to the right. He will find himself on a sloping stance, perhaps two clubs further from the green. Thus the audacious are rewarded.

In other places, the defences of the course have been substantially strengthened. The 15th hole, for example, is a straightaway par-5 of 520 yards which rises to a crest in driving range, then falls down to a rather shallow green protected across the entire front by a fairly wide pond. Not many years ago, it was found that modern players, with the wind behind, were driving to the crest and finding the ball kick forward some 30 or 40 yards, bringing the green within range of a mid-iron shot. How to prevent this? The idea of a bunker as defence was rejected in favour of mounds which brought a greater risk element to the drive taking a line on the right. If a ball was to kick wildly right from one of these mounds towards the adjoining 17th fairway, the green would be partly hidden by woodland. If it kicked left, two pine trees on the left side of the fairway would compromise the second shot. In all, the drive down that wide 15th fairway became an altogether more risky shot and the 15th became a much more subtle hole. Then again on the 18th hole back in the 1960s,

there were no fairway bunkers on the left side, from one of which Sandy Lyle played his famous 7-iron shot on the final hole of the 1988 Masters, a stroke which brought him a birdie and victory. It is said that the need for bunkers in that location arose after Jack Nicklaus hit a wild hook from the tee wide of the fairway and was given a free drop – the grouchers said an advantageous drop – from an area in which the gallery had been walking. Now the twin bunkers there, with high crests, are about as severe as any fairway bunkers on the course. Yet for all the hazards, all the defences, all the redoubts at Augusta, stretched to more than 7000 yards for the tournament, the low Masters round is 64, the low winning total is 271 – 17 under par. What is the poor architect to do with these fellows? The fact is that the best of the modern players, say the top 15 or 20 in the world, are so powerful, so precise in their play that they can destroy any "monster" even if it be 8000 yards long, if the course is soft, the conditions still.

The Augusta National club, and the Masters tournament, and Gleneagles Hotel, have much in common, and above all one thing – television. Televised golf, starting in the late 1950s, caught the end of the clinical, almost surgical, Ben Hogan, and the entire career of the dramatic ebullient Arnold Palmer. These players helped elevate the Masters tournament to Grand Slam status, to which manifestly it does not belong, since it remains an invitational and not an "open" event. Yet since the greatest days of Palmer, more and more foreign countries have shown the CBS telecast pictures of the Masters. In the same way, Gleneagles has become widely known internationally from televised events and such tailored-for television series as the BBC's *Pro-Celebrity Golf*. They are both beautiful places. In early April when the Masters is played, if the weather has been right and the club's gardening staff has got it right, the Augusta course is aflame with the flowering shrubs of a Georgia spring – azalea, dogwood, flowering cherry, magnolia and the rest. And where could a man find more delight than at Gleneagles in the long hours of a Scottish summer evening, the whole place ringed around with distant mountains? These courses have a dimension above and beyond the playing of golf. It lies in a certain, collective public conception of them, created from direct experience or from television pictures, sustained by conversation, reminiscence, by word of mouth – an odd dimension of innocent but continuing publicity.

The sensible golf architect, particularly when faced with a tract of virgin land, will say, "If you want to see my course at its best, come back in 25 years," meaning that grass and trees and shrubs must be given time to grow to maturity. Golf is a marvellous game in that it is played in the great outdoors, with all courses different, laid out over differing landscapes. On the whole golf architects should avoid trying to improve on nature – seldom can it be done. Certainly, the Augusta National golf course may have given more people more pleasure, even vicariously, than the Fruitlands nursery, but who would dare say it is more beautiful?

In the midst of all this stands the golfer, the golf player, and the truth may well be that the golfer gives little thought to the overall design of the course, or its designer for that matter. He will be mainly concerned with the shot in hand, in playing it properly, striking the ball well, since by the highest standards he is incompetent. And he will be concerned simply with avoiding the hazard between his ball and where he hopes it will be going, not with the quality or the location of the hazard. What does concern him, in the sense that he might give it a moment or two of contemplation once the round is over, is an overall, subjective impression of the course, the landscape, the environment, the weather, his total experience and the pleasures, or pain, that he has experienced. In that impression will be elements of the whole thing – the travel to the course, the welcome and service of the club staff, the locker room, the bar, the drinks, the meal, the companionship, and the post-mortem. In all of this, the golf course architect may well be a very distant figure and may even be completely overlooked, but if the golfer has been privileged to play and experience one of these great golf courses, he will be indebted to – the golf course architect.

*16th Hole*

# SWING THE CLUBHEAD

*"The Prime Necessity"*

**Bobby Jones**

*The secret of the perfect golf swing lies in the Atlas primary cervical vertebra.*

**T**hat is the vertebra at the top of the spine, the one which doctors say "holds the head up". It provides the nodding and turning movements of the head. What a splendid proposition – that the entire, complicated business of striking a golf ball correctly focuses on one little bone at the back of the neck! Very well – it's a lie. It's a lie for two reasons: first, there is no single secret to the golf swing; and, second, there is no such thing as a universally "perfect" golf swing. But there is such a thing as a perfect swing for each individual golfer, for each one of the foot-soldiers in the world of golf's vast army of supplicants, an army which without exception has been in search of the perfect swing since baffy was first put to feathery, indeed since man first swung a stick at a stone and there has been no shortage of instruction as to how it is done. By the way, don't forget the "Atlas". We'll come back to it.

For more than a century, a torrent of golf instructional books has poured down on the innocent golfer, seeking to lead him along the paths of righteousness, and more recently radio, film, television and now video have been part of the teaching media. As far back as 1687, Thomas Kincaid of Edinburgh set down a list of golfing instructions. Towards the end of the 19th century, with the gutty ball well established, the game increasingly popular and spreading quickly beyond Scotland, Chambers published *Golfing* in 1887, and following Sir Walter Simpson's *The Art of Golf* came the famous Badminton Library *Golf* by Horace Hutchinson and others, in 1890, with such chapter headings as "Elementary Instruction", "On style – various styles", "Out of Form – a Chapter for Adepts", "On Nerve and Training", and "Hints on Match and Medal Play". Since then, almost every champion golfer has written at least one instructional book.

**The swing sequence of Harold Hilton.**

Golf is basically about a man or woman hitting a ball with a stick. This involves a series of physical actions and reactions, from a state of rest back to a state of rest. The purpose of the golf swing, to paraphrase John Jacobs, one of the game's finest teachers, is "to deliver the face of the clubhead squarely to the ball along the target line at speed". The faster the clubhead strikes the ball, the further the ball will fly. The trick of the whole thing is to put together a series of physical actions which will allow us (a) to strike the ball correctly, and (b) to enable us to repeat that correct action. To hit the ball correctly and consistently, we need what Ben Hogan described as "a correct, powerful, repeating swing". But how to learn this? Well, one rational thought might be to observe and copy the master players. These champions have two things in common – they hit the ball very, very hard and they remain in balance throughout the entire action. Alas, for the eager observer, these are probably the *only* things they have in common. The Sandy Lyle swing is different to the Severiano Ballesteros swing. The Greg Norman swing is different to the Lee Trevino swing. Jack Nicklaus, Tom Watson, Raymond Floyd, Bernhard Langer, they are all different. But they are all champions and each of them has evolved a method of "delivering the face of the clubhead square to the ball along the target line, at speed". Not only have they done that, but some of the greatest players and champions – for example Byron Nelson, Jack Nicklaus, Raymond Floyd and more recently Nick Faldo – have made major changes to their swinging actions in the middle of active careers. For the observer, the student, the learner, all this is perplexing. But the procedures of the golf swing, the various physical movements which combine as a continuous action, are not chiselled in stone and handed down. These actions have been changed and modified by the improvements in the golf course and in golf's equipment, in particu-

187

lar those of the ball, but there are some abiding fundamentals to the operation, and in this chapter we propose to look at some of them and how some of the great players and teachers look at them, and the emphasis they may have put on this or that. These fundamentals are generally agreed to be The Grip, Stance and Posture, the Backswing (perhaps better expressed as the Back and Upswing), and the Downswing (perhaps better expressed as the Down and Through swing).

The grip is the golfer's only connection with the club. It governs the attitude of the clubface as it contacts the ball and therefore throughout the entire course of the swing it must not change. The fingers neither loosen nor tighten their hold on the club but remain constant in position on the club, and in pressure, from the instant of the first physical movement until the finish of the swing. This is an essential factor in the playing of the game. Three types of grip have evolved – the "Vardon" grip, the "interlocking" grip, and the "baseball" grip. The first was established, if not quite invented, by Harry Vardon, and it took him the best part of a year to get it right and feel comfortable with it. This is the grip in which the little finger of the right hand rides over the index finger of the left hand as they join on the club, and the "Vs" created by index fingers and thumb of each hand should point somewhere between the shoulders. Vardon believed he should grip tightest with the left thumb and index finger, with the right hand gripping firmly. Ben Hogan, by contrast, claimed that the main pressure in the left hand should be applied by the last three fingers and that, in the right hand, the two middle fingers should grip firmly. Hogan was very suspicious of a grip which applied excessive pressure with the right thumb and index finger. Bobby Jones, like Hogan, felt that control of the club rested in the three little fingers of the left hand, and that the other fingers should grip the club comparatively lightly. Jones, incidentally, for some years after he had retired from competitive play, was contracted to write twice a week a widely-syndicated golf column. From his writings, expressed in language at once prim and formal and precise, it is clear that few champions have given such intense intellectual attention to the game in all its aspects as he did. Vardon and Hogan might just have matched Jones in this. Tommy Armour, an outstanding player and an outstanding teacher, agreed with pressure from the last three fingers of the left hand, but insisted that the right thumb and forefinger should be as tight and snug as they could be, because they allowed the golfer

to whip the clubhead through the ball at impact. Many teachers have resisted this right-thumb-and-forefinger-at-impact on the grounds that if it is overdone – and that is the temptation – it will smother the shot, and that in any case there is an involuntary, subconscious tightening of the whole grip at impact. Armour, by the way, when it came to the subject of teaching, said that the highest achievement of the golf instructor may not be in the teaching, but in getting the pupil to learn!

The interlocking grip means what it says – the fingers are entwined, with the little finger of the right hand hooked between the index and middle fingers of the left. The Jack Nicklaus grip is the classic example, used by him because he has "small hands". Gene Sarazen and Francis Ouimet also used the interlock grip. The two-handed baseball grip has the hands touching, but with all the fingers on the shaft, neither overlapping nor interlocking. It was commonplace amongst all the golfers in the last century, through the periods of the feathery ball and the gutty ball, up to Vardon's development of the overlapping grip. Incidentally, Vardon grieved at the passing of the gutty ball. By 1911 he was persuaded that the game was deteriorating and he insisted that he was four shots a round(?) worse off than with the gutty. Perhaps the great man was being nostalgic and maudlin – he won the Open Championship of 1911 with the "new" Haskell ball!

Photographs of 19th century golfers at the top of their backswings, using the two-handed grip, are terrifying. The club is almost released by the fingers, left elbows are bent, the legs seem to be collapsing, the shafts lie way down their backs. It is hard to imagine that they could somehow re-grip the club and get the clubhead back to the ball with any consistency. Among more modern players, Abe Mitchell, a mighty hitter, used the baseball grip, but above all Dai Rees is perhaps the outstanding example of a successful golfer using this grip. Dai played on nine Ryder Cup teams, captained the winning team of 1957, won the Match Play championship four times, was second in the Open three times, and was a successful tournament player into his 60s. Yet at the top of his long backswing his fingers were all over the place, almost like the players of 100 years earlier. As his career shows, Dai knew very well how to get the clubhead back to the ball. Harry Bradshaw from Portmarnock, another tournament winner and Ryder Cup player, went to the other extreme as some kind of super-overlapper. He had huge and powerful hands ("Oi could kill a man wid dat hand!") and had three fingers of his right hand riding over those of his left, so that the whole fearsome apparition looked like a big leg of mutton. But Harry made it work.

The grip is the glue that must hold the entire swing together. As we have seen, expert players grip the club in a variety of ways. Golf is a two-handed game, but the two hands must work together as a single entity to deliver the clubface square to the ball. All expert players have grips which enable them to do this, and give them control over the flight of the ball. Powerful hands are clearly an asset in striking the ball faster and therefore sending it further. Arnold Palmer had immensely powerful hands. When he clamped them round the club, it looked like a toothpick, and one felt that no force on earth short of a nuclear explosion could have made him release his hold on the club. Yet Palmer was doing no more than holding it firmly, as opposed to tightly.

Great players, of course, work along fine margins. Ben Hogan, on coming out of the Army at the end of the 1939–45 war, made slight changes in his grip which certainly contributed to his exceptional championship achievements. He had become concerned at a certain looseness in his hands at the top of a rather long backswing and a powerful grip which left him with a tendency to hook the ball. He turned his left hand to the left, anti-clockwise so that the thumb went straight down the shaft. As he joined his right hand to his left, he let the little finger hook over the knuckle of his left index finger rather than having it ride on top of it, as in the pure Vardon grip. And, as he closed his grip, he let his right index finger and thumb ride high on top of his left hand, so that the V they formed pointed straight up the shaft. In appearance, it was a totally integrated grip which, held firm at the top, enabled him to make a correct and very powerful contact with the ball.

A correct, efficient grip is the first fundamental necessity, the "prime necessity" as Bobby Jones called it, in allowing the golfer not to *throw* the clubhead, not to *hit* with the clubhead, but to *swing the clubhead*.

Yet again, all that this proves is that, even with the most expert of players, there is no absolute, perfect, common or universal golf swing, even in its details. The first action of the golf swing is to take the clubhead straight back from the ball. If the golfer continued to do that he would plainly fall over. So at some point in this backward movement of the clubhead, the golfer must turn. He must turn his trunk and allow his arms to swing round and up. By initiating this backward swing with his left shoulder, left arm and hands keeping the shaft

and clubhead in a straight line, since he wants the widest possible arc to the swing to give it maximum centrifugal force, his left shoulder will move under his chin, and his right hip turn backwards. In order to do this, not to mention reversing the process when he has to swing down and through the ball, the golfer must stay in balance, and this is where we go back to our "Atlas primary cervical vertebra". The word "balance" is hard to define. It can mean keeping things in equilibrium. On the backward swing, much of the golfer's weight will move on to his right foot; on the down and through swing, it will move back to his left. To keep these physical actions smooth and fluid – which the golfer must do if the swing is to be controlled – the swing must be "centred", the golfer must remain "centred". There must be one still, small centre that is the core, the hub of all movement, to which all the movements of the hands, arms, shoulders, hips, legs, feet relate, and on which all depends. "Keep your eye on the ball" is an old golfing cliché which means more precisely "Keep your head still", which means even more precisely, "Keep the top of the back of the neck still". Having said that, it must also be said quickly that very famous golfers are exceptions to the rule. Peter Thomson, the Australian champion, and Joe Carr, the famous Irish amateur, moved their heads perceptibly, an inch or two to the right, at the start of the backswing. Among contemporary players, Curtis Strange is another example, but these men were expert enough and practiced enough, to have it back in position on the downswing and before impact. Indeed the physical action of turning the trunk round to the right probably means that all golfers move their heads *imperceptibly* to the right. Perhaps we are not doing so well with the dogmatic statement.

The golf swing is a series of unnatural movements. Ben Hogan has said "There is no such thing as a natural golfer." The bowler in cricket, the javelin thrower, indeed any thrower, delivers the ball or the javelin directly to the target with their upper bodies facing along the line to the target at the moment of overhead release, all the explosion of power and energy applied from behind, directly along the target line. The golfer, standing at the "side" of the ball, must swing the club back then return it to the ball in order to apply any force, and to do that effectively he must turn his hands, arms and body. Unlike the bowler or the javelin thrower he does this from a state of rest. Thus his preliminary stance and posture are very important. They cover a variety of purposes. They relate the golfer to the target line,

set up his aim. They put the body in balance. They "arrange" the body so that the sequence of physical movements in the swing can be properly initiated and completed. They prepare him for the conduct of an action which will allow him to make a proper contact with the ball. In a word, in terms of swinging the club, they make him ready. His 'sensors" in all of this are the feet and the hands – the feet because they must be the anchor, the foundation which supports his action and his balance, the hands because, with the aid of the shaft and the head of the club, they connect him with the ball.

Given that the golfer has settled on a grip which is comfortable and effective, he then stands to the ball with his feet square to the target line and the ball positioned slightly forward of centre, more or less opposite his left instep, the better to strike the ball forward and upward. The feet should be comfortably apart, say at about shoulder width. Even in the simple business of foot position, there have been differences of opinion. Most golfers take a stance with their feet turned slightly outwards of square, but Henry Cotton, throughout his career, kept his left foot rigidly square to the target line. He was an advocate of hitting "against the left side" so that at impact his left leg was straight and locked as he went through the ball and up into his follow through. What that did to the tendons and ligaments of his left ankle and knee doesn't bear thinking about. Ben Hogan by contrast came to believe that his right foot should be quite square to the line of flight, his left turned slightly towards the target. Having his right foot in this position controlled the turning of his right hip, prevented him from moving it laterally, and in the inner muscles of his right leg created tension and stored energy which would be applied on the downswing.

The golfer seeks movement in balance. The ideal golf swing must have ease, rhythm, tempo, smoothness, balance. The only purpose of the backswing is to put the golfer into a position from which to make a powerful downswing. Delivering the downswing requires a complete reversal of movement, which implies that, somewhere on the backswing, the motion stops and goes into reverse, as it were. Since the swing should be continuous, that seldom happens, although some fine players believe in a pause at the top of the backswing. Gordon J. Brand, the successful British tournament player, comes to a complete stop at the top of his backswing, and seems

**Nick Faldo bravely remodelled his swing then won the Open and the US Masters.**

none the worse for it. The golfer does not hit the ball on the backswing – a fast backswing is a waste of energy as well as being a menace to balance. Thus Jack Nicklaus says 'It is impossible to swing too slowly over the first 18 inches of the backswing", and Bobby Jones insisted on a long, slow backswing (he had a very full shoulder turn) so that there would be no need to "hurry" coming down. If the golfer doesn't hit the ball with his backswing, neither does he with his rhythm, tempo, balance or smoothness. They help him hit firmly through the ball, but he must strike it with the face of the club, thus he must swing the clubhead. And he must know what the clubhead is doing throughout the swing. He controls it through the "feel" in his fingers, and alas, like rhythm and tempo, feel cannot be taught. It must be learned through practice and experience. One of the most famous of all golf teachers, Ernest Jones, was the apostle of swinging the clubhead – "Swing the clubhead and all else will follow." At the age of 18, he had been an assistant professional at the Chislehurst club in Kent and became a fine player who could win tournaments, but in 1916, on the Western Front, he was very badly injured when a grenade exploded near him in a trench. In fact John Jacob's father Bob, who was nearby, helped to save his life, but Jones lost his right leg below the knee. In the 1920s, Jones went to America, and in a seventh floor loft in Manhattan he became a very successful golf teacher and animated theorist on the game, illustrating his insistence that it is possible to hit only with the clubhead by attaching a pen knife to the end of a handkerchief, swinging it, and demonstrating centrifugal force. He disliked "hitting" the ball and preferred the word "striking", since it better implied swinging.

The other Jones, Bobby, talked of much the same thing when he said he liked to think of the golf club as a weight attached to his hands by a length of string. He liked to feel he was throwing it at the ball with the motion he would use in cracking a whip. And Bobby Jones never much cared for the expression "hitting the shot". He thought that implied aggression. He preferred to talk of "playing" the shot, which had rather gentler, smoother implications. Ernest Jones was much opposed to any thought of "leverage" as a concept in the golf swing, claiming that in leverage the power applied and its object moved in quite opposite directions, whereas, in the golf swing, the power applied (through the hands) and the object (clubhead/ball) both moved in the same direction. Jones preached that the clubhead cannot move faster than it was swung and was persuaded that hands, fingers and clubhead were the keys to the entire action and that all other body movements followed them. This philosophy was completely opposed to that of Percy Boomer ("swing inside a barrel") who with his brother Aubrey was installed at the famous Racing Club at St Cloud, Paris, for many years. Percy was concerned with the movement of hips and shoulders, and above all the pivot, believing that hands and arms would follow naturally.

Of course, the more sardonic of golf teachers will tell you that 90 per cent of the mistakes the average golfer makes are made before the swing starts simply because of the carelessness and lack of logical thought, on the part of the player, with regard to grip, stance, posture, swing and just what he is about to do and how he should do it – the classic difference between strategy and tactics. On the other hand, the poor man has so much to think of, since he's not sure he is about to hit an effective shot. Yet, in fact, he should be thinking of only *one* thing. Sam Snead, once asked what he was thinking about during his swing, said, "Nuthin!" During a World Match Play Championship at Wentworth in the 1960s, several champion golfers were asked the same question, or rather what they were thinking of in that final millisecond before they started the club moving – they had taken up grip and stance, looked up the fairway, taken a few waggles with the club, settled their feet, then put the clubhead behind the ball. Within a fraction of a second, they would start to move. The question was "What are you thinking of at that precise moment?" Arnold Palmer, without hesitation, said "Hit the ball." Gary Player said, "Hit under the ball," which was interpreted as meaning hit the back of the ball. Roberto de Vicenzo, the greatest of the Argentine players, said "Tempo." Billy Casper said, "Nothing." When challenged on the grounds that *Homo Sapiens* in his conscious moments is perhaps incapable of thinking of "nothing", Casper rejected that. He said he had hit so many thousands of golf balls, played so many hundreds of rounds of golf, that he virtually did not have to tell his body, consciously, what to do. Peter Thomson, the Australian, said that he was thinking of where the ball was going, its destination, its target, where it would land, where it would stop, perhaps substantiating the John Jacobs teaching credo on the seeing of "ball to target", rather than "clubhead to ball". Thomson wrote later, and perceptively, of the golfer coming to the tee of the final hole of a great championship, in the lead, and of how his mind would be concentrated entirely on

a little patch of fairway, perhaps only 20 square feet where his final tee shot, perhaps the most important golf shot of his life, should land. The average player then should note that these great champions had only one single thought in mind during the swing, or in the case of Snead and Casper, no thought at all. The average golfer by contrast has a mind in a frenzy. He is thinking of grips, stance, posture, balance, rhythm, head still, eye on the ball, slow back, where is the damned thing going? Will I reach that bunker? What will the wind do? And so on. There is a powerful element of fear here, fear of the consequences of failure. The club golfer must contrive to "fill the mind with vacancy", and do no more than swing the clubhead.

As the club is swung back and up from the ball, the wrists will break and "cock" naturally at around waist level, carrying the hands on and up above shoulder level until the shaft of the club lies behind the head, parallel with the ground. The left hand will be slightly under the shaft, with the wrists still partially cocked. This top of the backswing position, particularly the hand position, is a key point in the golf swing, just as important as that initial move away from the ball. But golf, as so many other things, remains a slave to the fashions and circumstances of the hour. In the 19th century, golfers played with hickory clubs, long in the shaft, shallow in the face. They needed long, sweeping swings to get the ball away. The change of ball from gutty to rubber core, permitted shorter swings. Harry Vardon, although still playing with hickory shafts, modified this action as he did the grip, and his ideas carried through the golfing generations of Bobby Jones and Walter Hagen, until steel shafts came into general use in the early 1930s. These shafts were more powerful, less subject to the torque and whip of the hickories, and enabled golfers to make a simpler, more powerful strike through the ball. Steel shafts were shorter, swings became shorter and more upright, and, as a generalisation, allowed players to stand closer to the ball.

Probably the first player to become truly expert with the steel shaft was Horton Smith, tall, handsome, studious, from Joplin, Missouri (he was dubbed the "Joplin Ghost" with good reason). He was quick to master the management of this more powerful, more consistent shaft, and for a few seasons in the early 1930s he may just have been the best player in America. In the winter season of 1929, he emerged from nowhere, won seven tournaments and finished second four times. He was an elegant swinger and an outstanding putter; he won the first

Masters event in 1934, repeated in 1936, and became in his time the youngest Ryder Cup player. After a broken wrist, he was never quite as good again – it has happened to many a talented player. But it was Byron Nelson, a few years younger than Smith, who brought a minor revolution to what Bobby Jones had called "the inconsequential performance of striking the golf ball". (It could never be inconsequential for a professional player.) Not satisfied with his swing in spite of the fact that he had won the 1937 Masters and was a Ryder Cup player, Nelson by trial and error and hard practice came in 1938 to what many people thought were strange conclusions about the golf swing. One was that it was not possible to stand too close to the ball, manifest nonsense in that if you stand close enough, you'll whack your toes on the downswing! But this was a result of his "new" wrist and swing action.

Nelson decided that his accuracy and control would be improved if he took the club straight back and low to the ground for as long as possible at the start of the backswing, with the blade of the club held square to the ball as it had been at address. At the same time, he moved his right hip laterally to the right, in contravention of all previous backswing thinking. Holding the blade square on the backswing meant that the wrists did not cock, the forearms did not rotate and that, halfway up the backswing, the club was lifted into an upright plane with, inevitably, the right elbow "flying" away from the body, and with the left wrist straight with his forearm and not under the shaft, at the top of the backswing. Nelson previously had had rather a flat swing. Now he was upright. And he kept that left wrist straight so that as he came into the hitting area, he held the back of his left hand square to the target line. If it was a rather mechanical swing, softened by a little personal "signature" of a dip of the knees at impact, it was immensely profitable for Nelson, as his subsequent achievements show. The long, lazy, fluid swings of the Jones era were under siege, and Nelson's swing was to have a profound effect on a generation of golfers.

After the Second World War, and after Nelson's astonishing playing record in 1944 and 1945, his technique, picked up by many other players, came to be called glibly the "new American method", and through the 1950s and 60s – long after Nelson had retired from competitive play – the talk was that this "square to square" method was the way to play golf, and the appearance of Jack Nicklaus in the early 1960s, with his near-vertical swing, crunching attack on the ball and flying right elbow, did little to count-er it. One voice crying out against all this was that of John Jacobs who, apart from anything else and considering the power which modern players were applying to the ball, saw it as a certain recipe for destroying the golfer's lower back and spine. Jacobs's preaching, in a sense going back at least in part to the Bobby Jones thoughts on the swing, had its effect. Jones, commenting on Jack Nicklaus's remarkable total of 271 in winning the 1965 Masters, had said, "Jack plays a game with which I am not familiar." This was later seen to have a double-edged aspect: Greg Norman and the young Ballesteros had taken the Nicklaus route with upright swings. Nick Faldo had an upright swing. All made changes, none more so than Faldo. In the midst of a perfectly successful career, Faldo, for the best part of two years, went into the wilderness of a complete swing change, to one that was more rounded. At the end of that time, he came out of the woods, and with a rock-solid, rounded swing, won the Open Championship of 1987.

The antithesis of all this was one Lee Trevino, a player of singular achievement. Trevino spotted the ball forward, opposite his left foot, took an open stance, and almost as soon as he took the clubhead away from the ball, he was opening the face of the club, turning it clockwise, letting his forearms rotate. Trevino's flight pattern was left to right through the air; with a slight dip at impact, he had a long, strong, right arm "through the ball" which gave him his distance, from a marginally outside-the-line swing. Trevino hit the ball up – he could use the same tee peg for a month. Like many a great player, Trevino thinks his way is the way to play, that everyone should play his way, and what's all the fuss about? – just tee it up forward, tee it high, sweep it away, get your right hand through and off it goes, starting left and drifting nicely back to the centre of the fairway. He would refuse to accept that he "sliced" the ball. Often, even the greatest of players have a clear idea of how they swing the club when in fact they plainly don't swing it that way. Bobby Locke at his peak would aim 40 or 50 yards to the right of the line from a closed stance, and the ball would come back on a parabola to the centre of the fairway. He would be incensed if you talked to him about a hook – "Just a little draw," he would say, and "I can play it the other way, you know, too," meaning that he could fade the ball just as easily. For the club golfer, they can be a wearisome lot, these experts, all with differing ideas, differing methods, differing styles. "Style" of course is mainly little more than personal mannerisms. Gary Player starts his movement with a

little inward kick of his right knee, so that his entire action is a reaction to that; Jack Nicklaus turns his chin to the right before starting the club back; Nancy Lopez, one of the best half dozen players in the history of womens' golf, starts with a barely-perceptible lift of her left wrist; and Mark James, the British tournament player, does the same. Sandy Lyle has a slow, almost leisurely swing. Manuel Pinero, his Ryder Cup compadre, has a long, fast, whipping swing.

In 1968, a unique book, *The Search for the Perfect Golf Swing* was published by Heinemann for the Golf Society of Great Britain, the brainchild of Sir Aynsley Bridgland. He was an Australian engineer who had fought in the 1914–18 war and came to London in 1929 with the modest ambitions of owning a Rolls Royce, becoming a millionaire and a scratch golfer. He succeeded in all three, saying he got most satisfaction from the last of them. The man was, in short, a rich golf nut, and among many other achievements he founded the GSGB and assembled a team of scientists to make a definitive study of the golf swing. The team and its work were co-ordinated by Alistair Cochran, an Edinburgh University graduate, atomic scientist and county class golfer. Cochran and John Stobbs, then editor of the magazine *Golfing*, wrote the book. The scientists looked at the fundamental anatomical, mechanical, physiological and psychological principles of the golf swing. They acknowledged that there was a whole other dimension to the playing of the game, a foggy area involving the subtleties of character, personality, the individual human shape, desire, motivation and so on, and noted that one had to guard against what Babe Zaharias described as "getting all fouled up in the mechanics of the game". The book discussed the "levers" of the swing action, the upper lever being shoulders, arms and hands,

the lower lever being the club. This would not have endeared the team to Ernest Jones. It found that a good driver can generate four horse power on the downswing; during a drive, the face of a driver is in contact with the ball for only one-half of one-thousandth of a second, and that the ball will leave the clubface at about 135 miles per hour – staggering facts for the club golfer to digest. There is one other factor to consider in all the teaching, the learning, the thinking, the talking that we do about the golf swing. We all have a subjective "concept" of how we swing the club. Yet it is often totally different to the way we actually swing the club. Seeing a film of our true action compared to what we *think* we are doing might be a salutary experience.

For all the minor differences which the great professionals manifest, they all have fundamentals in common – a sound, positive, unchanging grip, a comfortable stance, balance and a regular tempo in the swing, speed through the ball at impact with the clubface square and, as important as anything else, uncluttered minds during the swinging action. And they all swing the clubhead and *allow* the clubhead to swing. When these experts play the "super" shot, the championship-winning shot – the splash-out from a deep, greenside bunker which finishes inches from the hole; the soaring iron shot which flies over the lake and spins down six feet from the flagstick – it is not from the inspiration of the moment. It is because they have practised the shot hundreds of times and have the "feel" of the shot, the instinct of what it requires. Somehow the club golfer has to acquire the same instinct, the "muscle memory" of Billy Casper, and the club golfer has to clear his mind of everything save making the swing as one continuous physical action, and above all else, to "swing the clubhead".

**Lee Trevino's unorthodox but famous open stance.**

195

# THE TOOLS OF THE TRADE

The gutty lasted 50 years, and the next major convulsion in the game came at the turn of the century with the advent of the "Haskell" ball, as we shall see. It was to lead to players getting better, courses becoming longer, the ball flying further, and, with advances in agronomy and course preparation becoming increasingly sophisticated, golf course designers were hard put to stay in step. The "Haskell" ball and its successors had a chequered time. It was made in various sizes, with various weights, by various companies, and it was not until the 1980s that the world's governing bodies at last agreed on a ball of uniform weight and size, and only after a good deal of squabbling between the British and the Americans.

Such had been the explosive growth of the game in America that it seemed no more than proper that Mr Haskell and his new ball should be American. In the great republic, the game was getting into an ample stride which was never to shorten, but yet again the "Kingdom of Fife" had a hand in its beginnings, in the distinctive persons of John Reid and Charles Blair Macdonald. Reid had emigrated, as had Andrew Carnegie, and around the same time, from Dunfermline, and established himself successfully in Yonkers, New York. In 1887, when Robert Lockhart, another Dunfermline man, was going back to Britain on a business trip, Reid asked him to bring back some clubs and balls. Lockhart very properly went to St Andrews, and in Old Tom Morris's shop bought a set of clubs and a supply of balls. Early in 1888, Reid and a few friends tried them out on a cow pasture, where they had laid out a few short holes. More clubs and balls were ordered – the first batch had been deemed a success. By springtime, the golfers had moved to a larger pasture, where they could lay

**Mark James with a set of Ping irons.**

out six holes. By November of that year, the end of the season, the half dozen or so friends sat down to dinner and formed the first American golf club, which they called St Andrews, and with Reid as president. If it wasn't specifically the first club that existed in America, it was the first to be formed and have a continuing, unbroken history to this day. As the membership grew, the club was forced to move more than once, until in 1897 it settled at Hastings-on-the-Hudson. Reid rather resisted the expansion of the club, holding that it should remain for a few friends, but for all that he was an out-going fellow, fond of his dram amongst other things.

After he died, they placed a bronze plaque on the wall of the clubhouse, which reads:

John Reid, Scotsman, American
The Founder of St Andrews Golf Club and its first President.
Born in 1840 at Dunfermline, Scotland. Died in 1916 at Yonkers-on-Hudson , New York.
A lover of men, of books, of sports; a loyal friend, a rare interpreter of the songs of his native land.

In parallel with this were the life and times of Charles Blair Macdonald, who, the name apart, was about as close to being a Scotsman as any American could be. Reactionary as the strictest Presbyterian, Macdonald was physically large and powerful, disputatious, stubborn and rich. At the age of 16 he had been sent to St Andrews – St Andrews in Scotland, that is – to study. His years there gave him the flavour of the gutty game, the old game, and impressed him in a way that lasted his entire lifetime (1856–1928). Macdonald became a first class player, and back home in Chicago he helped fund, organise and build two 18-hole courses, the first in the "West". By 1884, with the game blossoming, representatives of five clubs,

St Andrews, The Country Club (Boston), Newport, Shinnecock Hills on Long Island and the Chicago Golf Club – among the delegates were John Reid and Charles Blair Macdonald – felt obliged to formulate rules for the game and conduct national open and amateur championships. They created the Amateur Golf Association of America. Since this would be the organiser of championships open to professionals, it was quickly changed to the American Golf Association, even more quickly to the United States Golf Association. Golf in America was off and running, indeed sprinting. By the turn of the century there were at least 1000 clubs in the country.

If the gutty ball back in 1848 had opened a door through which many more people were enticed to take up the game, the rubber-core ball brought golf to the world, and the ball manufacturers, the rubber companies, were quick to meet the demand. The first decade of the new century was a time of much experiment for them, in making the core constant, in getting the right tension on the rubber windings, in the markings on the cover – bramble, dimple, mesh, recess and the like – but above all in finding a ball that would combine length with durability. Balls marketed as "Baby Kite", "Dunlop Junior" and "Baby Zodiac" were more tightly wound, heavier and smaller, and Harry Vardon, who had said that the early Haskell ball had put 20 yards on his drive, now claimed that these later, heavier balls would go 40 yards further. The "small heavy" offered a great advantage to the stronger player, particularly into wind, particularly if the course was soft, and lighter balls were preferred for downwind play and if the course was at all fiery. This was no more than a throwback to feathery times, when players carried balls of different weight and size and used them according to conditions. Thus there were rubber-core balls which varied in weight from 1.48 oz, which floated, to 1.70 oz, which did not.

John Laing Low, who made his mark on the story of golf in several ways, including course design (See Chapter 5), was a member of the Royal and Ancient Rules of Golf Committee and in 1903 had resisted the advent of the Haskell ball. When he became chairman of that committee in 1913, he resolved once and for all to establish some proper evidence as to the merits or otherwise of the "new" ball, in particular the small heavy. It was arranged that on the 2nd of April, 1914, the *Daily Mail* would sponsor a match between gutty and rubber-core at Sandy Lodge G.C., north of London. J. H. Taylor and James Braid, playing gutties, tackled Harry Vardon and George Duncan, playing rubber core, over 18 holes in the

morning, the same partnerships switching balls in the afternoon. Over the day, the rubber core won nine more holes than it lost. It averaged 40 yards further in the drive. The best round with the gutty was a 72 from Braid, with the rubber core a 69 from Vardon. All were agreed that the gutty was much better on the greens, but required much more accuracy in striking. If there was little between the balls at the hands of champions, the rubber core was clearly better for the average player – it was easier to hit, and mis-hit, and it travelled further. For the average player this was more than good enough.

But what was this small heavy ball doing to the defences of the golf course? Low was less than satisfied with this. The 1914–18 war put a stop to the discussions, but in a 1919 Victory tournament at St Andrews in dry weather, when some professionals were driving almost to the 16th green (350 yards), Low re-opened the whole bag of worms. On the 23rd of September that year, his Rules of Golf Committee passed the following resolution:

> The Rules of Golf Committee is of the opinion that in order to preserve the balance between the power of the ball and the length of the hole, and in order to retain the better features of the game, the power of the ball should be limited. Such investigation as the members of the committee have been able to make leads them to suggest that in the present circumstances this object would be obtainable by fixing a minimum limit of size for the ball. The committee proposed to consult the United States Golf Association and other bodies interested before submitting a definite proposal to the club.

Consulting the Americans, many later came to believe, was a mistake. However, if there was to be uniformity throughout the golfing world, these two bodies had to agree. Low wanted to limit the distance of the ball, particularly the small heavy, and had influenced his committee to achieve this by establishing a minimum size. He was perhaps less interested in specifying the "better features of the game". Ordinary golfers were little concerned with all this. They wanted then, as they still do, a ball which was easy to hit, would travel further and be close to indestructible, in short the best of all possible worlds. But Low's committee, perhaps as all golf legislators must, approached the ball problem from the position of the first-class player, the scratch player.

In May 1920, to consider the whole problem of the ball, British and Americans met in London, at Muirfield during the Amateur Championship, and again in London. The British team included Bernard Darwin, golf correspondent of *The Times*, the Americans George Walker, their president and subsequently donor of the Walker Cup, and Bob Gardner, the pole vaulter who fought an epic Amateur final against Cyril Tolley at Muirfield. The rather surprising fact is that, until this time, there had been no such thing as a "standard" specification for golf balls. From the beginning, golf balls had been made in a variety of weights and diameters. The meeting decided:

That the weight of the ball should be not greater than 1.62 ozs avoirdupois and the size not less than 1.62 inches in diameter. The Rules of Golf Committee and the Executive Committee of the USGA will take whatever steps they think necessary to limit the power of the ball with regard to distance, should any ball of greatest power be introduced.

After 20 years of trying, Low had at last restricted the power of the ball and found some accord with the Americans. But within the enclosed world of the day in golf this caused something of an outcry, if not an uproar. The ball was still too small, still too heavy. The Americans had insisted that they would accept only the American-made Spalding 30, and produced an American newspaper advertisement giving the weight of that ball. When the ball was weighed later, it was found to be appreciably heavier than 1.62 oz! Taylor, Vardon, Hilton and Duncan all weighed in with their opinions. The letter columns of *The Times* and other papers groaned with the weight of argument and counter-argument, most of it claiming that the ball was still too heavy – Taylor wanted a maximum of 1.5 oz. Yet Low's ball persisted.

When an American amateur team, including Bobby Jones, visited Hoylake in 1921, they were totally unable to stop the ball on greens baked by the driest, hottest summer of the century. Buckets of water were poured round several of the pins in perhaps the first instance of watering in the UK principally to help players to control the ball. The Americans were inclined to go their own way. By 1923, their experiments led them to stay with a ball of the same size, but lighter, at 1.52 oz. Through 1924 their experiments continued and they moved to a larger ball at 1.68 inches and marginally heavier at 1.55 oz. The ball manufacturers were surely having a

grand time keeping pace with all of this. The British stuck with "Low's Ball". The Americans declared in May, 1929, that they wanted a ball that was "an easier and pleasanter ball for the average golfer" (the first time *he* had been mentioned in all of this), and that from the 1st of January, 1931, to the 31st of December, 1932, the ball would be not less than 1.68 inches, not more than 1.55 oz in all USGA competitions. In fact from the 1st of January, 1932, they fell in with the British in terms of weight. From that date, the American ball has remained at 1.68 inches, 1.62 oz in weight. The Canadians adopted the same ball in 1948.

In 1938, the British were still fidgeting – "for the long hitter, the three-shot hole was a thing of the past; fairway wood club play was a thing of the past; courses were being stretched to more than 7000 yards with walks from green to tee of as much as 100 yards, and what the game needed, in economic and maintenance terms, were shorter courses. A 'shorter' ball would help." This was the attitude. The 1939–45 war put this into suspension, but in 1946 the R & A sub-committee proposed a larger ball, the American-sized ball. This was rejected by the club as being "too precipitate, too soon after the war". They decided to defer it for three years. In all this long saga, the British may be seen as having been more disputatious, more reactionary, the Americans more pragmatic. They wanted more scientific evidence on which to base decisions. By 1941, they had developed their "Armour machine", a testing device which produced results which allowed them to declare that, after the 1st of January, 1942, "no ball will be legalised if it exceeds an initial velocity of 250 ft/sec (at 70°F and sea-level)." This was the resilience factor. And by 1967 they were concerned with the "Overall Distance Factor", and, following a series of tests on a more sophisticated driving machine, the "Iron Byron", concluded that no ball should travel more than 280 yards with a 6 per cent margin – this was the first precise restriction on length, a factor which Harry Vardon had proposed a good 40 years earlier.

Within a decade of the war, the big ball, the American ball, was agitating the British again. Largely responsible for reviving the issue was John Jacobs, who has had an exceptional, embracing career in the game. In his time, Jacobs has been a senior club professional and a successful tournament and Ryder Cup player; he was managing director of a company which pioneered driving ranges and golf centres in the UK; he has designed golf courses; he was prominent in the separation of the PGA European Tour, the tournament players, from the

PGA itself, and through the first half of the 1970s was its supremo. He has been an outstanding thinker on, and teacher of, the game on a personal level and through the media of magazines, books, film and television. And he had long been an advocate of the bigger ball, holding that it demanded a much more accurate strike through the ball, and therefore would effect an improvement in the golfer's overall technique.

Jacobs was helped in his preaching by such as Henry Cotton and Dai Rees, not to mention a string of defeats for the British in the Open Championship and against the Americans in Walker Cup, Ryder Cup and Curtis Cup competitions. When the Americans came to play in the Open, they would switch to the British ball, profit from its extra distance, and with their ingrained swinging techniques manage it perfectly well, play it comfortably and successfully. The golf ball manufacturers, needless to say, resisted this campaign. The entire world outside North America was a market for the "British" ball, the smaller ball, and although they did manufacture smaller quantities of the 1.68 inch ball, these were inferior to the American product, and it would take them some time to match it in quality. But in the mid-1960s, the tournament professionals opted for the bigger ball in all their events, the R & A decided that, starting in 1974, the bigger ball would be obligatory for Open Championship play, and have decreed that as from the 1st of January, 1990, there will be one size of golf ball, the 1.68 inch. Since Coburn Haskell toyed with rubber threads at the end of the 19th century, it had been a tangled tale. And to this day, quite unabashed, manufacturers still market their product as "the ball that goes further". Back in 1934, Cotton's round of 65 was looked on as astonishing and the low aggregate of Cotton and Sarazen in the Open Championship was thought untouchable. Fifty years on, the low Open round, done by more than one player, is 63, the low aggregate is 268. Little thought may have been given that it was reasonable to expect that the best golfers would simply get better in time, as had competitors in all the quantifiable sports in Olympic and World Championships.

By contrast, the evolution of the golf club in this century has been more tranquil. In the 1920s, a tubular steel shaft was developed in America, and by the early 1930s it had eliminated hickory from

Nick Faldo changed his putter for the last round of the 1989 US Masters. He went on to win, helped in part by some spectacular putting.

club-making. Rustless chrome steel was used for iron heads. Following the 1939–45 war, when supplies of seasoned persimmon ran low, laminated wood heads came into use, and further experiments have seen shafts of aluminium and carbon fibre, clubheads of glass fibre and other materials, producing the quaintly-named "metal woods". As the supply of natural products diminishes, or is not enough to meet the demands of a game which continues to grow, no doubt the time will come when clubs and balls are made entirely of man-made materials.

All the problems concerning the tools of the trade seemed resolved, but in the 1980s a hiccup – to the average golfer it was surely nothing more – disturbed the tranquillity of the scene. It arose when Karsten Solheim, an American club manufacturer, started to make clubs with U-shaped grooves on the faces, the so-called "square grooves", in place of the traditional V-shaped grooves. Depending on one's point of view, the resulting hoo-ha took on undertones of either Machiavelli or the Marx Brothers. The whole fracas needs some explanation. Before 1900, the faces of golf clubs by and large were smooth. With the coming of the Haskell ball, punch marks and grooving were introduced to the faces of iron clubs. It was thought that they gave players more control of the ball, and in particular more backspin to shots pitched directly onto greens. Jock Hutchison won the 1920 Open, after a play-off against Roger Wethered, with irons which were so indented as to be punch-drunk, and by 1924, the first time in fact that the subject had ever been mentioned in the Rules of Golf, the R & A banned deep grooved clubs. As with the Walter Travis Schenectady putter 20 years earlier, it was probably a knee-jerk reaction – there was no definition of what was considered "deep". By 1942, the USGA had a definition. With the R & A, they had long accepted that grooves on the clubface could influence the behaviour of the ball. They commissioned an engineer to establish a formula for clubface markings. It resulted that the grooves should be V-shaped, the angle at the bottom of the groove should be 90 degrees, the width of the groove would be not greater than 0.035 inches, and that the space between the grooves should be at least three times the width of the grooves – all very neat and tidy, but perhaps a touch arbitrary.

The fact was that no one was precisely sure of what effect grooves had on the flight of the ball, and therefore to what extent they were "helping" the golfer. Dr Alistair Cochran, the scientist who co-authored the technical treatise *The Search for the Perfect Swing*, did some tests which suggested that the spin of the ball was not, after all, much affected by grooves and that the shape of the grooves was not very important. The next element in all of this came in the 1970s, when manufacturers abandoned the well-established but labour-intensive forging of iron heads and switched to the investment casting method. It is a process that does not lend itself to precisely-calibrated grooves. Thus the existing regulations on grooves were put out of kilter by a manufacturing process which also compromised the practicality of measuring the width of the grooves. The process left grooves of a cross-section closer to a shallow U. Thus, in 1984, detailed legislation concerning V grooves and much of the specification concerning them was dropped from the Rules of Golf.

The governing bodies of the game, as reasonable men, have always tried to work closely with the manufacturers, and have required them, if considering any radical changes in the tools of the trade, clubs or balls, to submit samples to them for approval. The Karsten Company of Phoenix, Arizona, was the first company to manufacture clubs with out-and-out square grooves. By 1985 there were reports that these new clubs were cutting up balls with balata covers, and the players assumed that this was giving increased backswing to the ball by roughing up its surface, rather as had been done to the early gutties. If this were true, more important if it was believed to be true, the top professionals would flock to use this new type of club, without much concern for its legality, constantly searching as they do to "improve" their equipment. The great advantage inherent in such clubs would be in shots from the rough, where blades of grass at impact are compressed between clubface and ball. The fluids in the grasses lubricate the ball, reducing the backspin on the ball as it leaves the face. The result is that, on landing, the ball will run on unpredictably – what the professionals call a "flyer". Paradoxically, at tournament level, this problem was heightened by a USGA policy of championship course preparation.

From the US Open of 1951, the USGA, with a championship rota of courses which had been designed in the days of the hickory shaft, saw the need to strengthen these courses against the power and skill of the contemporary players. When they called in Robert Trent Jones, the architect, to modernise the Oakland Hills course for that year – Jones believed that the players had become able to overcome the defences of most courses – he set precedents which have been followed by and large to this day. Fairways in the driving zones, around 240–250 yards, were compressed to a mere 15–20 yards across; the rough would be graded, a few inches high for a few feet adjoining the fairway, then as much as two feet deep in places, and greens would be protected by re-positioned and more severe bunkers, altered slopes. In some cases, rough was grown almost to the putting surfaces. In many cases, a collar of rough would surround greens, even forming a barrier to the entrances. Apart from anything else, this compromised the skills of chipping and running shots into the green. More and more the American game became a through-the-air game; more and more the players expressed themselves as less than happy with US Open golf courses; more and more they got flyers with their recovery shots.

The Karsten Manufacturing Company was the creation of Karsten Solheim, a Norwegian immigrant, an engineer who in his 40s started making golf clubs in his garage with a borrowed $1000. The Ping putter was his first successful product, with a long blade and a distinct cavity in the back, and so called, no doubt, for the sound the ball made when it was truly struck. The cavity back was also a feature of his iron clubs, "copper clubs", which traditionalists deemed downright ugly, but which came to sell some 500,000 sets per annum world-wide. The rules on clubs insisted that "markings must not have sharp edges or raised lips", so there had been a rounding of the angle where the groove meets the face of the club. Solheim sought to reduce the tearing effect of his square groove clubs by extending the radius of this rounding, and he did not choose to submit a specimen club for USGA approval. There was no doubt in his mind that his clubs conformed. The width of the grooves was not really an issue – the USGA believed that the rounding of these edges formed part of the groove, and that this reduced the distance *between* the grooves. Solheim insisted that they were not, and did not.

All of this produced a controversy, much of it acrimonious – Solheim is a stubborn man. Most of the rest of the golf trade felt that Solheim was wrong in so far as there had to be a governing body, and that everyone in golf should respect that, and comply with it. In June of 1987 the USGA announced that they were developing a new system of measurement for clubfaces. Later, it announced that square grooved clubs would "be considered non-conforming at USGA events in 1990, and non-conforming at all events played under USGA rules in 1996." The US PGA Tour – conducting the American professional tournaments – proposed to ban the use of square grooved clubs from the 1st of January, 1989. The

R & A announced that it would fall in line with any new USGA measuring system, and the PGA European Tour declared it would follow any R & A Rulings.

This convoluted story might well have seemed positively arcane to the average golfer, whose main pre-occupation is with actually making some kind of contact with the ball rather than the degree of spin he can apply to it. But it poses wider questions of concern to everyone involved in the game. It puts stress on what Peter Thomson called the third dimension of the game, which is, after direction and distance, judgement – judgement as to how far the ball will actually roll after landing, taking into account, wind, ground conditions, weather, and the type of club and shot that has been applied to it. This has always been a critical factor especially in British golf, a game played by and large over ground in a "natural" condition, and for so long with a small, lively ball. On the other hand, the American game for long has been played through the air, in "unnatural" ground conditions, that is to say on courses which have lush turf and growth, arising from the fact that they have had to be artificially watered to preserve and sustain the grass in very high summer temperatures. Jack Nicklaus was one of the first players to "measure" golf courses (it is now commonplace among the leading players) so that he knew after his drive had come to rest exactly how far his ball was then from the flagstick. Jack of course had the power and the talent to hit, say, a 1-iron shot through the air so that it would pitch on the green itself, and stop quickly on a watered surface. There is a school of thought that British courses, in particular links courses, are following too closely those of American courses in these respects.

Finally, in golf as with any sport, but more than most, there must be a governing body, and in this respect the game has been well-served. If the USGA and R & A have not always marched with the same pace, they have marched in the same direction, with the well-being of *all* golfers as their philosophy. Uniformity in the size and weight of golf balls and the form and shape of clubs is essential. Incidentally, in 1967, the Du Pont company produced a synthetic material, Surlyn, for golf ball covers. Surlyn is virtually indestructible, if lacking the "feel" of balata, and is used to cover the "two-piece" ball which has a rubber core, but not rubber windings. The next offering of the researchers may well be the "one-piece" ball, which takes us back to where we came in, or back to where the gutty came in, almost a century and a half ago.

*18th Hole*

# THE CRITICAL STROKE

On the 16th hole of the last round of the US PGA Championship of 1972, played over the Oakland Hills course in suburban Detroit, Gary Player, tied for the lead, sliced his drive into rough. The hole is a par-4 which doglegs to the right, and can be reached routinely with a drive to the left side of the fairway and a short iron shot to the green. Player was 20 yards off the fairway to the right and faced two complications with his second shot. There was a stand of mature, weeping willow trees facing him, between his ball and the green. Beyond the trees, there was a lake defending the front and the entire right side, Player's side, of the green, edging right up to the putting surface. There were three bunkers behind the green, and the entrance to the green was clearly designed for a shot from the left side of the fairway, which is where Player was not. The lie was good, since gallery movement had flattened the grass, but Player was 150 yards from the flag. His challenge was to get the ball high enough to clear the trees, far enough to reach the green, and also somehow find a way of holding the ball on the putting surface. He could have played the ball out to the fairway, and hoped to make his par with a shot to the green and a single putt. At that stage of the competition, it was not the Player decision. He hit an immense, an exceptional 9-iron shot, the critical shot, which cleared the trees, pitched on the green and stopped four feet from the hole. He holed the putt and went on to win the championship by two strokes. It was not the only critical shot Player had hit in his time – in the last round of the Open of 1968 at Carnoustie, battling with Jack Nicklaus for the title, he hit a 3-wood second on the par-5 14th hole which stopped just two feet away for an eagle which won him the championship.

In the US Open of 1972, Jack Nicklaus, leading the championship in the final round, hit a 1-iron shot to the 17th hole at Pebble Beach, a par-3 of 218 yards, played that day dead into wind. The Nicklaus ball, wind or no wind, flew straight at the target. It bounced a few inches short of the hole, struck the flagstick and flopped down, a few inches away. Nicklaus won the championship.

Then came Jerry Pate. For the 1976 US Open, the Atlanta Athletic Club's 18th hole was re-modelled. From being a rather nondescript par-5, it was shortened to become a more severe par-4, more severe because it now turned slightly left in the driving zone and because it was menaced by water. A lake covered the left side, then the entire front of the green. A drive too far left might catch a bunker, or the water; a drive too far right would be in tenacious rough. After 54 holes of the championship, Jerry Pate had been two strokes behind the leader, John Mahaffey. On the 18th tee of the final round, Pate held a one stroke lead over Mahaffey, Tom Weiskopf and Al Geiberger. Both Pate and Mahaffey, paired together, drove into the right rough; Mahaffey, pressing for the birdie he needed, tried to force a wood shot from there and failed. His ball splashed into the water, short. The hole on the 18th green was cut on the left, on a little peninsula that poked into the pond. There was a bunker behind the green. Pate found a clean lie in the rough and hit a 5-iron, smooth as silk. The ball soared over the lake, came down softly two feet from the flagstick – the critical stroke. Pate holed the putt and won the championship by two shots. It was his first tournament success.

Perhaps the most critical stroke of recent times is the 7-iron which Sandy Lyle struck from the fairway bunker on the left of the last hole at the 1988 Masters tournament. The ball was picked perfectly from the sand, flew over the flagstick, then ran back down the green, leaving a straight, downhill putt of some ten feet which Lyle holed, and with which he won the Masters.

These illustrations pose two fundamental ques-

**Sandy Lyle's critical stroke; the famous pitch out of the bunker at the 18th in the 1988 US Masters.**

Jerry Pate's critical stroke came during the 1976 World Match Play Championship.

tions. First, can there be such a thing as the single critical stroke when a championship may be won with a total of 280 or 290 strokes, long and short, large and small? And, second, what strange amalgam of qualities – luck, intuition, technique, chemistry, virtuosity – permit a man to make such a shot at such a time? Doug Sanders of the ridiculously short swing, but a player of quality, missed a three-foot putt on the final green which would have won the 1970 Open at St Andrews, and will be forever remembered for it (he lost the play-off to Nicklaus, 72–73). The result of that is that many other relevant facts about Sanders have been forgotten. He had to pre-qualify for this championship, then, on the very first hole of the very first round, he scored six, having dumped his second shot into the Swilken Burn, and incurred penalty shots (nevertheless, he finished in 68). And in that last round, at the height of the battle, he hit his second shot at the 17th into the fearsome Road bunker. Playing from there, and

getting the ball on the putting surface, much less close to the hole, is perhaps the single most difficult shot on the course. Sanders played a quite exquisite explosion shot to within a few inches from the hole to save his par-4 and went happily to the last tee, one shot ahead, one hole to play. He did not win the championship, but under the circumstances at the time his shot from the bunker on the 17th was surely a critical shot.

How does the "critical shot" happen? What strange power permits the golfer to produce this, the essential shot? When Billy Casper was asked what he was thinking during that final moment before he moved the clubhead away from the ball at the start of his backswing, he answered "Nothing". (Snead, asked the same question, gave the same reply.) Casper was saying in effect that "muscle memory" had taken control; the fact that he had repeated that physical action thousands of times in practice and competition meant that it no longer had become necessary for him to think consciously about it. He was surely therefore calling on his "unconscious" to swing the club. Thus he was talking about the virtuoso, the person "skilled in the mechanical part of a fine art". A musician, given enough practice, can learn how to play a piece of music "with his eyes closed", so to speak. And the more he practises the skill, the less aware he will become of his talents in displaying that skill.

An experienced car driver, on a road with light traffic or on a familiar route from home to work, simply functions without thinking about it. But, if he runs into heavy traffic, he will concentrate immediately, consciously. The inexperienced driver by contrast must concentrate all the time. The greater the mastery one has of a skill, the more automatic it becomes, so that the whole thing happens below the level of consciousness, of awareness, and the more one practises, the more one enlarges the "habit" portion of the unconscious.

In the 19th century, there was much disputation about the nature and function of the unconscious. The Behaviourists were inclined to the belief that habit-forming was all, was essential, and that original thoughts emerged from the unconscious in a random fashion. Other schools held that the unconscious, the largest realm of the mind, was like the bulk of an iceberg: below the surface, and vast. And the thinking was that the unconscious mind was like an enormous computer stored with all of one's human experience, habits and memory, and programmed to produce and send upwards, back into the consciousness, perfect responses to the downward stimuli of the conscious mind and its demands. We are at the mercy of language in trying to express obtuse philosophies in simple terms. But when we consider, for example, Darwin's propositions on the origin of man and of natural selection, many of the elements were already in place, from the work of Lamarck and Malthus. It was not a matter of sudden, blinding revelation, more one of Darwin's reasoning, so much so that Darwin's friend and associate Huxley said, "Why didn't I think of it – it's so simple!" It had simply been a question of seeing how all the elements fell together. Much of the achievement of another genius, Freud, was helped along by the work of Breue, Chalcot and Fliess.

So we come to Gary Player, for instance, standing over the ball before he plays his second shot, his fateful second shot to that 16th green at Oakland Hills, at a critical stage in a great championship. Player has decided that he must hit the ball over the trees, over the lake, go for the green. No one can calculate in absolute terms the effect of a bounce, or of the wind, on a golf ball. If Freud says "there are no accidents", he'd better not tell that to the golfer who sees a fine shot pitch in a small divot mark and spin off into a bunker. Player has been hitting golf shots every day of his adult life. He can hit a 9-iron shot "with his eyes closed". He is saturated in the game, but now he summons memories asleep in the dormitories of his mind.

Into the front of his mind, his conscious mind, comes an awareness of the importance of the moment, an awareness of the externals. Can he be inspired – animated by some mental or spiritual influence? Can he be lucky – the "fortuitous happening of events affecting the interests of a Person"? Perhaps not. Now he must simply divorce himself from the lie, the trees, the lake, the wind, the noisy silence of the gallery, the circumstances of the competition and the total environment, and focus himself entirely and utterly on the ball, the small, white ball and the purity and the power of his contact with it. Emerging from his unconscious, from that fertile underground, is an upsurge of what amounts to an act of creativity. He plays the shot, the critical stroke. But the foundation of the stroke remains the habit, created by the practice of the shot 1000 times over, drawn from the depths of his life's experience and becoming, for only a few enchanted seconds, a creature of his consciousness.

# THE GREATEST MATCH EVER PLAYED

## Preface

Match play golf, man against man, was the original form of competitive golf before the coming of the Open Championship in 1860, and the greatest contemporary exponent of this ancient game surely has been Gary Player of South Africa. Against the outstanding players of his time, through the 1960s and 70s, he won the World Match Play Championship five times in seven years.

Player always recognised that the clash of personality and character was just as important as the shotmaking involved in such matches. In his book *Grand Slam Golf* (Cassell, 1966) he writes of his epic match against Tony Lema in the 1965 World Match Play Championship, when he recovered from being seven down with 17 to play, five down with nine to play, and won on the 37th hole.

The chapter entitled "The Lema Match" seems to us to be an extraordinary revelation of the mental processes and pressures which are experienced by golfers of the highest class, at the highest levels of the game, and we reproduce it here, by permission, and with much pleasure.

**Tony Lema during the 1965 World Match Play Championship.**

**M**y match with Tony Lema, in the semi-final of the Piccadilly World Match Play Championship, at Wentworth, near London in October of 1965, has been called the greatest match ever played, by many people who were there – and I daresay by many people who were not there, but who read of it, or saw it on television. Now that is a big statement, a very big statement, but I am tempted to agree with them. It was certainly the most fantastic head-to-head match I have ever played in. I was one up at nine, six down after 18, seven down after 19, five down with nine to play, all square at the 36th. And I won on the 37th hole. Lema was 67 for his morning round, on a course measuring 7,000 yards; I was 68 for the afternoon round. These facts alone will give you some idea of the high drama, the remarkable swing in fortunes and the quality of play that each of us produced. Other people have said that all through 1965, in the big events, I played in a state of enchantment and that may well be true, but this day, the day of the Lema match, was one of the most astonishing in my life. I have looked back on it and come to see in it a summation of so much of my character and personality, good and bad, so much of a reflection of the pattern of my life, that it has become for me a strange, unnatural distillation of all it means to be Gary Player, all that Gary Player is. Simply, it contains my whole life story, and it is full of significance for me.

To illustrate this, I think the match is worth spelling out in detail, but there is a preamble to it, an overture that came just 12 months earlier on the same golf course, in the same event, in the same round. In 1964, Arnold Palmer beat me eight and six in the semi-final. You can say he thrashed me. In the first round, I was drawn to play Ken Venturi, who had won the U.S. Open that summer in dramatic style, in fierce heat and sapping humidity at the Congressional Club in Washington, D.C. I had a pretty good match with Ken, and beat him four and three. In Arnold's opening match, he beat Peter Butler on the 36th green, so it was to be Palmer–Player in the semi-final. Now not only was I not nervous at the prospect of meeting Palmer, not only was I certainly not afraid of him, but I felt quite confident of beating him.

Arnold and I, before this, had played something like 37 matches against each other all over the world, in exhibition matches, television matches, play-offs and so on. Some were in Japan, some in South Africa, some in Australia, some in Britain, most in America. And the result was a dead heat, an absolute dead heat, with each of us winning 18 and one tied. So there was no reason for me to be worried about shaping up to Palmer. But when he started his afternoon round eagle, par, birdie, birdie, birdie, I was gone, and I suppose anyone else would have been gone, too.

Driving back to London that evening, I realised that there had been really no way I could have beaten him that day. When I faced up to it, threw off my shock and shame and started analysing the whole thing, I had to conclude that with my attitude to my game and my life, it would have been totally impossible for me to have beaten Arnold Palmer at that time. I had been playing against one of the best players who ever lived, and certainly one of the most powerful, on a big course, when he was driving with a driver and I was driving with a 3-wood. In fact I was giving a man like Palmer a 60 yards advantage off the tee and expecting to beat him. There was some reason for me playing a 3-wood off the tee. Wentworth is a narrow golf course, and I had thought myself into a state of mind in which I was convinced I was straighter with a 3-wood than with a driver. This is not to say that Wentworth's West course is a ferociously tight and narrow course. It isn't, but if you hit a loose one you are quite properly punished, and it is a course on which a man has to hit into precise positions all the time. Face to face with Palmer, I brought out a 3-wood and a defensive attitude while he was flourishing his big driver and had aggression bursting out all over him. All of the nonsense on my part was a direct consequence of simply doing too much in 1964 – playing too many tournaments, too many exhibitions, rushing here and there, travelling thousands of miles all over the world, trying to be too polite to too many people too much of the time. I was very tired. My nerves were shot.

But this defeat was probably the finest thing that happened to me in 1964 and it probably made a golden 1965 possible. Although it sounds ridiculous, I almost enjoyed it, because I know now that I shall never again go back to using a 3-wood off the tee unless the hole is a lay-up, and particularly tight at that. And I suddenly saw very clearly from this defeat a pattern of behaviour that I would have to follow. First, I would have to plan my year's schedule more carefully, more ruthlessly. Second, I had to be really fit at all times. It was quite ridiculous for anyone of my age to be tired. And third, I would go with a driver off the tee at all times when it was possible. I had to have every inch of yardage possible against these big fellows. I know that if I had beaten Arnold in that match, I would have gone on persuading myself that all was well, and I should probably have persisted with these bad habits and wrong attitudes to my work. And I also doubt very much if I would have won the U.S. Open. Riding back to London in the car that night, I made a quiet vow to myself, that I would win the World Match Play the next year – and I did.

Rather less quietly I said to my manager, Mark McCormack, that I was feeling nervous, that my nerves were shot and that I had tried to do too much that year. I'm inclined to be a bit of a hypochondriac when it comes to health, but health is basic to my business. Without fitness, I can't do my job. So I got down to work on my physical condition and sought the advice of Roy Hilligenn, who formerly held the titles of Mr America and Mr Universe, and who laid down a body-building course for me. I went at it religiously. I built muscle all over my body, putting an inch and a half on my thigh muscles, for example, and I also built a lot of muscle on my nerves. I felt I built up a deep, strong nervous reserve, a good deal of nervous stamina, and a lot of confidence flowed from this improved physical condition. It is beyond dispute that when a man is physically well and fit, he will think more clearly, more simply, more precisely. All this I aimed at, and worked hard at, and achieved. It made 1965 possible for me.

When I came back to Wentworth, 12 months later, I was South African Open champion, U.S. Open Champion, winner with Harold Henning of the Canada Cup, and personal winner of the Individual Trophy, and a couple of weeks after Wentworth I was to become the Australian Open Champion to round out what might be called a fairly successful year. If my experiences on Wentworth's West Course in 1964 were relegated to history, they remained very much in my mind in 1965. The draw for the World Match Play put Tony Lema and me in the same half. If I beat Neil Coles, the British Match Play Champion, and Tony beat Peter Alliss, the British PGA Champion, in first-round matches, we would meet in the semi-finals. And this fact produced an odd preliminary. The day before the tournament started I was playing a practice round with Ted Dexter, the former England cricket captain and an amateur golfer quite good enough to lead Britain's Walker Cup team in the future, if he puts his mind to it. We had just finished the fifth hole when I noticed Tony Lema coming up behind, playing on his own. We waited and asked if he would like to go on by himself, or if he would like to join us. He said, "I'll come and play with you fellows." We drove off the sixth, and as we walked the fairway, Tony said, "You

and I have never played each other, man to man, in a match play event, have we?" I said, "No." Now I felt at this stage, thinking of a Lema–Player match, that I would have everything to lose and Lema nothing much to lose, because I was the reigning U.S. Open Champion and at that moment in time enjoyed a much better record in golf than Lema did. In addition, you never know when these fellows are firing psychological darts at you, so I thought quickly and carefully, searching for a sensible get-out. I said, "No, we haven't, but I hope we do meet – at least it will mean that I have won my first round match." With that, I felt I had held my end up modestly and reasonably; the point was never mentioned again and we played out the round.

In first-round matches, both Coles and Alliss went down five and four. It was to be Player–Lema in the semi-finals. I had no ambition to lose to Tony Lema. For one thing, in the States he has always knocked the Big Three – Palmer, Nicklaus and Player. In fact, he has criticised us quite severely. I don't blame him for this, I don't criticise him for this, because he obviously wants to be one of the Big Three, or perhaps he even wants to be the Big One, and there is nothing wrong with that. But I felt that he wanted to get through with publicity as much as achievement, and I am convinced that the only way to greatness in this game, or any other game, is in the record book. There is no such thing as a great player who doesn't prove it, by winning championships. On top of all this, I had heard in London that Slazengers had signed Lema on a world-wide contract, and that really was an incentive to beat him. I was with Slazengers originally and as far as I am concerned they showed little loyalty to me. I travelled everywhere for them, played exhibitions, made store appearances, all over the world for them, and when I had a bad period, a slightly lean period, they just dropped me completely and took Jack Nicklaus because he was having a great year. I would make an exception here and say that Slazengers Australia have treated me very well and out there I have one of the finest contracts and friendliest relationships with a company that anyone could have. But I was always unhappy with Slazengers U.K. and Slazengers South Africa and disappointed in the way they ran my affairs and handled the products. I felt I had been entirely loyal to them. If there is no love lost in war and business, well, that explains why I am not a very good business man. There is too much sentiment in me for that. And I certainly don't think I live with revenge. That is a dangerous word, and if you believe in God, as I do, there is no room for revenge in your thinking or in your emotional processes.

Nevertheless, there was a good deal of spice for me in the prospect of meeting and beating Tony Lema at Wentworth – my experience with Arnold Palmer a year earlier, Tony's remarks during the practice round, his sniping at the Big Three, Slazengers and so on.

I also knew quite well that the prospect of Lema–Player must have been fascinating to the public mind, a shocking contrast in character, temperament, personality, appearance. On the one hand Tony Lema – tall, handsome, dashing, nonchalant, an elegant swinger with a slightly sardonic air and the sharp dry connotation of the champagne image. The name "Tony" has something of the man about town in it, the name "Lema" is all latin and Mediterranean. On the other hand Gary Player – small, dark, deliberate, painstaking, the feeling of the man without talent who has done it all by sheer hard work and nothing else, a highly-strung faddist who bores the ears off you with weight-lifting and diet and nuts and raisins and talk of God, dark clothes, sombre under the big-peaked cap, and above all, a little fellow, a little man. And the name Gary Player? A plain honest Anglo-Saxon pairing, good enough name for a golf player but without any identifiable flavour to it – non-vintage. But there is a little more to Master Gary Player than that.

As it happens, I believe that Tony Lema is a very nervous guy. Behind the façade of relaxation, of being a very cool customer, I think he is very nervous, but I also think he is a very fine golfer who has very good control of his nerves. He is impressive. I had no illusions. In these affairs, one must always calculate that it will be close, very close, with two top players playing each other, even if one is a good deal better than the other. If you compare Arnold Palmer's record and achievements with that of Tony Lema, then Arnold's is ten times better. But that doesn't mean that Arnold could go out there and thrash him. If he beats him over 36 holes, by any margin, even one up, it's a pretty good performance. So in these affairs you have to depend on all your skill and experience and determination to win, and also hope for a few breaks at the right time. I really felt in my heart that I was going to beat Lema, I was bloody determined to beat him.

For the match, we had one of those beautiful English autumn days, a one-sweater day, with a slightly early haze which the sun burned away during the morning, and the temperature rose pleasantly into the sixties. The course was in prime condition, the crowds were huge, the television cameras were

poised and birds sang. What could be better than this?

We halved the three opening holes in careful par figures. I won the fourth hole with a beautiful eagle three. At 497 yards, Wentworth's fourth is on the card as a par five, but in truth, we could all reach it in two hits, so my eagle was really a birdie. But it tasted good. Wentworth's fourth hole is a blind tee-shot down a hole that falls and turns regularly to the left. The drive is over perhaps 100 yards of broken ground, heather and paths, then the fairway swings away dramatically down into a big amphitheatre. Out in front of the green, to be carried with the second shot, are a ditch and a ridge; there is a big banked and deep trap at the left front, and a flat, shallow bunker on the right middle. The green gathers from right to left, or more accurately from right front to left rear. If the second shot flies and pitches just right, it will be brought sweetly into the pin, usually cut behind the left front bunker. If not, it can be trapped either side, or carried right through the green. My 4-iron second did exactly as it was told and came up five yards short of the stick. I spent a good deal of time on the putt, and made it. That was really the only difference between us on the front nine, and if it wasn't breathtaking golf, it was fairly substantial play, me with 34, Tony with 35 against the card par of 36.

In retrospect, the 10th hole seems very significant. This is a 190-yard hole, hitting to a high green which is oblong, lying across the line of the shot, and which is totally screened by a line of big pine trees. You have to hit it far, and fly it high to carry the trees. I hit a 5-iron about eight feet from the hole. Tony's 5-iron caught the top of the trees and bounced down under them, in scrub and long grass.

At that point, after we had hit, it was 99 per cent certain that I was going to be two up. Lema fashioned a good shot, scrambling it out of the scrub and up the bank some 20 feet past the hole – and holed it. I missed from eight feet, so I was still only one up. From there on, I lost seven holes in a row. What happened was that I became too greedy. I had let Lema off the hook, let him get some of his confidence back. His tail wasn't between his legs as it should have been. It had risen a little. Instead of letting the thing go at that, I became greedy and told myself that I had to win the very next hole just to really flatten him before he got too confident. The 11th, from a high tee, is a fairly straightforward drive and pitch, but it turns slightly to the left into the green, with trees down the left side. I tried to play it fine, and drove it hard down the left side – too fine. My ball caught a branch and went clumping and clanging into the forest. When I reached it, all I could do was squirt it out on the fairway, then pitch it into the green, but not close enough to make the putt. Tony played a neat drive and wedge and had two putts for it. The 12th hole, 480 yards, he played perfectly with a drive and 4-wood and two putts. My 4-wood to the green caught a little bank on the left front, and I didn't get my chip close enough.

At the 13th, another dogleg, again I flew it too close to the left side, again was caught in the rough. I had to chop at it again, and that cost me yet another hole. Two down. The 14th is 183 yards, all the way uphill to a two-level green. Tony, really flashing now, had his 4-iron tee-shot two feet away for a birdie. If I had him on the hook at the 10th, he was certainly off it now. The 15th, 16th and 17th he birdied, and instead of hitting the ball moderately well, he was hitting it right in the middle of the screws and playing super golf. And getting birdies. He won seven holes in a row, with five birdies. Now I don't believe my nerve went, at any time in this morning round. I just couldn't get birdies. I was getting pars, and he was getting birdies, and when anyone throws super golf at me like that, I don't mind. When a man plays well, he deserves to win holes. So what could I do? I could hang on for dear life and try, try, try, knowing that the birdies would come to me, sooner or later. In fact, what almost everybody missed – I certainly never saw it written about or heard it discussed – was that I had to hole a very stiff 15-foot putt on the 18th to save myself going in to lunch *seven* down. I really tried on that putt as much as I knew. I felt that all the putts I had ever hit in my life, under pressure, in tournaments and championships, for all the money I ever won in golf, were built into that putt. I poured all of myself into that putt, and I know, I just know that 90 per cent of golfers, 95 per cent, 97 per cent of golfers, would have missed that putt. And I tried on it as though it would have won the match for me.

Now as we came off the 17th green, where Tony Lema went six up, he started to talk. He said something like "it's funny how golf goes, isn't it?" Tony Lema is a modest boy. He didn't say that he had beaten me already and that it was all over and all a formality. He went on about what the odds were of any top player winning seven in a row from another top player, and it was too bad that it happened to you and so on. I am sure he was not thinking that it was all over, but I'm equally sure that he was convinced he was going to win. He didn't say I had no chance – but I got the impression that he was thinking that,

ever so slightly. For these few seconds, he was a compulsive talker. He was just caught up in the tensions of the thing. little did he know it, but at that very moment I still believed, indeed I *knew* that I was going to win that match. I can't prove that to you. It is the simple truth. it is a truth based on an early and very hard lesson that I got as a young professional golfer, when I was four up with four to play on a fellow in the South African PGA Championship – and lost. Dormie four, and lost! That is branded into my mind. I shall never forget it as long as I live.

I had a quick, light lunch and set off for the practice tee. There had been a little hook at the end of too many shots in the morning, and I wanted to straighten it out. Tony Lema was sitting having a perfectly relaxed lunch. He had no plans for practice, and I don't suppose I would have had if I'd been in his position. But there it was.

I spent a good half-hour on the practice tee, working hard on straightening out the hook. The strange thing is that under pressure I never hook. I am more prone to cut the ball, if anything. When I started in golf I would hook, but now that my game is more developed, under pressure I would be more afraid of hitting a big slice. So I work on it, floundering around on the practice tee. Then I walk over to the 19th tee, and what do I do? I snap-hook it, right into the rough on the left. The fact that I did practise at least declared to the world my faith in myself, that I was still very much in the match. But you can imagine what a blow it was to me to hook that first drive, lose the hole, and go seven down.

Some of the gallery started to leave. They had written me off. Those who did stay hung back a little further, as though their presence might be embarrassing me. But the gallery didn't by any means abandon the match – the British really enjoy a fight, more than any other people in the world they really appreciate a hard struggle. This is something that is in their blood and I felt that this was another, an additional challenge, to me. I said to myself that I could do it, if I really could recover from this disaster, then these people really would see what courage was. I don't want this to sound like the big deal of the whole world – after all it was only a golf match – but this was my world, and this was the biggest deal in my world, do you follow? In any event, I won the next two holes with birdies, the second hole, a short one, and the third, which I played perfectly. The third is one of Wentworth's prettiest holes, 457 yards slightly uphill, through a long avenue of woods and rhododendrons, to a two-tiered green with the pin, of course, on the upper level. I had it on the top level, about nine feet from the hole, with a drive and a 3-iron, and holed the putt. We halved the fourth, and I won the short fifth with another birdie. That made me four down; something of an improvement, and outside the disaster zone now. Don't think Lema wasn't trying. On the fifth, 192 yards, I hit a three-quarter punch with a 4-iron about 12 feet from the hole. Tony was at least 30 feet from the hole with his tee-shot, but his first putt actually hit the hole and broke away. I got mine in and now we were at the sixth again, where we had that little chat during the practice round. We drove, pitched on, and he two-putted. As we played the hole, I thought that if I could get another one back by the ninth, he would be back to three down after a huge lead, and psychologically that would be a hell of a thing for him to wrestle with. I was convinced that I could detect, on that sixth hole, a slight colour change in his face. He looked a little more pale, and his cheeks had gone in slightly, and I knew I had him worried even then.

I thought of Lema all the time, Lema, Lema, Lema, of how he was thinking, what he was thinking, of this steady change in a situation which, an hour earlier, he had under complete control, and I knew quite well that if it had happened to me, I would have been just a little jumpy. So my strategy was to keep gnawing at him, keep the pressure on him, try to get one more hole back before the turn. A freakish little incident had happened as I walked down the fairway which underlined the significance of this sixth hole yet again, and makes me think now that it held the key to the entire match. I heard one of the spectators behind me say to his friend, "Let's go and watch the match behind – this one will be all over, at least five and three." I didn't say anything. I have long since learned to keep my mouth shut since I believe that when a man has paid his entrance money he's entitled to voice an opinion and say what he pleases, within the bounds of decency. But this fellow went on and on about it. His friend would say, "Well, just let's wait, you never know what can happen" and the first fellow said, "Don't be silly – what do you expect, miracles?" At that I turned round and said, "Sir, you obviously don't play golf or you would know a match is never won until the last putt has been holed, so stick around and you might just see something that will surprise you." I was very sharp with him. And I must say I'd be delighted to have a chat with that man today, because I hope he might

**Gary Player showed extraordinary tenacity and courage throughout the match.**

have a different outlook as far as his own weekend golf is concerned, if he does play the game.

Tony was in for four on this sixth hole, I putted about two feet past the hole – and missed the little one! As soon as I hit the ball, I knew I had missed. I almost wanted to get it back, and hit it all over again. It was unthinkable, missing from two feet in such a match, but I did it. Perhaps I had been thinking too much, about everything, on this sixth hole, and right there and then was the only time in the entire match when I thought I might not win. I thought dammit, I've let the whole thing go. But yet again the conversation with Lema in the practice round came back, and the one thing that buzzed in my head was that I had more to lose than he had.

As we walked from the green to the seventh tee, a most extraordinary thing happened to me. it was as though I was in the midst of a revelation, some spiritual experience which had a physical effect on me. This is almost impossible to explain, but I suddenly felt drenched in adrenalin. My mind became perfectly clear, my memory was sharp and precise. I became totally aware of my physical condition, my physical strength and the one thing I wanted to do was to get to that tee and play golf like I had never played before, like no man had ever played before. I felt tremendously charged up and yet absolutely calm and self-possessed at the very same time. It was a very strange experience.

We halved the next three holes, and at the ninth, I had to hole a hard 15-foot putt to make the half. So it was five down, nine to play, instead of three down as I had hoped for, and to any rational person, it was all over. My father told me afterwards that when he heard the radio news at that point, the 27th hole, he thought well, that's over. At the very same moment, as I walked to the 10th tee, I thought of him, and wondered if he would be getting the news. And I thought of my country, South Africa, maligned, misunderstood, pilloried by people who can tell us how to order our affairs from a range of 6,000 miles without ever coming down to South Africa and seeing for themselves, and trying to understand. I thought of my friends, the people who have helped me along the way, and all this added to my incentive to win this thing and put a fantastic achievement in the record books. Everything seemed to be tying up, in my mind, with the fact that I simply *was* going to win.

On the short 10th, Tony missed the green again and this time didn't make three. Four down. At the 11th, where I had come unstuck in the morning, I poured the drive right down the middle, pitched it

up to about five feet, and holed the putt for a birdie. Three down. The 12th we halved. Three down. Six to play. Better. On 13, again I was down the middle with a stinging drive. Tony snap-hooked into the bushes, knocked it about 40 yards down the fairway, and I had to play next. This is one of the hardest challenges in match play, when your opponent has made a mess of things, to get down to it and have the guts or character or nerve or will-power or whatever you like to call it, to play the shot, to get down to it and take the advantage that has been offered to you by getting down and playing a perfect, or at least a telling shot. So often when you think you have the thing in your hands, you in turn make a mess of it and hand the advantage right back to him. it's like needing a four on the last hole to win a tournament. That's what makes match-play match-play. It happens all the time. This time I hit a ripe shot with the 5-iron, finishing some 10 feet from the hole. Lema pitched it on, but at the front of the green and a good 25 feet away. And by crickey, he holed it. A real lifesaver. That is exactly what Tony Lema was thinking. After we had hit our tee-shots, and after I had hit my second, he was convinced he had lost another hole. Now in goes a beautiful putt, and he thinks he is off the hook again. My putt is going to break a foot to the right. After his saviour putt, I have to hole mine, I just *have* to hole it, there is no other way. And I did. I aimed a foot to the left, and it swung in smack in the middle of the hole. Just when Tony's spirits have risen a little, I have crushed him down again. Two down, five to play. Better and better.

Now Tony Lema is very worried. He's long since stopped talking, and now he is thinking all kinds of things. He is thinking, probably for the very first time, that it is possible for him to lose the match. And at the same time he is working very hard on resisting that very thought. He thinks he might lose and he refuses to think he might lose, at one and the same time. His thinking is confused. He's trying to make himself think positively, but in the depths of his mind there is a little negative pulling at the positive. On the other hand, I am now thinking very clearly, very positively at this stage, over the next two holes. I have only one thing, positive, working for me. All I have to do and think about is go, go, go. Keep on going. You have him. You have him worried and muddled and confused, and you have five holes in which to nail him. These next two holes, 14 and 15, we halved. Two down, three to play. Now the gallery is swarming round us, as we go to the 16th tee, a tight drive and pitch hole at which I have used a 3-wood because of the precision needed from the tee. The 16th at Wentworth is definitely not a driver hole. Lema had played a 3-wood in the morning round, and in that practice round. It was my honour and I thought – all this flashed through my mind very quickly – "take a driver and really bash it right down the middle and that will really shake him." Then I've got him, really got him. So I step up on the tee and take out the driver with a flourish and belt it like a bullet right down the middle of the fairway, right into position A. Now comes Lema. He's thinking and wondering what to do, the 3-wood or the driver? Even if he didn't think that way, this is how I think he is thinking, if you follow, and this is how my own confidence is being solidly stiffened. And if he does elect for the 3-wood, no force on earth, after my big drive, will prevent him hitting a fraction harder, to get close to me. Tony took his 3-wood, and snap-hooked it right in the trees. And he has to play another off the tee and eventually concedes the hole and I am one down, two to play. The crunch is nigh. The crowd is in near-hysterics.

The 17th hole at Wentworth is something of a hoodoo for me. That's not entirely true either – I don't believe in hoodoo holes – but I have never, let's say, played it particularly well. It is 555 yards, turning to the left, downhill, then uphill slightly, with a little dip in front of the green and a bank down from the right side of the green. In the landing area for the drives the fairway slopes from left to right and it is something of a monster hole, mainly because of that. I hit two very big shots, the second with a 4-wood, and came up about 15 yards short of the green. With a 3-wood, Tony was some 80, 90 yards short and he hit a gorgeous wedge shot, about 12 feet from the hole. How do you follow that? Well, my nerve was still good. I pitched my ball inside his, about eight feet from the hole, a good missable distance, but still inside his. Advantage still to Player.

Now I began to think that Tony Lema had to be so flustered that he would be doubting if he could hole *his* putt. But here again I was very lucky. Suddenly my mind filled with a tip my father-in-law, Jock Verwey, gave me when I was a very young boy starting professional golf in South Africa. He was a great match player – he won the South African Match Play Championship three times – despite the fact that he was a rather poor striker of the golf ball. He was probably the worst driver of a golf ball that I ever saw, he couldn't drive worth a toffee, but he was a great battler with the irons, and a tremendous chipper and putter and above all, he was a great thinker about a match and had tremendous guts.

He always said that in match play you should never anticipate mistakes from the other man, never rely on him missing a shot, missing a putt. You must always expect your man to make every putt, so that when you go up to putt, you are convinced in your mind that the other fellow will certainly hole his. Thus it flashed through my mind that Lema, no matter what strain he was under, would hole this one – and dammit, he did. But I still felt strong enough, confident enough, to go up and knock mine right in on top of him. Now if I had missed that putt, the match would have been over and I would have been out of the World Match Play Championship.

So we come to the 36th hole. I am one down, one to play. The entire drama of this long and momentous day seemed to have been packed into that putt on the 17th, the 35th hole. Now it was maintained and transferred to the 18th, the 36th. By this time I must have been absolutely exhilarated. Many people might have thought how terrible to be one down, with one to play. But after being six down the last time I played this hole, and seven down at the 19th, I just had to be feeling exalted.

We both hit probing drives down the centre of the fairway. Lema was away, and he hit rather a poor, low, hooked second, about 50 yards short of the green, with a bunker between his ball and the pin. I really launched myself into my second, with a 4-wood · the hole is 495 yards – and everyone screamed and yelled at what a great, great shot it was. Apparently, on television, it looked like the shot of a lifetime, but in fact it just proves that you never can tell in these matters. When I hit the ball, I thought it was an awful shot. I came off the ball a little bit, and it seemed to go through the top of the trees (trees from the right side on this hole at Wentworth crowd right in on the line of the second shot) instead of just narrowly missing them, as I had planned. It looked to me to be slicing, but it went through the trees, pitched short of the green, took a break to the left, squeezed past the right-hand trap, and took the curve of the ground nicely down until it finished about 10 feet from the hole. The result was magnificent. Of course, I was swinging a golf club, and not firing a rifle, but the ball had taken a line some eight feet to the right of the one I had hoped for. However, it had a perfect ending.

Tony Lema swung into his third shot – and was a little unfortunate. He hit a good-looking low pitch at the green, over the bunker, but it bit into the front of the green and stopped. Now if you look at that green at Wentworth closely, you will see that the front of the green is invariably a little more damp than the rest of it. This was certainly something I had noticed in practice, and Tony may have missed. If he had played a high pitch right at the hole, or pitched it short of the green and made it run, he might have been more successful. He didn't hole the putt, I used my two for it carefully, and we were all square. Unbelievable. We went into extra holes.

I have had something of a little complex about play-offs in the past. I think I had a streak in which I lost eight or nine tournaments in play-offs in the States and I got to thinking that they were unfair. You battle through 72-holes of medal play, come up level with someone, and then the whole thing may be on one hole of golf. I have always felt that an extra nine holes would be more fair rather than sudden death, since on one hole a duffer can beat a champion, and there is just too much involved in it when a man is trying to make a living. At the same time, I felt I had broken my streak of non-success in these things. I had beaten Kel Nagle in the U.S. Open play-off, and earlier I had beaten Arnold Palmer and Miller Barber at Pensacola in a play-off. And apart from all that, this was match-play, the raw blood and guts of golf, and extra holes are an intrinsic part of match-play.

The 37th hole. Two normal drives, my ball finding a slightly cut lie on the right side of the fairway. Tony low-hooked his second again, into a deep bunker at the left front of the green. I knocked mine on the front of the green. Tony exploded out, way past the pin. He failed, only just, with the putt. I had two to win one of the most astonishing golf matches ever played. I hit my first putt two feet past the hole – and made the return. I had won.

I shook hands with Lema, and then for the first time in that long, hard day, I felt shot through with nerves. I started to tremble like a leaf in a storm. My wife Vivienne came galloping across the green like a madwoman and hugged me, but I hardly knew about it. When I got to the edge of the green, I sat down and actually lost consciousness for quite a few seconds. A Dr Volkavici, from Cape Town, was there, and he made me stay down, and put my head between my knees. Then he took my pulse, and said all was well. When I stood up, my legs were like jelly, my hands were trembling. Not once throughout the day during play did my hands tremble on any shot – but they did when it was over. The only other time in golf when I felt just remotely as faint as this was in a Miami Open at Bayshore when I came up to the 72nd hole, a par-5, needing a four to beat Arnold Palmer and win. I hit my second into a bunker about 45 yards short of the green, leaving myself without doubt the hardest shot in golf, the most exacting – a long shot from a bunker. If you hit too far behind the ball, you'll be short of the green. If you hit too close to the ball, man, you will fly right over the green. I hit this one about eight feet from the hole, got the putt down, and won the thing, and I felt very faint then. In fact Harvey Rainer of the American PGA had come to me with smelling salts.

When I was able to start back to the Wentworth clubhouse, the ovation I got from the crowd helped me to feel better and recover very quickly. All the way back down the fairway, right to the clubhouse, to the very door of the dressing-room, they applauded me. it was something I appreciated very much. And something else which I appreciated deeply was the manner in which Tony Lema took his appalling defeat. His manners were simply outstanding, he was a great loser and I was immensely impressed with him, as a man, after I had beaten him that day. But it wasn't really until I had changed and was being driven back to London that the enormity of the thing closed in on me, and I realised just what I had done. I had in fact given a man of the class of Tony Lema six up over 18 hole, seven up over 17 holes, five up over nine holes – and beaten him. Why, the thing hardly bears thinking about! By the time I got back to the hotel, and had dinner in my room and got to bed early, I was very excited. It was difficult to get to sleep. Then I had to think of reasons why I wanted to beat Peter Thomson, in the final. I had to start right from the bottom of the ladder again and try to work up enthusiasm and determination and the will to go on and complete the job. My obvious problem was combating the feeling that almost anything that could happen in the final would simply have to be an anti-climax to the Lema match.

I have gone into this match at some length because it seems to me to tell the story of Gary Player aptly enough as a climax to the most remarkable year of my life. It contains, in its essence, this Lema match, the saga of the little fellow who set out from South Africa all those years ago with long hair, uncreased pants, a golf swing as ugly as anything you have ever seen, but also with a consuming ambition, with an endless bounty of guts, and with the determination never to quit, never to give up, never to surrender until the last putt of the last hole of the match dropped; with the plain intent of becoming the best golfer in the world.

# PICTURE ACKNOWLEDGMENTS

Associated Sports Photography: pps 124, 129, 137, 208, 214
David Cannon/All-Sport: pps 6, 17, 138, 142, 171, 204
Peter Dazeley Photography: pps 14, 18, 20, 22, 35, 148, 152, 156, 164, 167, 182, 194, 206
Michael Hobbs: pps 12, 26, 29, 33, 36, 40, 42, 46, 48, 51, 59, 60, 63, 64, 76, 80, 112, 119, 174, 178, 187
Hulton Picture Library: pps 10, 43, 53, 54, 67, 70, 73, 84, 90, 96, 104, 109, 117, 122, 127
Lawrence N. Levy: pps 132, 146
Phil Sheldon Photography: pps 4, 25, 162, 177, 190, 196, 200

Colour Section
Simon Bruty/All-Sport: pp 6 *left*
David Cannon/All-Sport: pps 3, 4, 7, 11
Steve Powell/All-Sport: pp 2
Peter Dazeley Photography: pps 6 *right*, 8, 9, 14
Michael Hobbs: pp 1
Phil Sheldon Photography: pps 5, 10, 12, 16

# INDEX

220

223